C000003777

Hard Poundıng:
The Story of the
UK Independence Party

*An inside story of the rise
of the UK Independence Party*

by

DR PETER GARDNER

Somerset Library Service	
1 9 5096938 4	
Askews	05-Jun-2008
	£9.99
324 .241	

The June Press

1 9 5096938   4

The Author

Peter Gardner has been a member of the UK Independence Party since its foundation. A Regional Organiser for the party in its early years, he coordinated the campaigns of fifteen party candidates in the 1997 General Election, in addition to standing himself as a candidate in that election. He was again the party's candidate in the Oxford East constituency in the 2001 and 2005 General Elections. He lives in Oxford, is married to Alicia, and is a member of a large Anglo-Venezuelan family. He lived in France for over four years. In this book he gives an insider's view of the rise of the UK Independence Party from small beginnings to a position on the national political stage.

June Press publications are not intended to represent a corporate view of developments in Europe. They are to promote and develop ideas and encourage individuals to express views on the EU situation, from a UK view-point, within the security and obligations of a stable and law-abiding nation. The views expressed in our publications are, however, the sole responsibility of the authors. We do not recommend any public support for any political organisation or to influence the voters in any referendum.

First published in 2006

by The June Press Ltd

UK distributor
The June Press Ltd
PO Box 119
Totnes
Devon TQ9 7WA
Tel: 44(0)8456 120 175
Fax: 44(0)8456 120 176
Email: info@junepress.com
Web: www.junepress.com

Copyright © Peter Gardner 2006

All rights reserved. No part of this publication may be reproduced
or transmitted in any form or by any means of electronic or
mechanical, including photocopy, recording, or any information
storage and retrieval system now known or invented, without
permission in writing from the publisher, except by a reviewer
who wishes to quote brief passages in connection with a review
written for inclusion in a magazine, newspaper or broadcast.

ISBN 0 9534 6974 3

This book is printed on environmentally friendly paper

Dedicated to David Lott, the unsung hero of the party, who has made such enormous efforts to steer it in the right direction

Contents

Acknowledgements   xi

Foreword   xiii

Preface   xv

Introduction   xvii

1 Counter Revolution   1

A Disillusioned European   1
Ideals, Despair, Treachery   8

2 Born at Bruges   27

The Bruges Group   27
Maastricht And The Establishment Parties   31
The Anti-Federalist League   34
The UK Independence Party   38
The 1994 European Elections   41

3 Building a Nationwide Party – 1994 to 1997   45

Grass Roots Rising   45
Coming Together   49
The 1997 General Election   51
UKIP And The Referendum Party   62

4 Internal Conflict and Recovery I – 1997 to 1999   71

The First Fracture Of UKIP   71
"Tirez Le Rideau"   71
Rebuilding The Party   81
The 1999 European Elections   94

CONTENTS

5 Internal Conflict and Recovery II – 1999 to 2001   **111**

Breaking The Consensus   111
The Second Fracture Of UKIP   116
Preparing For The 2001 General Election   148
The 2001 General Election   152

6 General Election to European Election – 2001 to 2004   **165**

A Long Preparation   165
People And Places   166
Moving Into Pavement Politics   175
Moving Onto Risky Ground   176
Goodbye Euro, Hello Constitution   178
The Opening Of The Second Battle   181

7 The 2004 European Election Campaign   **183**

Crash   183
Three Outsiders   183
Organisation For The Campaign   190
The Party's Policy Stance In The Campaign   193
A Pensioner Fires The Opening Shot   195
Kilroy-Silk Brings Up The Heavy Artillery   199
"Our Time Has Come"   203
Of Cranks And Gadflies   207
Coming To The Boil   212
Champagne And Then To Wreck?   220

8 European Election 2004 to General Election 2005   **227**

The End Of The Beginning   227
The House On The Rhine   228
Kill The Tories   233
The North East Says 'No'   241
Return Of The Curse   247

CONTENTS

9 The 2005 General Election Campaign   263

Great Hopes   263
Organisation For The Campaign   265
The Party's Policy Stance In The Campaign   266
A Final Parting Of The Ways   271
The Penny That Didn't Drop   274
The Question Unveiled   276
The Elephant In The Room   278

Postscript: "No More Europe"?   285

References   289

Acknowledgements

This book draws heavily from media articles published over the period which it covers, official UK Independence Party publications, internal correspondence, and personal recollection. It began as a diary in 1996 and then was turned into this book from 2003 onwards. It has greatly benefited also from the comments and personal recollections of David Lott, Nigel Farage, David Wilkinson, and others, who are due thanks for this and for the way in which they refrained from attempting to influence the text when it was perhaps not entirely kind to them.

Thanks are also due to Derek Bennett, Mark Croucher and John Harvey for photographs supplied by them, to the *Guardian*, *Daily Telegraph* and *Sunday Telegraph* for permission to reprint some photographs. Also to Keith Carson of the June Press who took on this project in the face of the feeling of some that "books on Europe" never sell. The comments of reviewers from literary consultancy Cornerstones helped greatly to push the text into what I hope is a more interesting style than the one in which it began.

As far as I know, the events related in this book are accurately described but I welcome corrections from those who may have better information.

Peter Gardner, Oxford 2006

Foreword

Our recent political history is littered with examples of new political parties that have foundered. All were launched with great optimism but hardly any were able to even achieve a few council seats. This book chronicles an exception, the UK Independence Party, which went from nothing in 1993 to securing 2.7 million votes in the European Elections of 2004.

It would never have been formed had it not been for the fact that our traditional parties all supported the UK's disastrous entanglement with the Exchange Rate Mechanism and, worse still, all supported the Maastricht Treaty. Dr Alan Sked's Anti-Federalist League had fought a few seats in the General Election of 1992 and from this, in September 1993, the UK Independence Party was born. The aim was clear, to get the UK out of the European Union.

However, it has been a tortuous journey for UKIP with splits and schisms threatening the very existence of the Party on more than one occasion. Political births are never easy and from the resignation of Dr Sked in 1997 to that of Robert Kilroy-Silk in 2004 there have been times when the future was seriously in doubt.

Dr Peter Gardner has done an excellent job in recording the peaks and troughs of UKIP's journey and has done so from a neutral position.

With our three major parties all still supporting EU membership and the public increasingly against, the UKIP journey is far from over. But for those who want to discover how the UK's fourth largest party came into being I thoroughly recommend this book.

Nigel Farage MEP

Preface

This book tells the story of how a determined group of individuals broke away from the political mainstream and built a new political party outside the realm of establishment politics. It is a story about true democracy in action, welling up against a complacent and overbearing political class attempting to insulate itself from the people it should serve and to whom it should be responsive. The book describes the creation and the struggles of the UK Independence Party over a period of nearly fifteen years, since the Maastricht Treaty prompted its formation. It has been a difficult time: we ourselves have been far from perfect, we have argued with each other, and have fractured and fallen out with each other. Only the most stubborn and persistent would set out to build and grow a new political party. This makes for difficult times. Nevertheless, I believe that our struggle has been a noble crusade and that the free participation of so many people is a reproach to the complacency of other people who are *too* cynical about politics. It is a story of people who are not "in it for themselves" and who passionately believe in the cause they are fighting for.

I can vouch for the truth of the contents of this book because I was there from the beginning. I was there when we first came together. I was there when we had our arguments, when the tables were banged in anger and the chairmen had to shout to bring meetings back to order. And I was there when we had our successes, when I felt, in my own small way, that I was walking with history.

I know the people involved and their motivations. Most of them would probably say that they would rather have done other things – we were not career politicians. But a job had to be done and we set out to do it.

Introduction

During the course of writing this book, I was advised that it should contain at least a short history of how Britain came to be where it is now in the European Union. So this introduction includes a condensed history of the European Union and a simple description of its current institutions. If you know, as I suspect, more than my advisor thinks you know, then skip this introduction and go straight to the first chapter. There, I take up the story in 1988 and also look at some of the lesser-known episodes that took place along the way which were at least partly responsible for getting us to 2006, our thirty-third year of membership of the European Union, and with the prospect of an EU Constitution to complete the process of absorption.

It is claimed that Britain was reluctant to join 'Europe'. This is only partly true. When the European Economic Community (EEC) or 'Common Market' was brought into being by the Treaty of Rome in 1958, it is true that Britain was not a signatory and that we had abstained from the negotiations that produced the treaty. But just a few years later, the attitude of Britain's political leaders changed dramatically and desperate attempts were made to join. A first attempt was made in 1961. It was vetoed in January 1963 by General Charles de Gaulle, President of France at the time. A second attempt was made in 1967. De Gaulle again exercised his veto. A third, successful, attempt was made in 1972, when Edward Heath, Prime Minister of the day, gave away so much in his desperation to get Britain in. The twists and turns of party politics meant that the Labour government elected in October 1974 held a referendum in 1975 on the issue of whether Britain should remain a member of the EEC. Following a campaign in which the 'yes' side overwhelmingly outspent the 'no' side, the electorate voted to stay in.

There was then comparative silence on the issue for ten years or so, until the next treaty, the Single European Act (SEA), was negotiated and signed in 1986. The Treaty of Rome established a common internal market within the EEC and a customs union and common commercial policy towards the rest of the world. It also set up the Common Agricultural Policy (CAP). The Treaty of Rome also established the current institutional structure, described briefly below. The Single European Act aimed to remove technical barriers – such as different national standards, for example – to produce a deepened internal market by 1993. To do this, a large expansion of the use of majority voting among the Member States was introduced. The SEA also took tentative steps towards a common foreign policy. But, already, even as the SEA was being finalised, ambitions for a further leap 'forward' were in the air. These ideas were for two separate negotiations on economic union and political union. Economic union meant, in short, a single currency, an idea already at least thirty years old by then – indeed, it had been around even in the early post-war years as an eventual aspiration of the EEC. The two sets of negotiations culminated in the Maastricht Treaty of 1992, which set out a detailed process for the establishment of the euro and which brought into being the European Union (EU), a new entity to supplement the European Community. The EU included further movement towards a common foreign and security policy – including an eventual common defence policy and EU armed forces – and cooperation in police and judicial affairs.

Maastricht and its single currency were a huge leap in the direction of a centralised European state – it was this which galvanised so many people and which led to the formation of UKIP and many other campaigning groups.

But even Maastricht was not enough for the committed federalist tendency: less than six years later, the Treaty of Amsterdam extended cooperation on police and judicial issues to create the Orwellian-sounding "area of freedom, security, and justice". Negotiated by the outgoing Conservative government, the treaty was signed by the new Labour government, with Labour additionally throwing aside Britain's opt-out in the area of social and employment policy. Amsterdam took the European Union into the areas of asylum and immigration – core issues normally associated with the sovereignty of independent states. Then came the Treaty of Nice, edging further into a common foreign policy and common judicial and police bodies. The Treaty of Nice also began the moves towards common EU armed forces, with its declaration of the need for a European Rapid Reaction

Force consisting of 100 ships, 400 combat aircraft and a force of 100,000 soldiers able to operate within a radius of 2,500 kms from Brussels.

Emboldened, the federalists came up with an EU Constitution with even more powers for the centre and which would have cemented and confirmed the supremacy of the centre over the Member States – the "capstone of a federal state" as the Belgian Prime Minister called it. Fortunately, that was sunk by the French and the Dutch referenda of 2004. But it is not off the agenda. Even as this book was being finalised, the whispers and the not-so-subtle hints about putting it back on the agenda had already started. French and German politicians, and prominent MEPs in the European parliament, to name only a few, are keen to bring it back in one form or another.

This is no surprise to those of us on the eurorealist side of politics, nor indeed to many interested members of the public. We know by now that the governing elites of the European Union are determined that the peoples of Europe shall have "ever closer union" whether they like it or not. Their only response to dissent is to attribute it to ignorance on the part of the people. They thus talk about the need to communicate more effectively with "European citizens" and to give us more information. What this means in practice is more propaganda. More propaganda in our libraries, in our universities, in our schools.

Indeed, we can widen out this theme: the European Union is only the logical conclusion, so far, of a process of divorce of politicians from the peoples they govern, on a continent-wide basis. How convenient it is for them to be able to band together across a continent and to create and sign all those treaties that give them the right to take decisions free of the democratic process and the consent of the governed. It's the dream of politicians and bureaucrats everywhere.

In Britain in 2006 an estimated 50 to 70 per cent of our laws are set by a foreign executive sitting in secret in a city that's not even in the UK, by people who we have never elected and who we can never throw out of office.

As for the structure of the Union, the three core institutions are the European Commission, the Council of Ministers, and the European Parliament. The Commission takes its orders from the European Councils, the special twice-yearly 'summits' of Prime

Ministers and Presidents of the Member States. The European Council sets the broad framework of action and the Commission implements those plans through EU legislation. Crucially, the Commission is appointed, not elected, and it is only the Commission that can bring legislation forward. Its as though the government in Westminster were perpetually in office, without the distractions of elections. Indeed, it is arguably intended to be that way.

Legislation can be of different kinds, the two more important types being the directive and the regulation. Importantly, in neither of these types of legislation is there any latitude for national governments: they are both obligatory. The only difference is that, with regulations, once signed, that's the end of the process – they are already law. Directives must be transposed into national law by each Member State producing its own legislation – but they are still obligatory. It is useful to remember this when one reads of various interest groups asking the government for an "opt-out". Should a government fail to implement a directive, the European Court of Justice exists to bring it back into line. Should a national parliament vote against a directive, that vote has no effect, which is why our government tries so hard to ensure that such debates never take place. Imagine the embarrassment if the pretence were exposed.

To be accurate, the above is a description of the workings of the European Community, rather than the European Union. The European Community can be considered the inner core and the European Union can be thought of as an outer layer around that core. The European Community is one "pillar" of the three-pillar structure of the European Union. Only within the inner core does the framework of Commission, Council, Parliament and Court of Justice hold sway. The business of the outer layer and its two pillars of foreign and security policy and police and judicial cooperation, is conducted by the Council of Ministers and is free of the authority of the other institutions – largely, and for the time being. It is, of course, the intention of the federalists to extend the power of Commission and Court to the whole Union. This the Constitution would have done, and may still do, if they get their way.

The patient building of this European Union over a period of 50 years has as its counterpart the progressive extinction of national democracies in Europe. Each time a policy area is transferred to Brussels, the possibility of ordinary people changing it becomes so small as to be considered impossible. And, once transferred, policy areas are never returned. The doctrine of the *acquis communautaire* is that power acquired is never given back.

This book begins in 1988, at a time when the EEC was about to make that dramatic leap forward at Maastricht, creating a European Union with overt political ambitions. That year was the centre year in the five-year period between the Single European Act and the Maastricht Treaty, the five-year period when one can almost say that the "old" EEC turned into the "new" EU of today. It was, looking back, a historic turning point. Margaret Thatcher's Bruges speech was a reaction against that turning point by one who understood what was happening. This book describes the speech, its background and the reaction to it at home and abroad, because it sets the scene for the story to come and because it gives a flavour of the times.

In the second part of chapter one, the book goes back forty years and presents an alternative view of the development of Britain's relationship with the European Union. In writing this sub-chapter, I wanted to discover for myself why the decision to join was taken. And, in thinking about that, I was interested not in the bare facts of what happened but in what real people were actually thinking. So I have looked at what opinions people actually had: at what the politicians thought, what the bureaucrats thought and what the public thought. I have also looked at the cynical attempts to manipulate public opinion that took place.

The two most important years in terms of the facts of Britain's relationship with the EU are probably 1973, when we joined, and 1993, when the Maastricht Treaty passed into law. But, as regards the *zeitgeist*, the unseen movement of opinion, the important years were 1960 and 1988, as I show below.

Having slowly come back to the time of the Bruges speech, the scene is set for my main story – the grass-roots formation of UKIP, its tortured and combustible progress over almost fifteen years, and the breakthrough of 2004 when we caught the popular discontent with mainstream politicians and the European Union, and blew a hole in the political consensus.

1

Counter Revolution

A Disillusioned European

For those who believed in the European dream, the year 1988 must have been encouraging indeed. The project was on the move again after years of only slow advance. The Single European Act of two years before had extended majority voting to many new areas and now Economic and Monetary Union – the European single currency – was again on the agenda and in the safe hands of Jacques Delors, the then President of the European Commission. Five years of European Councils – the summits of the political leaders of the EEC member states – had been spent dealing with the objections of Margaret Thatcher on issues such as British financial contributions to the EEC, the size of the EEC budget, and the Common Agricultural Policy, but she had eventually agreed to the Single European Act. Spain and Portugal joined the EEC just before the Act was signed. The following year would add the Social Charter, a set of rules on employment and social issues, to the European agenda.

In Britain, in particular, events were moving in directions helpful to the project. The Labour Party had radically changed its 1983 policy of withdrawal from the EEC and was moving towards an overtly pro-European policy. A speech by Delors to the Trades Union Congress in September 1988 cemented the equally dramatic reversal of opinion of the British unions, who had decided, after the trade union reforms of the Thatcher governments, that their objectives could be achieved more easily through Brussels. Opposition to the project within the Conservative Party was minimal with only a few die-hard opponents. Thatcher talked tough at European Councils yet always came to a compromise in the end.

But, by early 1988, Thatcher, who had campaigned for the 'yes' side in the 1975 referendum on whether Britain should remain in the EEC, and who in 1984 still thought of herself as a European idealist, though with different ideals from most Continental politicians, was becoming increasingly wary of the direction of the Community. She had noted that the increased powers that the European Commission had received in the Single European Act had only increased its appetite for more power. The Community seemed to favour bureaucratic rather than market solutions to economic problems and the federalist theme had begun to re-emerge. She understood that the emerging single currency project would eventually mean political union, an opinion reinforced by the speech of Delors to the European parliament on the 6th July 1988 in which he predicted that, within ten years, 80 per cent of economic and social legislation would come from the Community and that there would be the beginnings of a European government.

In the second volume of her autobiography of 1993, "The Downing Street Years", Thatcher recorded her feeling that she had been deceived over the nature of the Single European Act. She wrote that the Act "contrary to my intentions and my understanding of formal undertakings given at the time" had provided new scope for the European Commission and the European Court to press forward in the direction of centralisation. A later passage refers to misunderstandings arising from different national traditions of law-making. Reflecting on the need to learn from experience, she noted that ever since Britain had joined the Community, the words of the treaties had been used creatively by European institutions to extend their powers. This included the Single European Act, where "new majority voting provisions intended solely to implement the Single Market were used by the Commission to extend its regulatory powers". Vague declarations had been subsequently pressed into service to extend Community powers further into national life. Reflecting on all this, she finally decided, in late 1988, that it was time to make a stand:

> The more I considered all this, the greater my frustration and the deeper my anger became. Were British democracy, parliamentary sovereignty, the common law, our traditional sense of fairness, our ability to run our own affairs in our own way to be subordinated to the demands of a remote

*European bureaucracy, resting on very different traditions? I
had by now heard about as much of the European 'ideal' as
I could take.*

A speaking engagement was already available for the speech
which she now decided to make, and it was in the heartland of
the European project – the Collège d'Europe in Bruges. The
college had been established in the early post-war years at the
urging of a Spanish intellectual, Salvador de Madariaga. The first
Rector of the college, from 1950 to 1972, was Professor Hendrik
Brugmans, a leading light of the European Movement of the day.

Drafts of the speech ping-ponged between 10 Downing Street
and the Foreign Office, which deplored the original text and
which sought to remove what it saw as its more confrontational
aspects. The final version was still a radical departure from the
European consensus and the British consensus on 'Europe' that
had existed since 1973.

Thatcher delivered the speech on the 20th September 1988 in
the old cloth hall of the mixed Gothic and Renaissance Halle
building in Bruges. In the audience that evening were the Belgian
Prime Minister, Wilfried Martens; the then Rector of the college,
professor Lukaszewski; and assorted ambassadors. A
commentator in the *Economist* magazine noted that the College
was a "den of federalism if ever there was one", and that most of
the believers in a United States of Europe were in the audience
that evening. The audience flanked Thatcher on either side of the
hall, the space directly in front of her being mostly unoccupied.

After the introductory preliminaries, Thatcher attempted to
lighten what she was about to say by joking that, if the audience
believed some of the things that had been said about her views on
Europe, they might think that her invitation to speak was
equivalent to Genghis Khan being invited to speak on the virtues
of peaceful co-existence.

She set out five principles that she believed should guide the
future of the European Community. The first principle
emphasised the centrality of the nation states of Europe. The way
forward was through willing and active cooperation between
sovereign countries – "to try to suppress nationhood and
concentrate power at the centre of a European conglomerate
would be highly damaging and would jeopardise the objectives

we seek to achieve". Europe would be stronger if France was still France, Spain was still Spain, Britain was still Britain. Centralisation was not the way forward; it would be folly to try and squeeze them into an identikit European model. Working more closely together did not require an appointed bureaucracy. In her mind was the difference between her vision of minimal government and the European consensus of state regulation and interference. In the most well-known part of the speech, Thatcher made the defiant statement that her government had "not successfully rolled back the frontiers of the state in Britain, only to see them reimposed at a European level, with a European superstate exercising a new dominance from Brussels".

The second principle was about hard-headed, practical Thatcherism, as opposed to the lofty ideals and pronunciations on the future of Europe of the European elites. Community policies, she said, should address practical problems such as the waste caused by the Common Agricultural Policy. Thatcher set out this approach more forcefully the following day in Luxembourg. Asked a question about Europe during a press conference, she said that she was one of the few people who was constantly asking "What do you mean by that? What do you mean by European Union? What do you mean by Monetary Union? What do you mean by a United States of Europe – what do you mean, what do you mean?"

The third principle was about the need for the Community to follow policies that encouraged enterprise. This "Europe Open to Enterprise" section of the speech was the longest of the five sections. Enterprise, she said, was the key to future jobs and prosperity. State-controlled economies resulted in low growth. Free enterprise within a framework of law was the better system – "the lesson of the economic history of Europe in the 70s and 80s is that central planning and detailed control *do not* work and that personal endeavour and initiative *do*". The Community should also avoid protectionism and should adopt liberalising policies in world trade negotiations. Britain, under Thatcherism, had pursued liberalisation at home – the Community should do the same on the world stage.

Lastly, European defence should remain anchored around NATO. The Western European Union (WEU), a post-war defence grouping of ten European countries, had been reactivated in 1984 as a step towards a common European defence. Thatcher thought that any further moves in that direction would destabilise NATO, which had kept the peace in Europe for over 40 years: "we should develop the WEU, not as an alternative to NATO, but as a means of strengthening Europe's contribution to the common defence of the West".

In her peroration, Thatcher said that it was not enough to talk in generalised terms about a European ideal. She said that her speech charted the way ahead in practical steps. The Community should not be distracted by Utopian goals. Above all:

> *Let Europe be a family of nations, understanding each other better, appreciating each other more, doing more together but relishing our national identity no less than our common European endeavour.*

Reaction to the speech from other European leaders and from EEC officials was, according to Thatcher in her autobiography, one of stunned outrage, beginning with arguments over dinner after the speech with the Prime Minister, Deputy Prime Minister, and Foreign Minister of the host country. Wilfried Martens, the Prime Minister, later said that a highly decentralised form of European government was preferable but that there would be, in the end, a European government. A senior European Commission official called Thatcher's remarks outrageous and unrelentingly negative and predicted that they would do great harm. An MEP commented that "there is a lot of Genghis Khan in this speech", and the Commission said that "there is no question of restructuring 1992 to meet British demands".

By the end of that week there had been a torrent of press articles commenting on and mostly decrying the sentiments in the speech. In Italy, *La Stampa* said that Thatcher was like an elephant in the china shop of Europe. In Holland, *De Volkskrant* said that she had caused more damage during her European trip than hurricane Gilbert did to Jamaica. In France, *Le Monde* said that the Bruges speech showed that the years running up to the completion of the Single Market in 1992 "will be difficult, laborious and marked by conflicts between the twelve". *Libération* pointed out the difference between the United States of Europe "so dear to Winston Churchill" and Thatcher landing on the continent "more Gaullist than ever, refuting the idea of a European superstate and claiming simple cooperation between sovereign states".

Other references to this supposed Gaullist approach occurred in *La Libre Belgique* which said "Margaret Thatcher plays at being De Gaulle" and *De Standaard,* according to which "Thatcher sticks to her Gaullist credo". Still in Belgium, *Le Soir* thought that Thatcher was pursuing a strategy to "defend the ultraliberal policies she has followed over the last ten years in the United Kingdom".

Reaction from other governments was equally vehement. Greece was fully in favour of economic and political union and regarded the transfer of national sovereignty to the EEC as inevitable. Andreas Papandreou, the Greek Prime Minister, thought that Thatcher was edging towards rejection of the Single European Act. West Germany said that Thatcher had not understood the process leading to the single market of 1992 and that, deliberately or otherwise, she was confusing longer term goals, such as a single European currency, with the single market process.

Chancellor Kohl said that it was inevitable that some national sovereignty would be transferred to the EEC. France and West Germany demonstrated their disagreement with the ideas in the speech when Chancellor Kohl and President Mitterrand met to discuss cooperation in military and financial affairs, with Kohl suggesting that the EEC should eventually have a common army and police force. Announcing plans for a joint Franco-German embassy, a French official said that "to have a joint military unit and a joint embassy is as far from the spirit of Bruges as you can get". Italy, West Germany, Belgium, Luxembourg, and the Netherlands, suggested that, if anything, the process of integration should be accelerated, with political union going ahead at the same time as economic union.

In Britain, also, the speech was criticised, the Labour Party having become pro-European after its anti-EEC policy of the early eighties. The Labour Party's foreign affairs spokesman said that Thatcher was like Boadicea making her disastrous way through the countries of Europe. The Social Democratic Party conference, being held at the time of the speech, unanimously approved a commitment to European unity. Paddy Ashdown,

Leader of the Social and Liberal Democrats (the merger of parts of the Social Democratic Party and the Liberal Party, which subsequently became the Liberal Democrats), thought that Thatcher was like a soccer hooligan on the rampage and that she was guilty of xenophobia in velvet gloves.

The *Times,* on the day the speech was delivered, was sympathetic to its content but complained about "the negative tone in which it may be couched". A week later, having considered further, it was less complimentary, saying that she had gone too far in attacking the "nightmare" of a European superstate since nothing of the kind had been proposed. The editorial complained that Thatcher had merely set up a straw man in order to knock it down in the hope of appealing to public opinion. It thought that the declaration by Jacques Delors that there would be an embryo European government within seven years was a mere flourish. The newspaper thought that European Union was a faraway issue:

> The Single European Act, which lays down the 1992 programme for the single market, affirms an eventual European Union. What is meant by union is an open question, and certainly not one whose answer is imminent...It is therefore regrettable that Mrs Thatcher should have confused the faraway issue of European union with the abolition of frontiers to which all EEC leaders committed themselves in the Single European Act.

Two years after her speech, Thatcher was forced to resign as Prime Minister, brought down by opposition from the Europhile wing of her party. The new Prime Minister, John Major, proceeded with negotiation and ratification of the Maastricht Treaty against which Thatcher had so determinedly fought. Maastricht greatly extended the powers of the European institutions, laying the basis for a common European Foreign and Security Policy and enshrining Delors' ambition of a single currency for Europe. As Thatcher knew, as the federalists knew and still know, a single currency demands a single government.

Ideals, Despair, Treachery

In his political autobiography, "Separate Ways", published in 2000, the Labour Eurosceptic and former Cabinet minister Peter Shore described the aftermath of the debacle at Suez in 1956, when Britain and France colluded with Israel to mount a military attack on Egypt to try and regain the Suez canal after Colonel Nasser, the Egyptian Leader, had nationalised it. The invasion was a complete failure and the two colonial powers were forced to withdraw within days. Shore said that, in response to this event, "a mood of deep pessimism started to settle in the Foreign Office". It was the time when US Secretary of State Dean Acheson said that "Britain had lost an empire but had yet to find a new role". Shore says that Acheson was no Anglophile and had, in fact, as far back as 1947, said that "the British are finished. They are through".

According to Hugo Young, in his history of the European issue in Britain, "This Blessed Plot", a major factor in the failure at Suez was the straight refusal of the Americans to support Britain when it needed help. In September 1956 £20million left the country, in October another £30million was lost and in the first week of November alone another £100million had gone (a total of around £2.5billion in today's terms). Harold MacMillan, Chancellor of the Exchequer at the time, begged his Cabinet colleagues to abandon the operation. All requests to the Americans for financial help were refused.

The humiliation at Suez spread doubt about the future throughout the political establishment of the time. Shore says that "something like a collective nervous breakdown, a loss of nerve", seemed to have afflicted the British establishment. This breakdown, this deep gloom and pessimism for the future, seems to have destroyed the whole basis of the Foreign Office's approach to the world. In 1948, for example, Gladwyn Jebb, who was British Ambassador to France from 1954 to 1958, said "the idea of an Atlantic Community was the thing and that of joining Europe was subsidiary. In 1948 this was a proposition which I did not really dispute and indeed there were few people in Whitehall who would have asserted the contrary", whereas, speaking after Suez, Anthony Nutting, Minister of State at the Foreign Office during the invasion, voiced the despair of the time – "it just left us in a total vacuum, resenting everybody...British foreign policy was left in a sort of void really, for several years, until we picked ourselves up and said, well, we have got to go in *some* direction".

Some concluded that joining the 'Common Market' was the new direction. Indeed, some saw no other way. Sir Roy Denman, a senior official at the Board of Trade, talking about the first British application to join the Common Market, said that "Our aim was to secure acceptable terms of entry. In one sense the terms of entry were irrelevant. No sensible traveller on the sinking Titanic would have said I will only enter a lifeboat if it is well-scrubbed, well-painted and equipped with suitable supplies of food and drink".

Coupled with the blow of Suez was the rise of people in the Foreign Office and the political establishment who had fought in the Second World War, who had seen its horrors, and who had decided that some kind of European political entity was the way to prevent war in Europe ever happening again. Edward Heath was prime among these.

Donald Maitland, who eventually became ambassador to the European Communities from 1975 to 1979, said "I came back from the war absolutely persuaded that the imperial idea – the idea of us ruling other countries – was finished.... We had to decolonise, and if we were going to do that, we had to have another kind of foreign policy". Michael Palliser, Maitland's predecessor in the post, who had fought in the Coldstream Guards, had similar sentiments – "simply taking a train journey from Berlin through the Ruhr and up to the Hook of Holland, you saw a place that was absolutely flattened...I came out feeling that this was something one simply can't allow to happen again. It hit you like a kick in the stomach".

The post-war Marshall Plan aimed to rebuild this flattened continent, in the American self-interest of rebuilding a strong and stable Europe as a bulwark against Soviet expansionism. But the aid came with the proviso that it should be accompanied by European unification. Announced by General George C. Marshall, US Secretary of State, the detailed planning was done by George Kennan of the State Department in May 1947, only two months after both the American Senate and House of Representatives had voted in favour of a United States of Europe.

In his report, Kennan said that the idea was to "force the Europeans to begin to think like Europeans, and not like nationalists, in their approach to the economic problems of their country".

The Marshall Plan was approved in March 1948. At the same time a committee was set up to press for European integration. The American Committee on United Europe (ACUE) was, according to Richard Aldrich in his book "The Hidden Hand: Britain, America, and Cold War Secret Intelligence", a conduit through which CIA funds flowed to federalist groups in Europe. The members of the committee were, according to Aldrich, a mixture of past and future CIA agents and those who had been most determined in getting the Marshall Plan approved. The committee included the Senator who had proposed the motions in favour of a United Europe. Aldrich says that, through ACUE, the CIA provided about $3.5million, and private business around $600,000, (perhaps $65million now) to the European Movement between 1949 and 1960, when ACUE was wound up. In 1949 the European Movement was almost bankrupt. After 1953, perhaps as much as two thirds of its income came from ACUE. A sense of the scale and audacity of this operation is given by Aldrich, who described it as one of the most elaborate post-war CIA operations in Western Europe. The CIA sought "directly to undermine British foreign policy in this area...and then financed a massive popular campaign to encourage support for European unity among European youth". It also "covertly funded British groups, even Labour MPs, who would oppose British foreign policy on federalism". Funds were also offered to "ardent British federalists who worked with the *Economist* in a campaign of influence designed to persuade key opinion-formers that a more positive line on Europe would pay dividends for British business".

This was not the only US-backed funding for federalist groups in Europe. The Economic Cooperation Administration, the body in charge of administering Marshall Plan aid, and the US Information Service, also funded numerous federalist groups.

In October 1959 the Conservative Party, now led by Harold Macmillan, was re-elected to government. Macmillan, as Foreign Secretary and then Chancellor of the Exchequer in the previous administration, had already been ruminating on the need for European integration for many years.

In fact, Macmillan had been thinking about the European question since at least 1939. He met Jean Monnet, in London, in 1940. He was a founder member of the British section of the European League for Economic Cooperation (ELEC), a pan-European organisation established in 1946 with the aim of bringing about political union in Europe. The various national groups working towards European unity coalesced into the European Movement and held their first pan-European meeting, the Hague Congress in May 1948. This was a gathering of eight hundred invited attendees, including eight former Prime Ministers and twenty eight former Foreign Ministers. Macmillan was an enthusiastic delegate and worked towards the main aim of the Congress, a Council of Europe. When the governments concerned acceded to this request and the first Council of Europe met in August 1949 Macmillan was one of the official nominees of the British government and a key player in the proceedings, along with Churchill. It was at this first Council of Europe that Macmillan began to work to bring into existence his vision of the Europe of the future. He cared deeply about the cause of European integration and especially wanted to solve the age-old problem of Franco-German conflict. But his vision for Europe was not that of a supranational state. Many times in his autobiography he states that his vision was of a confederation, not a federation. Indeed, he referred to the federalists as extremists:

> *While nearly all of us were averse to the federal concept which a few extremists enthusiastically promoted, we accepted that sincere partnership in the common task of rebuilding Europe must involve some surrender of sovereignty and the creation of some form of political organisation, if European institutions were to avoid a regime of pure technocracy.*

Macmillan's concept of a confederation is described in detail in a passage where he explains his exasperation with the Foreign Office approach of the time:

> *We could not, of course, join a federation which would limit our membership of the Commonwealth or our association*

with the United States. But federation was not the only form of constitutional association between states. There could be a confederation, based on continuous consultation between governments; a Consultative Assembly could be used to create a European public opinion; European currencies could be linked individually or collectively to sterling; a European preferential area could be created, interlocking with our own system of Imperial Preference; and specialised but not supranational authorities could be set up for such matters as defence and heavy industry.

Moreover:

'Federation' of Europe means 'Germanisation' of Europe. 'Confederation' (if we play our cards right) should be British leadership of Europe.

But gradually, the route that Macmillan wished to follow, a confederal grouping working through the Council of Europe, became sidelined by the federalist path as implemented, first, in the Schuman Plan for a European Coal and Steel Community (ECSC) and then in its wider counterpart, the European Economic Community (EEC). As he saw the federalist conception of Europe beginning to dominate, he regretted the lack of early British participation: "what folly there has been during the vital and formative years! The absurd constitution-making of Schuman and Monnet on the one side; the isolationism of Bevin and the Foreign Office on the other, have brought this about".

As it became progressively clearer that the EEC was to become a reality, Macmillan became gloomier and gloomier about the prospects for Britain. Such a continental grouping might lock Britain out of trade with the EEC and could lead to the resurgence of German aggression. Then, "the long-term future might be grim indeed" and "this would be a serious, perhaps a mortal, blow". By February 1956: "I do not like the prospect of a world divided into the Russian sphere, the American sphere and a united Europe of which we are not a member". And later, in 1960, when Macmillan was edging towards acceptance of British membership of the EEC:

Shall we be caught between a hostile (or at least a less and less friendly) America and a boastful, powerful Empire of Charlemagne – now under French but later bound to come under German control? Is this the real reason for 'joining' the Common Market (if we are acceptable) and for abandoning (a) the Seven (b) British agriculture and (c) the Commonwealth? It's a grim choice.

It must have been difficult for someone born at the height of Empire to come to terms with the straitened circumstances, economic and political, that his country was then in.

Hugo Young says of him "so this was a European", though he qualifies this by saying that he was a tormented and indecisive one. Ernest Wistrich, a leading British federalist, called him a committed European.

Macmillan was at the centre, both politically and temporally, of the change of mind of the establishment on the European question. Young notes how, during the 1950s, Macmillan was "agonising for Britain". If there is one period of time that can be identified as the tipping point, when Macmillan and his Cabinet switched, however reluctantly and, apparently, without acknowledging to themselves the full consequences and gravity of what they were doing, it is surely the period from mid-1960 to mid-1961. Why, after ten or more years of opposition to federalism on the part of both Conservative and Labour governments, did this change of heart happen? There were several possible influences but it is difficult to decide which of these influences had any effect.

The possible influences include a sense of inexorable decline for Britain on the part of those in power and a consequent attitude of defeatism. Another influence was overt American political pressure in favour of a federal Europe, with Britain as a member, and the covert campaigns and money involved in trying to advance that cause. Another was home-grown pressure for a federal Europe, from continental and British politicians. Another was, presumably, that, once the Common Market had been formed, then, quite simply, something had to be done about it. Another was the concentric circles picture of British foreign policy and the sense of some that, somewhere in this picture, there should be a place for Britain to retain its position as a great power. With America now assuming a dominant role in the world, the power balance in the transatlantic relationship was changing. So the dominant position could not be there. Neither could it rest in the Empire because that was in the process of dissolution. Perhaps it could be found in the Common Market, by assuming its leadership (a naïve proposition, as it happens)? But at the centre of these influences – the entity that was subject to the influences – was Macmillan and his Cabinet.

So the confluence of forces, the quirks of personalities and even the randomness in events that surely exists, came together to produce the decision that has been the most fundamental influence on Britain for fifty years. In late July 1960, Macmillan, evidently having made his decision, reshuffled his Cabinet to place known federalists in key places. To the Foreign Office went Edward Heath, as deputy to the Foreign Secretary and with a special brief for relations with the Common Market. To Agriculture went Christopher Soames, to Commonwealth relations went Duncan Sandys. Both the latter were long-term federalists. Even before these changes, Sir Frank Lee, another federalist who was influential in the advice that he gave to the Cabinet, had been put in place as joint head of the Treasury in January.

In December 1960 Heath consulted Lord Kilmuir, the Lord Chancellor, on the legal and political effects of joining the Common Market. His answer was clear and unambiguous: sovereignty would be lost because Common Market law would be higher than UK law and the European Court of Justice would be able to overrule UK law and even Acts of Parliament. Sovereignty would also be lost because the Common Market would acquire treaty-making powers in some areas. Kilmuir said that "it will not be easy to persuade Parliament or the public to accept them" but he thought that the issues should be brought out into the open because, otherwise, "those who are opposed to the whole idea of joining the Community will certainly seize on them with more damaging effect later on". Prophetic words indeed.

Douglas Jay was a senior Labour politician who fought the federalist project with all the energy he could find. With Peter Shore, he was one of the leaders of the 'anti-Marketeers' group of the 1960s and 1970s. He believed in the redistribution of wealth by progressive taxes, and heavy state intervention in industry. The General Strike and the depression and unemployment of the 1930s had brought him into the Labour Party. Yet he had an unmovable attachment to democracy and the principle that individual citizens should only be bound by legislation debated in public and enacted by a body that they had elected. To him, that was the ultimate principle of parliamentary democracy. He was profoundly shocked by the numbers of eminent and educated people in the academic and the professional worlds who were ready to abandon this principle with hardly a thought. He compared it to the establishment backing for appeasement in the 1930s and quite likely suffered the same despair that Churchill admitted to when, despite all his efforts, he could not convince people of the approaching danger.

Jay's thoughts on the establishment conversion to 'Europe' differed from Shore's. Jay thought the loss of Empire couldn't account for the conversion. Similarly, he thought that economic difficulties and the supposed failure of the British economy were also not sufficient reason. As for the aim of preventing war ever happening in Europe again, he thought that that prospect was already outdated by the 1960s and 1970s. He referred to the "sentimental internationalism" of some who couldn't understand that the EEC was not just another international organisation. He called the "cold bath" idea, according to which competition within the EEC would improve the efficiency of British industry, "at best sheer nonsense, but at worst a dangerous delusion", and simply a propaganda argument.

Jay arrived at his reasons for rejecting the arguments recounted above by rationally analysing the situation. But was anyone else reasoning rationally?

For Jay, the conversion of the establishment was based on three motivating factors. He believed that the Conservative Party, the City and business circles saw the prospect of lucrative profits arising from the Common Agricultural Policy if Britain were to enter. He believed the Conservative Party wanted to turn the clock back on income redistribution by increasing indirect taxes on the less well-off; that employers would be able to squeeze labour and clamp down on strikes; and that the freedom of movement of capital promised by the Treaty of Rome also dangled the prospect of profits before international companies.

He, like many today, believed that the enterprise of European Union served, intentionally or unintentionally, to reverse the movement to universal suffrage begun in the 1832 Reform Act. That was implicit in what he called the "almost frenzied passion of the Foreign Office after 1966 for joining the EEC at any cost". This positive obsession would lead to immense prospects for the Foreign Office bureaucracy. It would be able to indulge in departmental empire-building and a huge increase of jobs and perks, if power were transferred to Brussels:

> *This sudden prospect of greatly enhanced departmental influence helps to explain, I believe, the almost unanimous conversion of the FO in the mid-1960s, and the emotional intensity with which it pursued the aim of membership at any cost. The issue of parliamentary sovereignty and the rights of the electorate seem to have meant almost nothing to the FO at all.*

Jay's view of the establishment closing ranks contains many parallels with the story set out later in this book. Comparing the years of appeasement and the Common Market issue he said that, in both cases:

> *One encountered a stifling orthodoxy; mysterious unanimity in the press (worse in the later case); a closing of ranks by the City, the publicity industry and the Conservative Party; a stampede of trimmers and wobblers onto the side of intellectual fashion; and a strong distaste by the big battalions for rational argument.*

Jay witnessed a famous October 1962 conference speech, on Britain and the Common Market, by Hugh Gaitskell, Leader of the Labour Party at the time. It was in that conference speech that Gaitskell made his remark about the end of a thousand years of history, but there is another part to the speech which would be understood by many today:

> *We are now being told that the British people are not capable of judging this issue – the top people are the only*

> *people who understand it. This is the classic argument of*
> *every tyranny in history. It begins as a refined intellectual*
> *argument and it moves into a one-man dictatorship. We did*
> *not win the political battles of the nineteenth and twentieth*
> *centuries to have this reactionary nonsense thrust upon us*
> *again.*

A remarkable document was released in 2002 under the 30-year rule. Foreign and Commonwealth Office (FCO) 30/1048 reads like a sophisticated suicide note. Titled "Sovereignty and the European Communities" it discusses the concept of sovereignty in rarefied terms appropriate to abstract academic study, concluding that, after all, it doesn't really mean very much in practice. The document reads like a gathering conspiracy to cajole and deceive the people into the path of self-destruction that the political elite had now fully hatched.

While stating that the British Parliament could, in principle, pass an Act taking the country out of the EEC, and asserting that Parliament, though it had delegated power to an external legislature, was still sovereign, it noted that "the loss of external sovereignty will however increase as the Community develops, according to the intention of the preamble to the Treaty of Rome", to "establish the foundations of an ever closer union among the European peoples".

In later sections, the document discusses public opinion, or "popular concern" as it terms it, somewhat dismissively. Concerns about national identity were to do with the British people being deeply conscious through tradition and upbringing of the distinctive fact of being British. But, foreshadowing later slanders, it refers to "another, less attractive" aspect of national pride – that many people disliked and mistrusted foreigners.

FCO 30/1048 at least admitted that entry to the Community would mean major change and loss of sovereignty, which latter phrase it put in inverted commas as though to suggest that this was an exaggerated popular concern. It thought that the phrase conjured up a "spectre of major and uncontrollable change and of adjustments that will have to be made which are deeply disturbing". It demoted the issue of loss of sovereignty to a simple fear of change and the unknown on the part of the public. The British people were also sadly misinformed about their status in the world – Britain was now no more than a middle-ranking power. The idea that it could do just as it liked in international affairs was mere illusion.

The study frankly concluded that entry into the European Communities would mean opting for a system of remote and "deeply strange" bureaucracy. Despite this, it would be in the British interest to develop the Community in the direction of a harmonised economic, fiscal and monetary system and towards a common foreign and defence policy. This would lead to a situation whereby, "by the end of the century, with effective defence and political harmonisation, the erosion of the international role of the member states could be almost complete". But this retreat into the status of a mere province of a fully integrated European political union was in the "major interests" of the country.

The document looked in more detail at this possible development and effectively declared that parliamentary sovereignty and national independence would have disappeared by 2000: "even with the most dramatic development of the Community, the major member states can hardly lose the 'last resort' ability to withdraw in much less than three decades". A prestigious and directly-elected European Parliament, which the paper said Britain should campaign for, would mean a weakening of the British Parliament and the erosion of its sovereignty. If the point was ever reached where Britain had lost the ability to renounce the Treaty then "sovereignty, external, parliamentary and practical would indeed be diminished". Diminished seems something of an understatement.

In this state of bureaucracy and declining democracy, the paper thought that political parties would have to avoid exacerbating public concern "by attributing unpopular measures or unfavourable economic developments to the remote and unmanageable workings of the Community". Finally, it would be necessary to set up a smokescreen to hide the loss of democracy that would occur:

> The transfer of major executive responsibilities to the bureaucratic Commission in Brussels will exacerbate popular feeling of alienation from government. To counter this feeling, strengthened local and regional democratic

> *processes within the member states and effective Community*
> *regional economic and social policies will be essential.*

Thus did the officials plan the end of their country's independence.

In the 1970 General Election, the Conservative Party Manifesto promised that "our sole commitment is to negotiate; no more and no less". Jay says that everyone at the time understood this to mean that, if negotiation was successful, a new mandate would be sought to actually sign the Accession Treaty. It was what Jay and others in the anti-Marketeers group had campaigned for: a mandate from the electorate, either in the form of a referendum or through a fresh General Election. At the same time, Edward Heath promised that he would only take Britain into the Common Market if he had the "full-hearted consent of Parliament and people".

When the negotiations were felt to be heading for a successful conclusion, a cynical government campaign set out to covertly influence public opinion in favour of UK entry into the EEC. The purpose was not to guarantee the outcome of a referendum – no referendum was granted on the issue of entry – but to indirectly convince MPs to vote 'yes' when the time came in the House of Commons. Shore said that "the normal standards of political and public service behaviour, of ministers, MPs, broadcasters and civil servants collapsed and were abandoned when government and people were faced with what was and remains the greatest single issue in our post-war history".

FCO document 26/1215 of February 1972 was written at the request of Anthony Royle, Parliamentary Under Secretary of State at the FCO, whose idea the campaign was. William Whitelaw, Lord President of the Council, was its main recipient, as he had had overall direction of the campaign. It is an account, classified secret and entitled "Approach to Europe 1970/71", of the clandestine collusion of the FCO, the British Council of the European Movement, the Federal Trust, the Confederation of British Industry (CBI), sympathetic Labour and Conservative MPs, including Conservative Central Office, and others, to persuade the public to back British entry into the Common Market. The document explains how the FCO and its

Information Research Department (IRD), established in 1948 to disseminate anti-Communist propaganda, set out to accomplish their task. It describes how, within days of the formation of the new Conservative government, FCO ministers realised that British public opinion had to be swung round and that "all the resources of the information machine should be brought into play". To this end, the FCO and the IRD began to concentrate on domestic opinion and to form links with the British Council of the European Movement (BCEM) and other pro-Common Market organisations.

The two-phase campaign consisted of an unofficial campaign from late 1969 to July 1971 and then an official phase from July 1971 to the first Parliamentary vote in October 1971. The aim was to "develop British press, radio and television contacts with a view to influencing them and encouraging them to use our publicity material". But this work would have to be "extremely discreet", in the form of unattributable support for "non-official" people. An open attack on public opinion by the FCO would not be helpful.

In late 1969 and early 1970, the FCO established a European Communities' Information Unit (ECIU) to deal with the propaganda effort abroad. In September 1970, Royle himself proposed a domestic public relations program. The ECIU was expanded to take on that domestic propaganda campaign along with the IRD. Royle says that at this time the ground was prepared "by the European Movement in consultation with FCO departments". A huge Ministerial speaking campaign throughout the country was put into place and Royle and Geoffrey Rippon, Prime Minister Heath's principal negotiator in the entry negotiations, gave unattributable briefings to senior editors and journalists in the provincial press, 'an exercise which had an excellent impact'. The European Movement also dramatically increased its speaking program. By the beginning of 1971, it was supplying 80 speakers a month in London alone. Speakers were provided to women's conferences and conferences of the trade unions and industrialists. The Federal Trust organised its own conferences in favour of British entry.

The ECIU made the media a prime target of its efforts, providing briefings to journalists to stimulate "favourable press comment on our application" and maintaining regular contact between itself and the producers of major current affairs programmes on radio and television. The FCO document singles out Peter Shore, Douglas Jay, and Neil Marten (a leading Conservative anti-Marketeer) for their media appearances: they had mounted a "heterogenous but effective campaign in the country and in Parliament against membership of the European Communities in principle".

More well-known, perhaps, are the so-called 'media breakfasts' where politicians, the media, pro-Marketeers, government and other interests, had weekly breakfast meetings at the Connaught Hotel. The breakfasts were the idea of Geoffrey Tucker and James Garrett, public relations advisers to the campaign. Royle's description of the campaign says that the breakfasts were an invaluable addition to the official coordinating organisation. Apart from Royle and Rippon, the core group included the head of Conservative Central Office and the Director of the BCEM. Other attendees included the Managing Directors of BBC Radio and ITN television; the Head of Current Affairs at BBC TV; the editor of the *Economist* magazine; and representatives from the Labour and Liberal parties.

The Connaught breakfasts were one of the subjects explored in an edition of the Radio 4 program *Document* in February 2000. Entitled "A Letter to the Times" for that edition, the program interviewed Geoffrey Tucker, Richard Aldrich and Sir Edward Heath, among others. The interviewer, Christopher Cook, read from Tucker's 1970 campaign plan: "nobbling is the name of the game. Throughout the period of the campaign there should be direct day-to-day communication between the key communicators and our personnel e.g. the FCO and Marshall Stewart of the *Today* program". "A Letter to the Times" revealed that Tucker succeeded in getting an extra five minutes added to the ITN evening news to explain EEC matters. Talking of the *Today* program, Tucker said the presenter at the time, Jack de Manio, "was terribly anti-European and we protested privately about this and he was moved...Ian Trethowan listened and de Manio was replaced". The interviewer pointed out that Trethowan, the Managing Director of BBC Radio, was a known friend of Edward Heath.

The regional press provided 'substantial and favourable

coverage' right through the campaign but it seems that television coverage in the final stages was dropping off. Southern and Granada TV had 'accepted assistance and mounted a useful series of interviews with local industries'. Scottish TV 'accepted pressure to do generally more than they had hitherto'. FCO 26/1215 notes that the German Embassy, in a careful assessment, judged that radio and television output in August was "contributing importantly and favourably".

The government campaign also included 1,000 visits a year from other European countries and an annual subvention of £7,500 to the European Movement (about £70,000 today). The latter asked its corporate members to include an EEC element in their advertising. The *Times* and British Leyland were two who obliged. The IRD kept up a steady stream of letters and articles to the press, in close concert with the European Movement, and the latter provided speakers and material for schools.

Anthony Royle noted with satisfaction that the campaign had only cost the government £461,400 and the British Council of the European Movement £250,000.

When Edward Heath left office in 1974, Royle was knighted, presumably for his services to the country.

But, according to Jay, this was not the only propaganda offensive going on. He claimed in his book that the European Communities Information Service (ECIS) had been at work since at least 1964 with an even larger budget. Starting with £1million in 1964, ECIS had ramped up its expenditure to £3million by 1971 and to £7million by 1975. Of this total, for the whole of the EEC, Jay says that about one third was spent in Britain, thus implying that the ECIS expenditure in Britain in the year of the debate on British entry was about £1million. Noting that in any earlier period it would have been considered "grossly improper" for such large amounts of political propaganda to be financed from abroad, he says that it was spent not only on leaflets and pamphlets but also on hospitality, visits, tours and free holidays to anyone considered in Brussels to be an opinion-former on the British political scene: journalists, officials, industrialists, trade unionists. He even claimed that secret "retaining fees" were paid to selected individuals.

And, again according to Jay, there was more. He records that the expenditure of the European Movement increased from

£41,000 in 1969-1970 to £105,650 in 1970-1971 and then to almost £645,000 in 1971-1972. The income of the Movement in that same year was almost £916,000, drawn from big firms, banks and wealthy individuals. Against this, his own organisation, the Common Market Safeguards Campaign, had at most £20,000 to spend in 1971.

FCO 26/1215 contains two remarkable graphs. The first shows the results of public opinion polls between February and August 1971 on the question of whether Britain should join the EEC. In March, public opinion was something like 70 per cent against and 20 per cent in favour. As the government propaganda campaign intensified throughout the Spring and the Summer the opinion polls began to shift dramatically. The 'no's began a steep decline and the 'yes's began an equally steep climb. By August they were at parity.

Was this the rightful result of a far-sighted government convincing its people of the merits of its case? No. The second graph shows what happened after August. Just as the 'no's and the 'yes's had dramatically converged to parity so, after August, they separated again, so that, by mid-October, when the Parliamentary vote took place, the 'no's stood at 47 per cent and the 'yes's at 32 per cent.

This was not 'full-hearted consent'. It was a blip engineered by a covert campaign of disinformation.

The six-day debate on the First Reading of the Bill to join the EEC ended in a majority of 112 for the motion. But this was not the decisive vote, the vote that would legally approve the Treaty of Accession. Further, no Treaty had been available for MPs to inspect. Indeed, the Treaty was only published a few days after it was signed by Edward Heath in January 1972. When the Bill came up for its Second Reading on the 15th February it consisted of a mere twelve clauses which declared that all past and future EEC legislation would have legal force in Britain. Jay called it a "legal conjuring trick": there would be no detailed consideration of each and every individual item of legislation that the Accession Treaty would bring in. When the vote came on the 17th February, the majority in favour was just eight: 309 to 301. At the final stage, the Third Reading in July, the majority was seventeen. Jay records that it then went to the House of Lords, that "historic defender of the British Constitution" and was passed "with platitudes in plenty but not a single amendment".

The Labour Party was elected to government in February 1974 and Harold Wilson, the Prime Minister of the time, ordered renegotiations on the terms of Britain's membership. James Callaghan, Foreign Secretary, had operational control.

By October of 1973, the opinion polls showed approval of British membership of the EEC at around 35 per cent compared to around 53 per cent who disapproved. But the story of 1971-1972 was to repeat itself – in more than one way.

Peter Shore, Douglas Jay, Neil Marten, Enoch Powell and others threw themselves again into the fight, this time as the official 'no' campaign. The European Movement, under the banner "Britain in Europe" were the official 'yes' campaign. Both sides received £125,000 of public money for their campaigns. But Britain in Europe raised £996,000 from donations and the National Referendum Campaign only £8,600. Also, as recounted above, the European Communities Information Service spent a round £2million on its propaganda eff o rt. The 'yes' side included almost all the media, both main political parties, and the government machine. Jay said that the 'yes' campaign succeeded in mounting a "deafening propaganda barrage".

But this was not the only way that the 1975 referendum campaign was similar to the 1971 covert effort. Once again, according to files released to the public in December 2005 and not to my knowledge so far reported on elsewhere, government mounted a campaign to change public opinion though, in fairness, the campaign of 1975 was less mendacious than that of 1971 and most of it was in the open. Within the Cabinet Office, a Referendum Information Unit (RIU) was set up to provide, so it was said, "factual information" to the public but also with the remit, much criticised in Parliament and the media by the anti-Marketeers' side, to provide the government's 'interpretation' of the renegotiations and general issues to do with the EEC. During the course of the campaign, the RIU spoke to national and local newspapers, television stations, national and local radio, political parties and organisations, private companies, magazines, foreign media, and MPs. On this occasion, however, it seems that these contacts were through the organisations and individuals approaching the RIU themselves, rather than through an active campaign attempting to influence opinion. The RIU produced weekly internal reports summarising media debate on the forthcoming referendum, even counting the number of column inches of newspaper coverage devoted to the various issues.

Within the FCO, a separate Referendum Unit was established which had 'propaganda' as one of the three items in its remit. However, at least according to the files released in 2005, the unit had minimal contact with the media or other organisations and no instruction to do so. It seems to have mainly fought for the FCO's desire that the government should actively press the case for a 'yes' vote – what it called the "third voice" of the campaign, as compared to the official 'no' and 'yes' campaigns. As in 1971, the FCO's effort was in close consultation with Britain in Europe and, this time, the Labour Committee for Europe.

But, separately from the 1975 documents, there is a hint also of continued CIA interest in the relationship of Britain and Europe. In 1975 Richard Body, a Conservative MP who worked with Jay, Shore et al, was joint Chairman of the Keep Britain Out campaign. Body says that in 1975 two Americans came to see him, bearing a large bundle of papers. The Americans said that they were CIA agents who were upset that their agency was going to interfere in the referendum campaign – "they said that a new head of station was going to be appointed who was not a normal CIA man. He was very well-known in the federalist movement and they (CIA) were going to intervene in different ways and they produced a substantial number of documents to verify what they were saying". The new head of the CIA London station was to be Cord Meyer Jnr, who had been a founder of the United World Federalists organisation in 1947. Body tried to publicise this information at the time but no newspaper took up the story. The only publication to print the story was the then new London *Time Out* magazine, which had a very small circulation. Body gave up talking about the episode.

By April 1974, when the renegotiation began, the opinion polls showed approval of membership steadily climbing and disapproval rapidly dropping. By October, the two lines of the graph crossed each other. When asked a modified poll question – "should Britain stay in the EEC" – after the campaign proper began, the 'yes' line rocketed up to over 60 per cent while the 'no' slumped to under 30 per cent. The referendum result was 17,378,000 in favour of continued membership (67 per cent) and

8,470,000 against (33 per cent).

In my opinion there are only two possibilities: either the massive propaganda spend of the 'yes' side successfully, and massively, swayed public opinion or, when the time came for people to focus on the question and make up their minds, they decided to vote for the status quo, perhaps now fearful of 'going it alone'.

Apart from a few lone voices, the issue then disappeared into obscurity, except for a few minor skirmishes at the time of the Single European Act of 1986, until Margaret Thatcher's speech in Bruges. By that time, the increasing powers of the EEC had begun to push the subject back into the public domain. At the time of accession the powers of the EEC, its influence on internal British politics, were minimal. By the time of the Bruges speech, EEC influence was becoming significant. In the words of Lord Denning, a former Master of the Rolls, commenting on European legislation in 1990:

> No longer is European law an incoming tide flowing up the estuaries of England. It is now like a tidal wave bringing down our sea walls and flowing inland over our fields and houses – to the dismay of all.

The Bruges speech reignited the question of Britain's relationship with the EEC and marked the beginning of a new phase in that relationship. Out of the Bruges speech came the Bruges Group, a forum for politicians and academics who profoundly disagreed with the federalist project. From the Bruges Group, as a splinter organisation, emerged the Anti-Federalist League. After two years the Anti-Federalist League renamed itself as the UK Independence Party. This book places the history of the party in a line of development that began in Bruges in 1988 and which is still unfolding today.

2

Born at Bruges

The Bruges Group

The Bruges Group was launched on the 8th February 1989. Its members were mainly academics and supporters of Margaret Thatcher and her economic and European policies. Lord Harris of High Cross, who was also chairman of the Institute of Economic Affairs, was Chairman of the group. Margaret Thatcher was its first president. It had an Academic Advisory Council that included Alan Sked, senior lecturer in international history and convener of European studies at the London School of Economics[†].

Its founder was Patrick Robertson, a 20-year old student of modern history at Keble College, Oxford, who, having heard Lord Harris speak at the Oxford Union, persuaded him to become chairman of the group, although Robertson had been considering launching such a group even before the Bruges speech. Quoted in the *Times* on the day after the launch, Robertson said that if the Community stuck to its original intentions of creating a single European market it would be "a power for good that no-one could reasonably quarrel with". But he warned that political integration was creeping up the agenda and that most people were unaware of the dangers. The Bruges Group, he said, wanted to start a national debate and ensure that the electorate could make its wishes clear.

[†]Brian Hindley, senior lecturer in economics at the London School of Economics (LSE), and Professor Kenneth Minogue, also of the LSE, were the two Vice-Chairmen. Patrick Robertson, the founder of the group, was its Secretary. Its Academic Advisory Council also included Norman Stone, professor of modern history at Oxford; Martin Holmes, senior visiting research fellow at Mansfield College, Oxford; and Patrick Minford, professor of economics at the University of Liverpool.

At the age of 12, Robertson had told his mother that he wanted to be a politician (she cried). A member of the Bruges Group later said that Robertson was too idealistic for that path. He also had a characteristic to be found in some other committed Eurosceptics – the experience of looking at their own country from abroad for a number of years. Born in Edinburgh, he moved with his family to France and Italy when he was young. He spent some years in Rome before being sent to Dulwich College at the age of 12.

After four years there he switched to Kingston College of Further Education and then went on to read modern history at Oxford. But after only a year there he became 'patriotic and het up' about European federalism. When he founded the Bruges Group, his family was still living in Italy and he had friends both there and in France. He once declared "my commitment to Europe is my life".

Alan Sked fitted the image of the genial don. He was born in Glasgow and was 41 when the Bruges Group was formed, was highly intelligent, with a cultured, almost establishment voice, and, at least a few years later, with a striking combination of white bouffant hair and blue eyes. He had followed a path of enthusiasm to exasperation on the European issue and was now passionate in his condemnation of the EEC, saying at around this time that "I was once a manic federalist but then my work convinced me it was ridiculous". Most of the members of the Bruges Group were from the right of politics, but Sked had a Liberal Party background. He joined the Scottish Young Liberals at the age of 14, later became President of the League of Scottish Liberal Students and stood as a Liberal candidate in Paisley when a postgraduate at Oxford.

The Bruges Group followed a two-pronged approach. Academic publications such as a series of pamphlets would take the intellectual road, while the group's members would also be public spokesmen for the group on television, radio, and at public meetings. Their concern was to highlight the way in which the EEC was taking on a much more political dimension in addition to the trade issues involved in the creation of the Single Market. Harris, elsewhere in the *Times* on the day of the group's launch, said that Thatcher's Bruges speech had broken the "conspiracy of silence" on the future of European cooperation. At last, he said, the debate was being joined in good time for the European parliament elections that were to be held a few months later. Harris said that the aim of the group was to "help inform voters' choice not only in Britain but on the Continent, where Mrs Thatcher's anxieties are more widely shared than may appear".

Sked was later to provoke a row with John Major, Prime Minister after 1989, after issuing a press release for the group asking whether "the overthrow of Mrs Thatcher [was] paid for with the blood of thousands of innocent Iraqis", a reference to what he saw as the resolute approach of Thatcher compared with the soft touch of Major over the massacre of the Kurds in northern Iraq after the Gulf War of 1991. Not content with that, he later criticised West Germany in a Bruges Group pamphlet entitled "Cheap Excuses" for its lack of action during the Iraq war, causing the West German embassy to deliver an official protest to the Foreign Office. On the European issue, Sked was less forthright in his views than he was to be later, saying that "we occupy the middle ground between federalists like Hugh Dykes and Edward Heath, and those like Teddy Taylor who want to come out".

The Bruges Group was not the first manifestation of opposition to the European project. In his book, "Euroscepticism in Contemporary British Politics", Anthony Forster relates the history of the 'anti-Marketeers' group which existed before 1988, and indeed the story of opposition from 1945, but shows that the Bruges speech brought into existence a new generation of opponents under the name "Eurosceptics". This analysis, of the old and the new phases of British opposition to the European project, is widely held. Writing for *Collegium*, the academic publication of the College of Europe, where Thatcher made the Bruges speech, Simon Usherwood agreed that the Bruges Group was amongst 'the very first of the current wave of anti-EU groups that sprang up in the late 1980s and 1990s'.

The group developed a parliamentary counterpart, the Friends of Bruges Group, whose first chairman was Bill Cash MP. This group had, by 1990, around 100 MPs as members. Forster says that it was seen by many as "an embryonic party within a party" and that, with financial support from Sir James Goldsmith, who would later found the Referendum Party, it had a turnover of £100,000. Cash explained in the *Times* in March 1989 that the group would describe themselves as "pro-European antifederalists" and that they believed that they were fighting "one of the most serious battles of twentieth-century politics, supporting the Prime Minister and the party in checking the spread of federalism and socialism throughout the EEC".

One of the ways in which the Friends of Bruges proposed to do this was to disseminate information to others in the Conservative Party, believing that backbenchers and even some ministers still didn't understand the extent of EEC influence on domestic policy.

The same *Times* article reported that the Bruges Group intended to set up Belgian and French counterparts, with Alain Madelin to be present at the inaugural meeting in Belgium. Madelin later stood as a candidate for the French presidency in 2002 on what was described as a Thatcherite free-market platform.

The group began a campaign in July 1990 to limit the powers of the European Court of Justice (ECJ). Lord Denning, former Master of the Rolls, and Roger Knapman, Vice-Chairman of the Conservative European Affairs Committee, were supporters of the campaign. It followed the decision of the ECJ in the Factortame case involving the 1988 Merchant Shipping Act. The Act had attempted to prevent Spanish fishermen registered in the UK from using British fishing quotas. The ECJ ruled that this was contrary to EU law on the freedom of businesses to establish themselves anywhere in the Community. It was one of the most high-profile demonstrations of the power of the European institutions to strike down British Acts of Parliament.

Roger Knapman was later a Conservative whip but subsequently joined the UK Independence Party in May 2000 and became its Leader in October 2002. Knapman noted ironically "I wonder if we are not just sitting here every day, making laws until the European Court decides to overrule them. In the light of that ruling, and the Single European Act, what exactly is the state of our sovereignty?" Sked wrote a pamphlet for the Bruges Group in March 1992 entitled "Time For Principle", the last paragraph of which condemned Prime Minister John Major and his Foreign Secretary, Douglas Hurd, for betrayal at Maastricht:

> *The Maastricht Treaty, therefore, about which Britain's political leaders are strangely silent in an election year, would, if ratified, very quickly not only undermine our*

*parliamentary democracy, but would in the course of a few
years set the seal on Britain's history as an independent
country and make us a province on the periphery of a
European unitary state with superpower pretensions. In
negotiating and signing such a document, I contend that
John Major and Douglas Hurd have betrayed not merely
their principles but their country's vital national interests.*

The new 'Eurosceptic' phase of opposition was to be more
virulent than that before, now that the consequences of Britain's
membership of the EEC were becoming clearer, now that the
deceptions of those involved fifteen years before were starting to
reap their inevitable harvest: a backlash against and an alienation
from a political system that had led them astray. Perhaps the
politicians of the seventies thought that, no matter what, the thing
to do was to get in. Any problems could be smoothed over
afterwards and it would all no doubt be manageable. The story
related in this book suggests that this was a historic mistake.
Forster, in his examination of the years 1979 to 1990, says:

*Opposition to European integration in the period before
1988 remained an elite concern, confined to Parliament with
the exception of the European parliament elections of 1979
and 1984 when the issues managed temporarily to break out
of the Westminster arena and engage the general public.*

After 1988, opposition took root outside Westminster and
away from the realms of the elite.

Maastricht And The Establishment Parties

Whereas the Bruges speech, with the Maastricht Treaty in the
background, marked the beginning of a new phase of
Euroscepticism, the arrival of the treaty in the House of
Commons marked the point at which federalist and antifederalist
sides came to real battle in the new phase of opposition.

It is not the aim of this section to recount in detail the passage
of the Maastricht Treaty through the Houses of Parliament. What
is relevant for this history is that none of the establishment parties
represented the views of those many people who disagreed

entirely with the principle of the treaty. The Conservative government negotiated the treaty and pushed it ruthlessly through Parliament, using strong-arm tactics culminating in the ultimate option of calling for a vote of confidence. The Labour opposition was, in fact, broadly in favour of the treaty and only argued against the Bill because the Social Chapter, setting out wide-ranging measures in the area of employment and social policies, had been relegated to a separate protocol to which Britain was not a signatory. Their decision to oppose the Bill was also motivated by a desire to create trouble for the government in the parliamentary debates. The Liberal Democrats were equally, if not more enthusiastic, with their Leader, Paddy Ashdown, predicting that the importance of the nation state would decline in the years to come. There was no party opposing the treaty as a matter of principle.

Opposition within the Labour Party was in some ways greater than in the Conservative Party. The Labour Euro Safeguards Committee claimed in 1990 that just under a quarter of Labour's 270 MPs were members. In the second reading of the Maastricht Bill, 61 Labour MPs voted against, despite the Opposition's official decision to abstain. At the third reading, with the Opposition again having officially decided to abstain, 66 Labour MPs voted against the Bill.

In the Conservative Party, the number of rebels was smaller but the issue caused far greater dissension because the government majority was only 21 and the hard-core rebels numbered about the same. At the second reading 22 Conservative MPs voted against their party line and 23 voted against a paving motion allowing the Bill to go to the committee stage. At the third reading 41 rebelled. In the final vote of the 18-month passage of the Bill through the House of Commons and the House of Lords, when Major turned the issue into a vote of confidence in his government, no Conservative MP voted against and only one, Rupert Allason, abstained. Rather unfairly, perhaps, Allason subsequently lost his seat at the 1997 General Election, arguably due to the presence of a UKIP candidate.

The official attitudes of the three main parties during the passage of the Maastricht Bill through parliament, in the European Communities (Amendment) Bill, are illustrated by the statements below, taken from the debate on the Bill during the second reading on the 20th and 21st May 1992.

Introducing the Bill, the Prime Minister made claims which are difficult to agree with, given events since then. The Maastricht Treaty, he said, marked the point at which Britain had begun to reverse the "centralising trend". Decision-taking had been moved back to the member states. A legally binding agreement had been reached on subsidiarity – the concept by which the Community would only act when Community actions were truly necessary.

Continuing with his theme, Major sought to allay fears about increasing moves towards a federal Europe:

> They fear that the institutions of the Community will increase their powers step by step so that, in the end, we create what we understand by a federal Europe: a strong, central Government in Brussels with some powers devolved to the individual nation state. I understand those fears, but that is not the route foreshadowed by the Maastricht Treaty.

Not long after the treaty was approved, the Commission proposed a directive limiting the maximum number of hours in the working week. Major claimed that Britain was exempt because of its opt-out from the Social Chapter. But in 1996, the European Court of Justice ruled that the Working Time Directive could be introduced under article 118 of the Maastricht Treaty, thereby circumventing the British opt-out. This caused Major, on the day of the judgment, to write to Commission President Jacques Santer, complaining that the ECJ was taking too broad a view of the scope of the article. In terms indicating a sense of betrayal, he said that:

> This is contrary to the clear and express wishes of the United Kingdom Government, and goes directly counter to the spirit of what we agreed at Maastricht. It is unacceptable and must be remedied.

It was not remedied – so much for subsidiarity.

In the second reading debate Major went on to say that "the old tendency among some of our partners to think that action by the Community was always the answer is diminishing". Speaking for the opposition in the debate, Neil Kinnock presented a characteristically verbose amendment to the main motion. Kinnock declared his party's support for the treaty:

> *The Labour Party has already made it clear that it broadly supports the treaty concluded at Maastricht because it is a necessary framework for the economic, social and political development of the European Community.*

But, in line with his amendment objecting to the opt-outs from the single currency and the Social Chapter he said that:

> *We cannot, however, extend that support to the Bill. We cannot endorse the Government's action in opting out from the agreements made by the eleven other European Community member countries on social policy and on the approach to economic and monetary union. Both of those decisions by the Government will disadvantage the British people. The social policy opt-out would be reason enough by itself to justify refusal to support the Bill.*

Paddy Ashdown, presenting the Liberal Democrat position, made his party's commitment to all things European plain and, replying to a comment by Peter Shore, said "he believes in the eternal utility of the concept of the nation state. Frankly, I do not". Responding to veteran Labour politician Tony Benn's restatement of the case that the electorate should always have the power to change their rulers, Ashdown, supposedly a liberal and a democrat, said:

> *The Right Hon. Gentleman is right that the Maastricht Treaty fails to provide such democratic accountability for the European institutions that it creates. Despite that deficiency, we shall vote in favour of the Bill.*

The Anti-Federalist League

In November 1991 Alan Sked, having come to believe that the fightback against federalism could most effectively be carried on by providing a vehicle for which people could vote in elections.

Sked left the Bruges Group and with a small number of sympathisers founded the Anti-Federalist League. The fledgling group recruited around 150 members from a letter that Sked sent to all members of the Bruges Group on the 3rd November. The letter said that the aim of the League should be to sponsor parliamentary candidates at the General Election in 1992 if none of the major parties opposed European political and economic union. The Manifesto of the League would call for a halt to further integration; proper accountability to national parliaments; a veto on the Maastricht Treaty; and a self-governing Britain rather than Britain as a province of a European superstate. The League would have to exert as much political pressure on the government as possible before the government surrendered British independence – John Major would have to be shown that "to sign at Maastricht will entail political suicide for him and his party".

Sked's departure from the Bruges Group was not amicable and followed his issue of the press release, mentioned above, criticising John Major's actions in the Gulf War. Kenneth Minogue, Chairman of the group, accused Sked of being an embarrassment to the Prime Minister.

In the April 1992 General Election the League put up 16 candidates, gaining only 5,007 votes – 0.55 per cent of the votes cast in those constituencies. Candidates included Sked, Helen Szamuely, Tony Scholefield, Sue Nelson, and Peter Compobassi. Results ranged from Martin Howson's 2,121 (3.4 per cent) in Staffordshire Moorlands to Helen Szamuely's 41 in Hammersmith.

After the election, Sked called together those who had been active in the campaign[†]. A National Executive Committee (NEC) was formed with Sked as Leader[††].

[†]These included Helen Szamuely, Tony Scholefield, Gerard Batten, Peter Compobassi, David Wilkinson, John Harvey, Hugh Moelwyn-Hughes, Nigel Farage and Gerald Roberts.

[††]Batten was Secretary and Moelwyn-Hughes was Membership Secretary.

Alan Sked's Newbury by-election poster 1993

UK Independence Party 1996 National Conference

The League made organisation for the 1994 European Elections its main objective while also deciding to contest by-elections. For the European Elections a target of £250,000 in funds was set in order to provide a candidate in every constituency. The League also turned its attention to setting up regional and local branches, settled upon the principle of not taking up any seats that might be won in the European Elections, and debated whether its platform should be extended to other policy areas or whether it should continue with its central policy alone. These issues were discussed at a meeting of the League at the London School of Economics on the 22nd May 1992. Sir Richard Body, Conservative MP for Holland with Boston, spoke in the latter, public half of the meeting. Attempts were made to bring in a speaker from the Labour Party but these were not successful.

The League, like its successor, had an internationalist outlook rather than the 'Little Englander' mentality imputed to it by its opponents. A meeting of the 9th July was addressed by Knud and Luise Pedersen of the Danish Vote No Campaign. They spoke about their experiences in the Danish referendum on the Maastricht Treaty, where the result on the 2nd June was 49.3 per cent for and 50.7 per cent against.

Additionally, in a Newsletter to members in August, Sked set out the League's non-discrimination principle:

> We now have to seek the widest possible political base in this country. That means that we must look for members from whatever background. We do not care whether they have voted Labour, Liberal or Tory in the past; whether they are white, black, brown, or yellow; whether they are Christian, Jewish, Moslem or Buddhist; whether they are straight, gay, or somewhere in between.

Between the 1992 General Election and September 1993, when the League became the UK Independence Party, the former contested two by-elections. At Newbury in May 1993 Alan Sked took 601 votes (1.0 per cent), coming fourth out of nineteen candidates. At Christchurch the following month Sked took 878 votes (1.6 per cent), coming fourth out of fourteen candidates.

The UK Independence Party

The UK Independence Party was formed from the Anti-Federalist League at a Committee meeting of the League on the 2nd September 1993[†]. The Committee discussed fourteen possible names for the proposed party and eventually decided on its present name. At the first meeting of the new party on the 13th November 1993, at the London School of Economics, the new Executive Committee[††] discussed the prospects of fighting the following year's European Elections and agreed a draft Constitution.

In January 1994 the party began publishing a bi-monthly Newsletter. In the first, Sked in an article, said that the party would contest as many seats as possible in the European Elections but that any seats won would not be taken up. This "empty seat" policy would be "a standing rebuke to the Eurofederalists" pretension to represent the British people. Maastricht is unconstitutional. The House of Commons cannot constitutionally deprive the British people of the authority to run their own affairs'.

Sked had reached independently the conclusion that many, including myself, had reached: none of the established parties, not even the Conservative Party, could be trusted on the European question. In my case, after watching the strong-arm tactics used by the Conservative whips to get Maastricht through parliament, I simply allowed my eight years of Conservative membership to lapse. The years of branch committee meetings in dowdy clubs, Executive Council meetings, Finance and General Purposes Committee meetings, and unofficial behind-the-scenes planning, slipped into the past. I abandoned a party which was betraying one of its key principles. So did several thousand others. This disillusionment and final decision to break away was reflected in the bitter words of Sked's article:

[†]Present were Gerard Batten, John Harvey, Hugh Moelwyn-Hughes, Gerald Roberts, Tony Scholefield, and Alan Sked. Nigel Farage sent apologies.

[††]The members of the new UKIP Executive Committee were Alan Sked, Helen Szamuely, Gerard Batten, John Harvey, Nigel Farage, Gerald Roberts, Hugh Moelwyn-Hughes, Ian Booth, Peter Compobassi, Nigel Greenwood, Melvyn Rendell, Tony Scholefield and David Wilkinson.

Speaking of other parties, the ratification of the Treaty by Tory leaders helped clarify matters enormously. There is now no point whatsoever in attempting to maintain Britain's independence through the Conservative Party. Nor can we rely on the so-called Eurosceptics within it. They could have brought down the government. They could have forced a General Election on the issue. Alas, they preferred to give their votes of confidence to Mr Major....If this country does become the province of a superstate, it will be because, when it came to the crunch, the Lady Thatchers, Lord Tebbits, Bill Cashs, Teddy Taylors, and all the rest of them, put the unity of the Conservative Party before the independence of their country. Let none of us make the same mistake.

Musing on "things to come", Sked was clear that the party would have a forward-looking ethos, something that its future critics would rarely be able to understand. As a historian, Sked knew that there was no rosy past to return to, just a hard slog for acceptance:

The press will want to know whether we are up to the task of setting the agenda for an independent Britain in the twenty-first century. So too will younger people who have absorbed the social changes of the last thirty years. Our programme will not therefore be one of turning the clock back to the 1950's or any other period in the mythical history of Merrie England. On the contrary, we shall have to develop policies which meet the challenges of tomorrow and we shall have to seek votes not merely from former Conservatives (this is not the Conservative rejects party) but from Labour and Liberal Party members and from anyone else who has a vote. This is a serious party and it will only deserve to be taken seriously if it can appeal to all sections of British society.

Both the individuals who were to stay longest in the leadership of the party and who were to most profoundly shape it were on board by the end of 1993. Nigel Farage helped Sked when the latter stood at the Newbury by-election, having met him at a public meeting about the Maastricht Treaty some time before.

David Lott read about the new party in the *Daily Mail*. Only two months into his retirement and with no experience of politics, a phone call to Sked was to take him into the role that was to dominate the next part of his life. Mark Daniel's "Cranks and Gadflies: The Story of UKIP" paints wry portraits of the personalities involved and what brought them together to form and fight as UKIP.

Nigel Farage

We were probably mostly, though not exclusively, ex-members of the Conservative Party. We believed in the right and the desirability of Britain governing its own affairs and could see that the Maastricht Treaty would severely compromise that right. We were, therefore, nationalists, in the sense that we believed that the nation-state was the right and natural unit for political expression. We were not nationalists in the pejorative sense that federalists and some on the left attach to the word. We were not anti-foreigner right-wingers, Sked least of all.

It was not the case, as is often claimed by some non-participants in politics, that we were looking for advancement or financial rewards. There is no place more desolate as regards these infrequent favours than a fledgling political party. The electorate is never more cynical than when receiving an advance from a newcomer on the political scene.

The 1994 European Elections

It is probable that the political establishment of the time was still largely unaware of UKIP and that, therefore, their decisions and manoeuvres were not affected by the party's existence. Nevertheless, there must have been some awareness of political pressure because, for example, in April the *Sunday Telegraph* allowed Alan Sked the platform of its centre-page political column to exhort the electorate to vote for the party in the European Elections. Additionally, a few days later, the *Times* also gave Sked a centre page article on the same theme and, in its editorial, opined that the question of Britain's membership of the EU was a "broken taboo". In the same edition of the newspaper there was a report that Prime Minister of the day, John Major, had ordered a toughening-up of the Conservative Party's European Elections Manifesto. We cannot know how much that decision was influenced by his party's own internal dynamics and how much by the existence of UKIP as a possible electoral threat. Most probably it was due to the former but, while politicians always deride the electoral prospects of smaller parties, they are always extremely sensitive to potential electoral threats.

In the context of requests for a referendum on the Maastricht Treaty, an issue that was the subject of the Campaign for a British Referendum while the treaty was going through Parliament, journalist Peter Riddell commented in the *Times* in May 1994 on the dislocation between the main parties' opinions and the opinions of voters. Riddell thought that there was a case for a referendum on Europe because none of the main parties reflected public opinion on the issue. The public had no real choice on Europe "apart from Alan Sked's UK Independence Party, and this has no chance of winning any seats". There was a genuine problem with this state of affairs and a referendum could be one way of resolving the issue, he thought.

Although the party subsequently (after the 1997 General Election) changed its approach to one of appealing to potential supporters in all parties, it initially concentrated on trying to win over supporters in the Conservative Party, as reported by the

Times later in May – "The nine-month old UK Independence Party, led by history lecturer Alan Sked, yesterday launched its anti-Brussels European election campaign with a call to disillusioned Conservatives to switch their allegiance".

UKIP was, according to a *Times* article just before the election, one of the "flights of fantasy on (the) fringe", grouped along with the Natural Law Party and four Raving Loonies among the 554 candidates from 65 parties contesting the elections. However, with candidates in more than an eighth of the seats, the party was eligible for a five-minute party political broadcast. The paper admitted that, for various reasons, many Conservative voters would abstain. Others would vote for opposition parties as a protest but would feel uncomfortable about electing candidates who were even more enthusiastic about Europe. Some voters might even "cast a quixotic vote for the UK Independence Party" because it was the only party in tune with their views. Altogether, many voters would feel deprived of a real choice in the election the following day.

We presented candidates in 24 of the 87 constituencies of the 1994 European parliament elections. Our platform was a simple one of opposition to continued British membership of the EU and a pledge not to take up any seats won. Sked's April article in the *Sunday Telegraph* told readers that the party refused to recognise the legitimacy of the European Union. Its principal aim was to repeal the Maastricht and Rome treaties and, as this could only be done through the Westminster parliament, its strategy must be to win a majority there. There was no case "in principle or practice for taking up seats at Strasbourg".

The Anti-Federalist League's commitment to all British citizens was carried over into the new party. The membership application form stated that "the UKIP is a non-sectarian, non-racist body with no prejudices against foreigners or lawful minorities of any kind" and the party's Constitution had an entrenched non-discrimination principle. Membership was open to non-British residents who shared the party's aims.

We gained 155,487 votes, 3.3 per cent of the vote in the seats where our candidates stood, and another 16 antifederalist candidates averaged 3.5 per cent where they stood. In four constituencies there were two anti-federalist candidates. Our votes were typically 5,000-6,000 in Euro-election constituencies of around 500,000 voters on a turnout of about 37 per cent. As a sign of electoral success to come, however, Nigel Farage took 12,423 votes in Itchen, Test and Avon, out of an electorate of 550,000.

Four by-elections were held on the same day as the European Elections. At Barking, Gerard Batten gained 406 votes (2.1 per cent), coming fifth out of six. At Dagenham, Peter Compobassi gained 457 votes (2.1 per cent), again fifth out of six. At Newham North East, Tony Scholefield gained 509 votes (2.6 per cent), fourth out of seven. At Eastleigh, Nigel Farage gained 952 votes (1.7 per cent), fourth out of six.

After the lull in politics during the rest of the summer the taboo referred to by the *Times* was explicitly broken by Norman Lamont, Chancellor of the Exchequer when Britain left the European Exchange Rate Mechanism (ERM) on 'Black Wednesday', 16th September 1992, who was reported to have sung in his bath after the event. At a fringe meeting of the Conservative Party conference in October, Lamont was blunt:

> *I suspect that I am not alone at having been surprised at how our membership of the European Union has turned out. We seem to have joined a club very different from that which we had in mind in the early 1970s. The forces for political integration have proved far stronger than was foreseen. We deceive the British people and we deceive ourselves if we claim that we are winning the argument in Europe. There is no argument in Europe. There is Britain's point of view and there is the rest of Europe. The only question at Maastricht was how much Britain could swallow and what special arrangements could be made for us. There is not a shred of evidence at Maastricht or since that anyone accepts our view of Europe.*

And then, perhaps thinking of his role in the fiasco of Britain's exit from the ERM, when interest rates were briefly hiked to 15 per cent in a desperate attempt to defend sterling's membership of the mechanism and billions of pounds were lost in the foreign exchange markets, he said:

Today, when we come to examine the advantages of our membership of the EU, they are remarkably elusive. As a former Chancellor, I can only say that I cannot pinpoint a single concrete economic advantage that unambiguously comes to this country because of our membership.

3

Building a Nationwide Party
1994 to 1997

Grass Roots Rising

The 1994 European Elections, though their outcome was modest
for the party, acted as a catalyst for our formation. Membership
increased to around 3,000 and, by August 1994 we had offices,
though rather cramped, at 80 Regent Street, at the top of premises
occupied by Tony Scholefield, who became manager of the office.
The Executive Committee[†] included David Wilkinson. Wilkinson
was tasked with setting up party branches throughout the
country, through the rather grandly-termed Branch Liaison
Department in Wallingford in Oxfordshire. It was through
David's persistence that I re-entered the world of politics,
knowing only too well what demands it would make. In
September we formed the Oxford branch of the party, with Sked
as special guest, in his own *alma mater* of Merton College. By
October 1994 the party had around 20 constituency associations.

By December 1994, we were able to fight the Dudley West by-
election with considerable resources and manpower – around 100
party activists helped in that by-election. For myself, it was a
return to the paper and poster-strewn offices of temporary by-
election campaigns. The rapidly-installed telephone lines snaking
across the functional carpet. The boxes of leaflets. The posters on
sticks leaning in the corner. The street maps stuck on the wall,
with colourings marking the streets that have been leafletted.

[†]The Committee also included Gerard Batten (Secretary), Colin Bullen
(Membership), Nigel Farage (Recruitment and Fund-raising), John Harvey
(Newsletter), Craig Mackinlay (Treasurer), Gerald Roberts (Manifesto).

We gained the support, of mixed political benefit perhaps, of Enoch Powell, the Conservative politician forever tainted by his infamous "rivers of blood" speech on immigration in 1968, which caused Edward Heath, Leader of the Opposition, to immediately sack him from his shadow cabinet. In the by-election, Powell said in a public statement that he hoped that the electors of the constituency realised how privileged they were to "speak for Britain before the rest of the country".

They could help to get rid of a government that persisted in selling out to Europe the country's rights to make its own laws and to levy its own taxes: "you will do this effectively if you support Mr Floyd". The result, in the event, was again disappointing, with the candidate, Malcolm Floyd, achieving 590 votes. Ron Dickinson, an energetic party worker who was later to be involved in the party's second major schism, was Floyd's election agent.

Among the new intake of members there was perhaps a naïve idea that the we only had to put up a candidate and the electorate would instantly respond to our message. After all, the media of the day were reporting widespread political disaffection over Maastricht. It was a first lesson in the difference between the views of the political establishment and media, and ordinary voters. The response from the electorate was one of apathy, bemusement, and a certain amount of hostility to an unknown party.

After Dudley West, we returned to internal development and the expansion of the network of branches. The next General Election was too far in the future to require immediate efforts and for a year or so the priority was to concentrate on the tasks of establishing a Manifesto; creating internal party democratic procedures; building party membership; extending the branch network; and improving the accuracy of the membership database.

In January 1995 Sked sacked Wilkinson from the Executive Committee on the grounds that funds and information had been withheld from London by the Branch Liaison Department. Branch development was switched to a system of Regional Organisers, each region consisting of a few counties.

David Wilkinson

In fact, according to Wilkinson, Sked had an intense suspicion that the former was trying to set up a party within a party. What followed was a concerted attempt, dubbed the "night of the long FAXes" by Wilkinson, to force him out, with defamatory FAXes being sent to all the branches. Wilkinson threatened legal action about accusations of misuse of funds and his accusers backed down. Not surprisingly, however, Wilkinson's loyalty to the party had been severely damaged. Just returned from Strasbourg on a mission to try and convince Sir James Goldsmith to abandon his idea of forming the Referendum Party, Wilkinson reconsidered his position. Within a week or so he had left to work with Goldsmith, as the Referendum Party's first employee, employed in candidate selection.

The job of the Regional Organisers was to promote branch formation in their regions. A National Organiser coordinated the efforts of the Regional Organisers, George Duthie in Hertfordshire being the first in that position and David Lott taking over in July.

For myself, I became Regional Organiser for the Home Counties North region. Oxfordshire, Berkshire,

Buckinghamshire, Bedfordshire and Hertfordshire had a fledgling network of just half-a-dozen branches. My efforts did not lead to a great expansion in the number of branches – it was a difficult job finding people to take on branch committee positions and the hard slog of long-term campaigning. Evenings spent phoning members on long membership lists would sometimes culminate in a nucleus that could be launched officially as a new branch. On a Saturday or a Sunday or sometimes a weekday evening I would turn up at a committee meeting of a new branch and try and paint a picture of where the party wanted to go.

In internal party procedures, a topic of concern to many members was the development of internal party democracy. Most grass-roots organisations are set up through informal appointment of the activists to various positions. However, with the membership at 3,000, a system of election was required, most notably in appointments to the party's National Executive Committee (NEC). This issue was one of the principal items of discussion at a meeting of the branches held in Huddersfield in January 1995.

The Huddersfield meeting was the first time that the newly-formed branches were able to meet each other. Around 50 members from 24 branches attended the meeting. Topics discussed included the party Constitution, the Manifesto, publicity and elections. A further meeting of the branches was arranged in Stratford-on-Avon for March and arrangements had already been made for a first national conference in June.

The Stratford-on-Avon meeting included further discussions on the Constitution and Manifesto. An interim Constitution allowing the party Leader to appoint the members of the NEC and vesting all real authority in the party Leader was presented by Sked.

Another disappointing by-election result was received at Islwyn in February 1995 when the party's candidate, Hugh Moelwyn-Hughes, received only 289 votes (1.2 per cent). Likewise, in Perth and Kinross in May 1995, when Vivian Linacre's 504 votes gave the same percentage result.

The by-election results of 1992 to 1995 were consistent with our later experience: difficulty in breaking through in England, with votes and branches stronger in the South and tailing off rapidly towards the North, even weaker in Wales and almost nonexistent in Scotland. Only Hartlepool, a decade later, bucked that trend.

Coming Together

The first National Conference of the party was scheduled for June 1995. By this time, we had around 50 branches but, in the event, the announcement did not generate sufficient interest and the conference was postponed to later in the year. It eventually took place on the 28th October at the London School of Economics. Attendance was about 400 and, apart from the novelty attached to a first national conference, the main message was the need to prepare for the next General Election by the adoption of candidates in constituency associations. The conference attracted virtually no publicity in the national media, apart from a rather ironic article in the *Daily Telegraph*. The coverage, though small, was helpful, despite the tone – "Unlike the gatherings of the main parties, though, the first national conference of the UK Independence Party had to end at 6.30 because the lights were going to be switched off...The omens were not good. The microphone was playing up, the media stayed away in droves, someone was drilling next door and the conference slogan – 'Set Britain Free from the European Union' – fell off the stage. But 400 people turned up and party coffers were swelled by £10,000". The Christmas 1995 edition of the party's Newsletter showed evident relief on the part of Sked that the party had passed a crucial first test.

> We are, as I always stress, a party of volunteers. We are not professional politicians. But we are so motivated by the purest patriotic beliefs and so determined to do well by future generations that we do not begrudge the effort required to save this country's democratic independence. What is more, I am now fully convinced that we can do it. The party conference gave us signal proof that there are enough of us, sufficiently well-organised, to allow us to claim that we are here to stay. We have already established a permanent political party on a national scale through the efforts of ordinary people. We are not dependent on the whims of a few individuals; we are not dependent on one

man's chequebook; we are not even dependent on the press.
We have made it and we have done so by our own fine
efforts. It has not been easy, but ours is a historic
achievement. We shall yet change the history of this country.

The conference brought us together psychologically as well as physically. It enabled the party, in a sense, to meet itself for the first time, and contributed to the gradual construction of a sense of identity, community and purpose.

In the following year, 1996, David Lott set off on a grass-roots campaigning tour throughout the country, hauling the message around in an old lorry with a loudspeaker on top (Verdi's *Chorus of the Hebrew Slaves*) and volunteers in tow. In November, he was in the West Midlands en route for Barnsley where there was a by-election in early December. I and Chris Cooke, Regional Organiser for the West Midlands and a refugee from the Social Democratic Party, joined him in the middle of the month for a leafletting tour around Birmingham and the nearby towns. It was the Longbridge car plant at 7.30am, shopping centres, the University, the railway station: leaflets and music. Then on the next day through West Bromwich and Solihull. We dropped in to take advantage of a Labour Eurosceptic public meeting where Peter Shore was speaking. Saturday was Burton-on-Trent, overcast and drizzling, where there was a meeting of the Regional Organisers to talk about organisation for the General Election. It was the first time the Regional Organisers had had such a meeting. I reflected then that, five years before, there had been nothing. Now there was a growing party with a developing infrastructure. But it seemed to me that another five years would be necessary before we became a fully-fledged party. It just takes that long to build a voluntary organisation from the bottom up.

In early December we were in Barnsley for the by-election. Days out at 9am leafletting, sometimes in the cold and an almost gale-force wind, with barely more than barking dogs for feedback. Count Nikolai Tolstoy was the candidate, a rather strange choice for the constituency, given the aristocratic background of Tolstoy and the working-class nature of the constituency. Alan Sked came to speak at a public meeting. Stage props, leaflets and posters were hastily loaded into a van and carted off to the school where the meeting was to take place. The chairs were scraped into rows. The BBC came and filmed. We closed up, loaded everything back into the van and Sked departed for London. Tolstoy headed back to Oxfordshire. Myself, Brian Alchorn, the campaign manager, Craig Mackinlay and John Whittaker went back to the pub where we were staying in nearby Hemsworth.

By-election results were still disappointing. At Littleborough and Saddleworth in July 1995, John Whittaker received 549 votes (1.3 per cent). At Hemsworth in February 1996, Peter Davis gained 455 votes (2.1 per cent). A slightly better result was received in South East Staffordshire in April 1996 where the candidate, Andrew Smith, was well-known locally as an independent councillor, but this was still only 1,272 votes (2.9 per cent). At the Barnsley East by-election, Tolstoy gained 378 votes (2.1 per cent).

South East Staffordshire was instructive, though disappointing. In the late stages of the campaign there was immense friction between the Major government and the rest of the EU over a ban on the export of British beef imposed by the European Commission. The Cabinet, it was said, was ready to bring about a confrontation over the ban. I was the campaign organiser in Staffordshire South East for seven weeks. Our campaign office was situated in the main shopping area on a busy street corner. I noticed no change at all in the attitude of the public at the height of the confrontation. And the result of 1,272 hardly demonstrated a wave of indignation.

The 1997 General Election

After the party conference of 1995 efforts were concentrated on the upcoming General Election[†]. Campbell Poulter, Regional Organiser for Gloucestershire, Somerset and Wiltshire, was appointed in January 1996 as a paid Candidate Recruitment and Support Officer (i.e National Agent). His job was to identify possible candidates, interview and select them, and train them in electoral rules and the basic elements of political campaigning. At that time we had Regional Organisers in about half of twenty regions covering all of the UK, with southern England the strongest area. In May 1996 a number of information and policy papers, covering such areas as the cost of EU membership, the

1996 Intergovernmental Conference, defence and crime, were made available to candidates. These were mostly written by Sked. Day-to-day contact with branch chairmen and chairwomen was maintained by Paul Sharp, a 19-year old volunteer in the Regent Street office.

Two additional offices were taken on, one at 93 Regent Street and one in Salisbury. The office at 80 Regent Street was the base for the election campaign. At 93 Regent Street, Sharp and Scholefield handled liaison with the National Agent and National Organiser, Regional Organisers and branches. The Salisbury office was provided by Tony Gatling, a Wiltshire activist. Later in the campaign, and also in Salisbury, a separate printing and distribution facility was provided by Michael Holmes, a businessman who had joined the party in October 1995 and who was to be the candidate for New Forest West in 1997.

Numerous public meetings were arranged, with speakers such as Sked; *Telegraph* journalists Christopher Booker and Bill Jamieson; and Count Nikolai Tolstoy. Meetings were held in Bournemouth during the Conservative Party conference and in Brighton when Sir James Goldsmith's Referendum Party held its rally. The largest public meeting took place at Salisbury on the 25th November when around 700 people turned up. Media coverage of the party and its campaign was increasing but the Salisbury event attracted no coverage at all, rather remarkably for such a large meeting. By December about two public meetings were being held each week. Party membership was approaching 5,000.

†An election team was put in place in August. Sked, Harvey and Mackinlay were in charge of the party political broadcast. Mackinlay was also to coordinate the public response to the broadcast. Batten, Poulter and Dickinson were to handle printing and distribution of election addresses. Scholefield and Dickinson were in charge of leaflets and publications. Sked and Mackinlay were in charge of media relations. Jane Bellamy was to raise funds. The financing of candidates, where candidates were not financing themselves, was the responsibility of Mackinlay and Poulter. Production of the Manifesto was for Sked and Roberts. The recruitment and training of candidates was for Lott and Poulter. Farage, Dickinson and Gatling took on the tasks of coordinating election addresses and liaison with candidates. Finances were scarce and virtually all income was kept by the party centrally so that some funds would eventually be available to candidates who could not otherwise run.

By this time Goldsmith's Referendum Party was drawing considerable publicity and we in UKIP were feeling angry and frustrated at having what small attention we had been getting redirected towards Goldsmith. All the more so because we had spent over three years building up a democratic party from the grass roots whereas the Referendum Party was essentially a one-man band, even if that one man had declared that he would spend £20million on his campaign.

At one stage it appeared that there might be an attempt to deny both us and the Referendum Party the chance of a political broadcast. The *Sunday Telegraph* reported in February that the Referendum Party was taking legal advice about a Whitehall document which appeared to suggest that the barriers to smaller parties would be increased. The document noted that small parties had the right to a five minute party election broadcast so long as they fielded a minimum number of candidates – 50 in a General Election or 8 per cent of the seats in local elections. The paper suggested that a change was being considered that would mean that, in future, parties would have to demonstrate "proven electoral support". In the event, no changes were made.

The *Guardian* reported in March that the Conservative Party, or at least some of its candidates, had tried to reach a deal whereby UKIP candidates would stand down for Eurosceptic Conservative candidates. Two Conservative MPs, Tony Marlow and Rupert Allason, had, UKIP claimed, contacted it to "offer political deals whereby independence party candidates would withdraw in their favour in return for a more Eurosceptic attitude on their part". Our electoral threat was probably overestimated, but Allason subsequently lost his Torbay seat to the Liberal Democrats by 12 votes with Graham Booth, the UKIP candidate, gaining 1,962 votes. Marlow lost his Northampton North seat to Labour by 10,000 votes but the UKIP candidate polled only 464.

On the 24th July we presented our first 100 candidates to the media, with the *Guardian* reporting that there would be an eventual 600. Sked was quoted as saying that he was confident that the party would win six or seven seats at the election.

Members of the UK Independence Party
with their leader, Alan Sked
The Guardian 24th July 1996, picture by Martin Argles

On the 24th July we presented our first 100 candidates to the media, with the *Guardian* reporting that there would be an eventual 600. Sked was quoted as saying that he was confident that the party would win six or seven seats at the election.

The second National Conference was held in October 1996 at Methodist Central Hall in Westminster. Nearly 1,000 members attended, and the great media coup was to be the defection to UKIP of the Conservative MP Teresa Gorman. Gorman had been one of the nine Conservative MPs who had rebelled over the Maastricht Treaty and who had consequently had the Conservative whip removed, and who John Major, in an unguarded moment, had called "bastards". In the run-up to the conference Sked had been in negotiation with Gorman as a possible defector to the party.

At the very last moment, Gorman changed her mind, necessitating a hasty reorganisation of the conference format. The *Independent on Sunday* reported that Major was facing renewed "Euro troubles" and that, though Gorman had denied that she was about to defect, the Press Association reported a UKIP source as saying that she *was* going to defect at the conference but that she had had second thoughts. The *Guardian* reported later that she had been "within an ace" of defecting to the party. Sked later used an interview on BBC Radio's *Today* program on 13th January to again call for her to defect to UKIP.

The recruitment of candidates for the General Election was the central theme of the conference, given that the election was at most seven months in the future. The conference gained a little more media attention than the year before in that the BBC's Political Research Unit provided a questionnaire for all candidates, there was brief TV coverage on BBC, ITV, Sky, and GMTV, and Sked was interviewed on the *Today* program.

Pro-Europeans like to imply that Eurosceptics harbour far-right sympathies. Indeed, it has been a consistent feature of the Europhile side that abuse and smear are used to the exclusion of argument. Another prominent trait is an assumption of superiority. William Wallace, a Liberal Democrat peer, showed this in a *Guardian* commentary in December:

> *The passionate anti-Europeans who are determined to save Britain from continental domination are an extraordinary crew. There are nasty undertones of xenophobia, even echos of fascism, beneath the coalition of malcontents who claim to be dedicated to the salvation of England.*

Wallace mixed in the conquests of Ireland and Wales and the union with Scotland and a claim that Eurosceptics saw themselves as quintessentially Anglo-Saxon. Having set up the straw man he then tried to knock it down with irrelevant facts:

> *Nor does the myth fit the motley collection of romantics who propound it. For a start, an astonishingly large number are not really English, in their own exclusive terms. The UK Independence Party's candidate in the Barnsley by-election was Nikolai Tolstoy – a name redolent of European high culture rather than the Saxons rooted in England since before the Norman Conquest. Sir James Goldsmith, who stems from a great European financial family, made his money largely in New York, and invests it from Mexico to*

France.

An earlier and more extreme example came when the European Movement was supposedly launching a counter-offensive against Eurosceptics. Giles Radice, Chairman of the Movement said in the *Times* of June 1995:

> *The antics of the Eurosceptics are no longer just damaging relations with our European partners; they are threatening our membership of the European Union itself. It is our duty to expose their backward-looking, xenophobic, nihilistic and fundamentally unpatriotic agenda.*

In June 1996 the *Independent* published a full-page article on the European issue which was of the opinion that:

> *Xenophobes are feeding off the undefined notion of European union. Britain must not buckle beneath their bigotry....the truth is that the main emotional force behind the anti-Brussels crusade isn't parliamentary traditionalism or democratic sensitivity. It is xenophobia – raw, potent and addictive.*

This example of the true nature of the liberalism of the modern Left was followed by a protestation of the newspaper's intellectual superiority: "We are a pro-European newspaper because we think that to be anything else is morally wrong and intellectually disgraceful". Somewhat inconsistently, however, the article went on to proclaim opposition to the single currency, opposition to political union on the grounds that it could not be democratic, opposition to the Common Agricultural Policy, opposition to the free movement of people within the EU, and opposition to the EU having full powers to set social policy. Both smear and superiority were used by Sion Simon in the *Daily Telegraph* a year after the 1997 General Election:

> *The foot-soldiers of the Europhobic army are just small-minded people who hate foreigners. There is no such ambivalence in New Labour. Blair is the prince of the quasi-intellectual, quasi-creative, liberal middle class for whom the*

pursuit of pan-European cooperation is paramount.

The popularity of the EU, or perhaps its perceived relevance, was shown by the by-election for the Merseyside West seat of the European parliament that took place on the the 12th December 1996. Turnout was just over 11 per cent and in Liverpool it dropped to 8.9 per cent. We did not field a candidate there because we did not realise the election was to take place until after nominations had closed.

By December about 140 candidates had been selected and in April the list was at 179. By the time the General Election was held, we had 194 candidates. Because of the roots of the party, many of those candidates were completely unversed in political practices. Many were political innocents who just felt they had to make a stand and fight. Campbell Poulter also took on the role of media officer and worked to develop contacts in the media in order to try and ensure coverage for the party in newspapers and on television. Sked was accorded a generous interview by Boris Johnson in the *Daily Telegraph* in December and was interviewed on BBC1's *On The Record* program on the 26th January, postponed from December when John Major had taken the original slot after several weeks of cabinet in-fighting over policy on the single currency.

Two opinion polls in January found that about 40 per cent of voters wanted Britain to leave the EU but, as the future would repeatedly confirm, this aspiration was actually well down in the overall list of voters' concerns.

We wanted to present as many candidates as possible in the General Election in order to be taken seriously as a political force. Publicly, we claimed that we would present 500 candidates. We also wanted to make entirely sure that none of our candidates held views which were at variance with the party's principle of non-discrimination – it was not to be a platform for racist or anti-foreigner opinions.

The *Financial Times* reported on the 1st February campaign launch, saying that a speech by Bill Jamieson was listened to by "an audience of 600 mostly retired, entirely white faithful packed into a lecture hall at the London School of Economics". This was, unfortunately, true. UKIP at the time – and still – has never been able to bring in large numbers from the younger generations or from the ethnic minorities, despite doing all it can on the latter issue, particularly, to make clear that it is not a party of the far right.

The natural tendency to exaggerate prospects was shown by Sked's claim, at the campaign launch and at the launch of the party's Manifesto on the 7th April, that we had 16,000 members, when 5,000 was nearer the mark. The rivalry between UKIP and the Referendum Party that was a pronounced feature of the campaign was shown by Sked's comment at the campaign launch: "we thank you Sir James, for spending £7million putting Europe on the General Election map, but you are a protectionist and we believe in free trade; you are happy to stand on a single issue, and we have a full Manifesto".

Bill Jamieson, UKIP candidate in Putney where Sir James Goldsmith was the Referendum Party's candidate, took up the image of the Referendum Party as a gathering of high society when he urged Sir James to "disband his tarnished glitterati of Belgravia apologists and throw his lot in with UKIP".

The Wirral South by-election on the 27th February was another disappointment for us. Despite the local council having given it the title EuroWirral and despite the constituency being festooned with EU flags, our candidate, Richard North, gained only 410 votes (1 per cent). I felt at the time that one could discuss interminably the possible reasons why voters haven't voted for you but the only way to really find out is to gather hard evidence. I devised a simple questionnaire and went back to the constituency to get the hard evidence from shoppers in the street. My small survey of 102 voters showed that only 44 had heard of the party. Only 12 of those 44 knew of the party's main policy. Five of those agreed with it and at least 3 of those probably voted Conservative. Hence, 1 per cent.

The *Sun* newspaper conducted a poll of 795 Wirral South voters over the weekend after the by-election and the poll showed that 'Europe' came low down in the list of voters' priorities.

In more carefully conducted national opinion polls, the *Daily Telegraph* reported a Gallup poll on the 18th April. It gave 50 per cent to Labour, 31 per cent to the Conservatives, 12 per cent for the Liberal Democrats, 3 per cent for the Referendum Party, and 4 per cent for "others". The article probably accurately reflected the public mood when it said that most people were aware of

Britain's EU membership and had views on it. But those views were seldom strongly held. Only a minority felt passionate about it. Most did not accord the issue a high priority. When asked about the most urgent problem facing the country the number mentioning Europe was rarely above ten per cent and was more usually two or three per cent.

The General Election campaign of 1997 in effect lasted about five months. Once into 1997 everybody knew that the election would take place by May at the latest, so all parties effectively began their campaign when the new year started. It was a frustrating campaign for UKIP because the media almost entirely ignored our existence, even though we put up almost 200 candidates. The treatment accorded to the Referendum Party was not much better, despite the fact that they put up 547 candidates and even though their National Conference on the 19th October had received generous TV coverage. Even right-of-centre newspapers seemed to want to disparage and belittle the party rather than concentrate on its message. There were accusations that Sir James Goldsmith wanted to buy his way into big-time politics for his own personal ambition. In fact, Goldsmith already knew that he was seriously ill with cancer.

Despite the combined 741 candidates of UKIP and the Referendum Party, there was essentially no mention of their existence in TV coverage. The Referendum Party gained, not surprisingly, more exposure than UKIP, but even this was limited to no more than a few minutes in total. UKIP was accorded, once, thirty seconds very late in the campaign as almost the last item in the election news. We were reported in the same section as an item about the Monster Raving Loony Party's "campaign".

Coverage in the national newspapers was better. Our Manifesto proposals were covered by a number of the national papers. The *Daily Telegraph* on the 8th April reported:

> *Under the gaze of a portrait of Sir Winston Churchill, the UK Independence Party launched its manifesto yesterday and claimed that Britain would be more than £20billion better off outside the European Union...The party published a 10-page manifesto and claimed that the net gain to the country from leaving the EU would be a 'bankable' £13billion with a probable further £8billion as the knock-on*

savings from trading with the rest of Europe began to benefit the British economy. The party, founded in 1993, promises to cut taxes, spend more on health and education and reduce the national debt with the savings.

The party political broadcast went out during the third week of April. Responses received as a result of the broadcast were fed back to candidates and Regional Organisers so that they could follow them up locally. Regional Organisers were central to our efforts to guide mostly inexperienced, ordinary people successfully through an election campaign. My own Northern Home Counties area produced fifteen other candidates apart from myself. Many were paying their own expenses, many would pay them if they could but simply didn't have the money. I put in bids for central party funds, such as they were, for those candidates who were really strapped for cash. Late in the campaign, the money I had asked for mostly came through. The closing stages were occupied by frantic phone calls and FAXes between myself, candidates, printers, Campbell Poulter and David Lott.

The party political broadcast was not well-received. It featured Alan Sked in something like a lecture to the viewers and an admiring Leo McKern, the actor who played a grumpy barrister in the well-known TV program "Rumpole of the Bailey". McKern had left the Conservative Party and joined UKIP in the run-up to the election. A caustic comment in the *Daily Telegraph*, on the day after the election, said "the aims of the UK Independence Party were clearer. It wanted Britain out of Europe, full stop. Its own broadcast was charming in its amateurishness. There sat the party Leader, Dr Alan Sked, with his extraordinary thatch of silver hair, like a Philip Treacy hat, taking turns with a thoroughly scruffy-looking Leo McKern to address the nation".

The Manifesto was launched on the 7th April during a rally at Redhill and on the following day the *Daily Telegraph* accorded Sked a prominent opinion article in the centre pages – "Vote UKIP to Quit Europe". The *Times* also interviewed Sked, and the rivalry between UKIP and the Referendum Party came out again: "the UK Independence Party is convinced that it has a firmer base of support than its direct rival, the Referendum Party". Sniping at its billionaire Leader, Sir James Goldsmith, Dr Sked said: "We have a democracy inside our party – it isn't about one chief with his chequebook".

An editorial article in the *Daily Telegraph* during the last ten days of the campaign underlined how the European issue had been the issue that the main parties all wanted to avoid talking about. At last, it said, "this election is getting exciting". It could be the first in modern times, it said, where the agenda would escape the efforts of the party leaders. It noted that John Major had described the single currency "as the most important peace-time issue this country has faced in living political memory" in his TV broadcast of the previous week. But it also noted that the sentiment had been forced out of him by events in the campaign and that both he and Tony Blair had hoped to get through the campaign without discussing the issue.

The *Times* said the same a week later – "both parties" had had to deal with the question that, above all others, should have defined the campaign. But both parties were divided on the issue, so neither had wished to discuss it. It had been left to a few brave British politicians and some careless Brussels bureaucrats to make Europe "the most invigorating subject on the doorsteps in these last electioneering days". But, instead of voting for either the Referendum Party or UKIP, the newspaper advised its Eurosceptic readers to vote tactically for candidates of one of the three main parties, giving a complex analysis of which one to vote for, depending upon the views of the candidates in the constituency. It went so far as to publish a list of Conservative and Labour candidates and their views on European integration so that readers knew where they stood. The same article then deployed the "wasted vote" argument: "Voting for one of the fringe parties, such as Sir James Goldsmith's Referendum Party or the United Kingdom Independence Party, may provide emotional release for sceptics but will not, in itself, help to shape the Parliament and government which will take the important decisions".

On the day before the election the *Daily Telegraph*, supporting its Conservative cause, used the same argument in an editorial comment. The key purpose of a General Election, it said, was to produce a government. Since neither the Referendum Party nor the UK Independence Party could realistically gain a majority, it would be a mistake to vote for either of them. The two parties represented honourable opinions on the most important issue of the day but voting for them would only let in more Europhile candidates.

The wasted vote argument is convenient for the established parties. If followed, it would ensure that no new party could ever make inroads into the status quo. It would entrench the major parties forever. If Kier Hardie had heeded this advice he would have refrained from taking votes from the Liberal Party and there would never have been a Labour Party. In any case, a minor party gathering hundreds of thousands of votes, even if no seats, assuredly affects the political calculations of the parliamentary parties. In fact, it can scare them out of their wits.

Our campaign was fought around the central issue of withdrawal from the European Union. We argued that this would free £19billion for spending in other areas. A further £8billion would be saved through not paying the UK's annual contribution. Release from the Common Agricultural Policy, by allowing imports of cheaper food, would reduce people's expenditure on food and lead to increased tax revenues as the saved money was spent elsewhere. Our policies of cutting back EU regulations in the economy would increase employment by one million, again increasing tax revenues and reducing the cost of unemployment benefits. Employers' National Insurance contributions would be reduced. £5billion of the £19billion would go on greater spending in health and defence. £7billion would go on tax reductions. Another £7billion would go to pay off government debt.

In the event, neither the Referendum Party nor UKIP won any seat. UKIP gained 106,001 votes, the Referendum Party 811,829. The result was profoundly disappointing. We had been clearly outspent (central party expenditure had amounted to about £100,000), we were still unknown to many, our central policy possibly did not appeal to many, and we had been portrayed by the media as a "wasted vote", and so failed to make any real impact. None of the six MPs that we had claimed as our ambition were elected. Only one deposit was saved, that of Nigel Farage in Salisbury with 3,332 votes (5.7 per cent).

UKIP And The Referendum Party

The existence of the Referendum Party in the 1997 General

Election campaign was cause for considerable vituperation and amusement in the national media and was a serious threat to the fortunes of UKIP, as the election results eventually confirmed. Before and during the campaign there was intense rivalry between the two parties, though it is probably fair to say that the rivalry – and resentment – was more deeply felt within UKIP. Many of our members resented the fact that, having spent almost four years in the painful process of building a national party from the bottom up, Sir James Goldsmith came along with £20million and was able to set up a national organisation in a fraction of the time and then to completely overshadow us in the media stakes.

Sir James Goldsmith was a businessman who, in 1993, had behind him, according to Yves Messarovitch, a "phenomenally successful business career". In what might appear as a paradox to those on the Europhile side, his family background took in names and places familiar from Continental history. Most of the Goldschmidt family, distant cousins of the Rothschild banking family, left Frankfurt when Prussian troops took over in 1866. Goldsmith's grandparents moved to Paris and then to London. Although the son of a German father and a French mother, he had dual British and French nationality and adopted Britain as one of his home countries. His father was a Conservative MP between 1910 and 1918 and a friend of Winston Churchill.

From around 1990 Goldsmith's business interest waned, and he moved into politics on a platform of environmentalism and economic protectionism. In 1994, with the French '*souverain - istes*' Philippe de Villiers, Charles de Gaulle (grandson of the great Leader), and others, he co-founded the Autre Europe movement in France and was elected as a French MEP in the European elections of that year, going on to become Leader of the Europe des Nations group in the European parliament.

The Referendum Party was formed by Goldsmith in November 1994. Goldsmith announced his intention on the BBC's *Breakfast With Frost* program on the 27th November when he said that he would finance a new political party aimed at securing a referendum in Britain on any further moves towards closer European integration.

Here, Patrick Robertson re-enters our story. Robertson had left the Bruges Group after a bitter falling-out with Sked and others in the group and had been taken on as Goldsmith's effective Chief of Staff. It is said that Goldsmith ensured that Robertsons was not actually employed by the Referendum Party. Instead, Goldsmith paid Robertson's PR company directly for the latter's work as a PR consultant. This way, so Goldsmith is reputed to have said, he would have greater leverage over someone who was perceived as increasingly erratic.

In January 1995, as already partly related above, Wilkinson went to Strasbourg to speak to a conference of the Europe des Nations group. Still loyal to UKIP, he wanted to dissuade Goldsmith from continuing with his Referendum Party idea. But the ball was already rolling and it seems that Goldsmith did not take the fledgling UKIP seriously. And, according to Wilkinson, there was also, though perhaps later, a feeling on the part of Goldsmith that he positively wanted to keep out UKIP members. They were *too* committed, *too* volatile, *too* raw, too difficult to control. Goldsmith wanted a professional organisation, with him at its head. And, according to Wilkinson, Robertson wanted a "sackable mercenary army".

According to Wilkinson there were, perhaps still are, two types of people in UKIP – the dedicated, passionate, committed and sensible members on the one hand and, on the other hand, some who were quite bonkers. The Referendum Party couldn't distinguish between these two types – the social climbers in the Referendum Party, and there was such an element, including candidates, thought Wilkinson, just wanted to be able to say at the golf club that they had met Sir Jimmy. To them, the oiks of UKIP were all just, well, oiks.

With Wilkinson's efforts at branch formation being trashed by others in UKIP, including Alan Sked, the former's loyalty to UKIP was in shreds. When, around February or March 1995, Goldsmith offered a year's contract to Wilkinson to work on candidate selection for the Referendum Party, Wilkinson left. During his year with the Referendum Party, says Wilkinson, Sked sent several FAXes to Goldsmith suggesting a meeting to discuss cooperation. Goldsmith was not interested and gave standard instructions to his staff to say that, unfortunately, Sir James was away in South East Asia and couldn't be contacted.

Also at this time, Sked wrote a letter to all UKIP members on the subject of the Referendum Party, clearly indicating that he was bothered by the electoral threat that it might pose. After lamenting that Wilkinson was being paid to "poach" UKIP members, he said that Goldsmith had claimed that he had spoken to Sked. This was untrue, said Sked, but others later indicated that such a meeting had taken place with a view to an agreement by which 75 Referendum Party candidates would stand down to allow UKIP candidates to stand on a UKIP/Referendum ticket. Goldsmith would also pay the party's costs. Mark Daniel, in his book, quotes Hugh Moelwyn-Hughes as saying that "both men emerged from the meeting looking thunderous". In fact, Moelwyn-Hughes told me, he was actually quoting somebody else whose identity he no longer recalls. Wilkinson says that no-one with any inside knowledge has ever claimed such a meeting took place and even suspects that it was a myth developed to discredit Sked.

Sked went on to say that, anyway, they had incompatible views on the subject. Goldsmith was a protectionist who wanted Britain to remain in the EU behind high tariff walls. Sked, by contrast, believed withdrawal was the only path and supported a liberal free-trading future for Britain: "nor can I view Sir James's plans with anything but regret" he said, "he has not consulted anyone and his strategy is barmy".

The letter went on to suggest that the Referendum Party was a one-man band and criticised its strategy of attempting to gain power, holding a successful referendum, and then dissolving itself. Sked ended his letter by objecting to the way that Goldsmith was trying to "use his billions to hijack British democracy". Sked placed his faith in British parliamentary traditions and said he had "no quick fix or magic wand to offer and certainly no billions – only the hard grind of traditional electioneering". Britain might be politically ill but Sir James's "quack medicine" wouldn't cure it. Only independence could do that.

There were more specific policy differences between Goldsmith and UKIP. The *Independent*, in a profile of Goldsmith in March 1996, pointed out that he actually wanted strong European institutions to control joint foreign, defence and environmental policies. This had caused difficulties with Tory "anti-Europeans", the article said, and had provoked Sked to dismiss it as "the politics of Sunset Boulevard practised by an ageing playboy plutocrat".

By October 1995 the Referendum Party was active in seeking

out possible General Election candidates and local organisers. It had a Statement of Aims that explained that Goldsmith was Chairman of the Europe des Nations group in the European parliament and that he had campaigned in France with Philippe de Villiers, Charles de Gaulle and others. It was the aim of the party to gain a majority at Westminster and to form a National Government made up of senior political figures of past and present from the main political parties. This National Government would be in power for no more than eight weeks. It would pass a Referendum Act, hold the referendum in those eight weeks and then resign and precipitate a fresh General Election which would lead to "politics as usual". The party would then dissolve itself.

In the *Times* in the same month an article by Peter Riddell showed the anger of the establishment when it sees something from outside its charmed circles attempting to move onto "its" territory. It also showed the continuing failure to realise that the European Union was not just a single issue on the fringes of British politics. Riddell said that Goldsmith "should save his millions", that the Referendum Party was an "antidemocratic and unnecessary initiative". Anti-Maastricht candidates in the previous year's European Elections had had relative success – the UK Independence Party had reached 3.3 per cent in the con-stituencies where they had stood but, at a General Election, voters were "deciding which party they want to govern the country rather than about a single issue".

The Referendum Party's January 1997 Statement Of Aims clarified the choice to be put in the referendum. The question would be whether electors wanted the UK to be part of a federal Europe or whether they wanted the UK to be what many thought they originally voted for – a "common trading market". In March 1996 a Referendum Party Newsletter said that the referendum they wanted would have to involve a full debate on fundamental issues. Anything else would be a "continuation of the fudge and subterfuge which has led Britain into a European construction diametrically opposed to that which was approved during the 1975 referendum on our membership of the EU".

The Referendum Party, and Goldsmith in particular, were savagely attacked by the media. Although the media complain about the establishment parties, they are particularly scathing of any new entrants. In the *Sunday Times* a few days before the 1997 General Election, A.A. Gill enjoyed himself at the expense of UKIP's party political broadcast:

> *The jingoistic little England UK Independence Party showed a home video from somebody's hideous home, fronted by Leo McKern, the actor who plays Rumpole of the Bailey, and its party chairman, who is a doctor or professor or something. The most rivetting thing about it was the professor's hair. He looked like Chewbacca, that hairy alien in Star Wars. I wouldn't be surprised if his head were a site of special scientific interest with rare orchids and Jonathon Porritt in it. His accent is suspiciously mittel European and McKern is an Australian. Maybe the UK Independence Party is entirely made up of foreigners.*

Private Eye referred to the "crackpot UK Independence Party". The *Times* reported on UKIP/RP rivalry on the 26th June in an article entitled "Rival Party Threatens Goldsmith". The text was accurate but a cartoon above the text, subtitled "Invasion of Platform by Tabloid Nationalists", pictured UKIP members as Colonel Blimps carrying banners saying "Achtung! Goldschmidt" and "Blitzkrieg Nach Osten".

In June 1996 UKIP produced a leaflet specifically about the RP in which Sked said that many people wrote to him about Goldsmith and that, as soon as he had seen Goldsmith interviewed by David Frost in November 1994, in which he had promised financial backing to any party prepared to fight for a referendum, Sked had FAXed him. There had been no reply, Sked said, he had merely received a standard letter a year later.

The *Daily Telegraph* reported in October 1996 on the Referendum Party's conference, laying emphasis on the supposed high society and celebrity nature of the event, and also noting the rivalry between UKIP and the Referendum Party:

> *Other supporters familiar from the gossip columns spotted at parties with Sir James included Frederick Forsyth, the novelist, and Jemima Khan, Sir James's daughter and wife of Imran Khan, the former Pakistani cricket captain. Meanwhile, last night the rival UK Independence Party*

attempted to steal some of Sir James's thunder by staging its own event at the Old Ship Hotel, close to the conference centre. But one of Sir James's supporters dismissed this as a 'dowdy irrelevance'. He added: 'I'm told that they are going to be parading some so-called defectors from our lot – but why would anybody want to leave to eat sausage rolls and drink poor white wine with the likes of Dr Alan Sked when we can drink as much champagne as we like and look at Jemima'.

In late 1996 our national campaign team made efforts to use RP media success to gain publicity for UKIP itself and also asked our candidates to identify RP opponents in their own constituencies with a view to encouraging defections. One such defection was that of John Bostock, a party organiser in charge of 71 seats in the North West. He cited organisational inadequacies and the changed form of the referendum question as his reasons for leaving the RP and joining UKIP. A number of newspapers covered the story. The *Guardian* reported that Bostock had resigned in disgust, complaining of amateurishness and of the weakness of the party on the ground, saying "the whole thing is a nonsense. It is just a complete and utter fallacy". Sked seized the opportunity:

We are a party of volunteers, not of amateurs. If we had £20million to spend like Sir James, we could make him look like a cowboy plumber. The Referendum Party is a mirror image of the European Union itself. It spends money like water, is highly centralised and still has no idea what's going on.

An article in a gossip column in the *Sunday Telegraph* was typical of another strand of approach by the media when it joked that news of another defection confirmed its belief that the UK Independence Party "would be the party to laugh at in 1997" as Leo McKern became the "latest, perhaps the only C-list celeb to join it".

Conversely, Richard North, the UKIP candidate at the Wirral South by-election on the 27th February, defected the other way, prompting Sked to complain in the party's Newsletter that it was only the RP's offer to provide generous election expenses that had caused the defection. It was "amazing how almost overnight a man can change his principles and party. In the end we are well rid of such people". UKIP was gaining so many converts from the RP that the odd one going the other way was of no consequence, he said.

The UKIP/RP rivalry and the disagreement of both with the Conservative Party was summed up in an article in the *Independent* of late 1996. Taking up the story of the defection of McKern it said that UKIP was "portraying itself as the only true vote for anyone wanting Britain to withdraw from the EU. Unlike Sir James Goldsmith's Referendum Party, the UKIP proposes withdrawal without a referendum".

The almost million votes for the two antifederalist parties were quickly forgotten by the media and the new political establishment, though the Conservative Party, in its post-election agonisings, argued about where the four and a half million lost votes had gone. Kenneth Clarke and Michael Heseltine argued that four million former Conservative supporters had switched to Labour or the Liberal Democrats to show their support for the single currency. Norman Tebbit, conversely, said that almost one million votes went to either the Referendum Party or UKIP and that almost three million had just stayed at home.

John Major, according to reports at the time, was already in favour of a referendum on the single currency but was opposed in this by a number of members of his cabinet. The historical verdict on Sir James and the Referendum Party must be that they ensured, through electoral pressure, that the Conservative Party did in the end promise a referendum on entry to the euro and that this in turn obliged the Labour Party to offer the same. Once the election was over and Sir James died, the party melted away. The efforts of the party's 547 candidates were forgotten but the achievement of putting a referendum, even though not the one Sir James had wanted, on the agenda of the main parties remained.

Here, Patrick Robertson leaves our story. The man whose phone calls to senior Conservative politicians would be returned within minutes, according to David Wilkinson, played no further significant part in politics. Volatile and with an explosive temper, the Thatcherite *wunderkind* burned brightly but briefly and then faded.

The existence of the Referendum Party and its successor, the Referendum Movement, after the General Election, when the former decided to become a pressure group rather than a party, was one of the factors that led to profound internal schism in UKIP, a schism which very nearly led to our complete self-destruction.

4

Internal Conflict and Recovery I
1997 to 1999

The First Fracture Of UKIP

Immediately after the General Election, an intertwined mixture of differences as regards the future of the party; destabilisation attempts by the far right jealous of the party's relative success; disillusionment and personal frictions, began to tear us apart. The troubles had been brewing well before the General Election and were only kept under wraps because of the need to show unity during the campaign. In reality, there were huge frictions between senior party members on a number of issues. There were rocky times ahead.

New parties seem to be peculiarly prone to internal disagreement, probably because anyone starting or joining such a party must be particularly strong-minded. We were once described by one of our own supporters as "8,000 members and 9,000 egos".

"Tirez Le Rideau"

Disillusionment was one factor in the rancorous split but perhaps not the main one. The two most important issues were the desire of some senior members of the NEC to broaden the party's cooperation with other groups, especially the Referendum Party, and assertions by Sked that the party was the subject of infiltration by the far-right British National Party (BNP). Farage was later to say that he did not think that Sked really believed these assertions, that it was merely a diversionary move to deflect attention away from the embarrassing Deavin episode, described below.

We enter murky waters here – the province of plots, conspiracy theories, suspicions, rumours and dirty tricks. Indeed, in a letter in January 1997 to branch chairmen, Sked had warned, in the context of the reception by party members of anonymous letters from the far right that, as support for the party grew, it should expect "dirty tricks of all kinds" from its opponents. But these attacks were a sign of the party's success, he said – "if we're not rattling someone, we are not getting anywhere".

One in-depth study of this episode claims that Sked had already unwittingly helped in one of those dirty tricks by appointing Mark Deavin, a Ph.D student under Sked at the London School of Economics, as head of a new research department of the party in October 1995. Deavin was indeed appointed to that position, as Sked had said in the Newsletter of that month. But Deavin was, unknown to Sked, involved with the BNP. One version of the story says that Deavin was part of an effort by that party to destabilise UKIP, the BNP hoping that they could somehow take over or destroy the party, mistakenly believing that we were in the same political arena as themselves.

In the shadowy world of conspiracy theories, there is always another explanation. The study referred to above went further and claimed that, in fact, Deavin was a security service plant intended to destabilise both parties. Conversely, a *Sunday Times* article of July 1997 claimed that MI5 acted to prevent far right infiltration of the Referendum Party. Who can say what the facts are? Perhaps they are filed away in a secure safe somewhere.

The Deavin connection with UKIP was revealed in a television program, the *Cook Report*, of the 17th June 1997. Sked was interviewed by the program and disowned Deavin, speaking of a "political, academic, and personal betrayal". On the same day, Nigel Farage met Deavin over lunch in a restaurant, possibly to discuss a legal action by Deavin against Sked. Farage told Deavin that joining the BNP was a very silly act. As they left the restaurant, a third person approached the two. Someone, unknown, took a photograph of all three. The third person was possibly Tony Lecomber of the BNP who had served two jail sentences for possession of explosives and an assault on a Jewish schoolteacher. Farage has always said that he did not know Lecomber was present.

The photograph, with accompanying text, was circulated anonymously to party activists at the time and was later the subject of an article in the *Times* in June 1999, just days before the European Elections of that year. This sorry saga of intrigue was related by Christopher Booker in a letter to the *Spectator* some years later.

In the aftermath of the General Election senior members of the party were thinking of the way forward, for the party specifically and for the wider antifederalist movement. David Lott, Nigel Farage, and Michael Holmes felt that the way forward consisted of bringing together as many groups as possible under a single antifederalist umbrella. In particular, they wanted to forge an alliance with the Referendum Movement and bury the hatchet of UKIP/RP rivalry that had existed during the General Election campaign.

Sked, during the Deavin affair, had been told by the *Cook Report* television program that there were other BNP infiltrators in the party (the in-depth study referred to above claims this was not true). It seems that Sked then conflated this report with the attempt of Lott, Farage, and Holmes to take the party in a direction different from the one he wanted. Some said that the conflation was intentional.

Michael Holmes

Holmes had, in 1981, been a candidate for the Liberal Party in the Dorset County Council election of that year and was later to say that he found the Thatcher policies of 1979 to 1981 "abrasive and divisive". Lott, an expansive and genial personality, seemed an unlikely member of the far right. Farage, a strong and direct personality and City commodity broker given to smart suits, was not known for espousing far-right views.

However, the grisly affair erupted. On the 14th May Lott wrote to the party's Regional Organisers to explain that he had been told by Sked that he was about to carry out a "cabinet reshuffle" of the party leadership. Sked thought, explained Lott, that there was evidence of right-wing infiltration of the party and that others were trying to reorganise the party behind his back. Most NEC members, and the Regional Organisers to whom he was writing, were to be relieved of their positions – and that included Lott himself.

In a more detailed letter on the same day, to Regional Organisers and former candidates, Lott gave vent to the anger and frustration he had felt at what he saw as a lack of organisation and sense of urgency during the 1997 campaign. He called for a thorough overhaul of the party's management, attacked amateurism in its operation and the failure of Sked to devolve the operation of the party to others, citing the disappointing party political broadcast as a fiasco of bad management. Moving onto the offensive, Lott went on to give details of a meeting intended as a first step in bringing together the various antifederalist organisations. He said that the party was just "sitting around waiting for something to happen" but that Michael Holmes had taken the initiative and was organising a meeting to explore future options. Candidates who had stood for UKIP and the Referendum Party in the recent General Election, together with others from other organisations, were to be invited to this 'brainstorming session' on the 7th June. Further, Lott would follow that with an approach by the party to the other twenty or so British Eurosceptic organisations with a view to forming a united front. Beyond even that, Lott proposed an opening to similar groups in other EU countries.

Sked wrote to Lott on the 15th May, saying that Lott's letter had saddened him very much. He complained that if only Lott had spoken to him, the party Leader, the former would not "have been taken in by the likes of Michael Holmes". Referring to the *Cook Report* program, Sked said that he had spent an afternoon in the television studio watching the tapes of the program and that these had alerted him to the fact that the party was being infiltrated. Was Michael Holmes an infiltrator, he asked rhetorically. He didn't know but "I do know he is a trouble-maker and intent on destroying the party as it now exists". Sked claimed that Lott had fallen into bad company and that this was all because he had failed to get his way in democratic votes in the NEC.

Reacting to the challenges of Lott and Holmes, Sked wrote to all members on the 19th May informing them that a rally was to be held at the London School of Economics on the same day as the Holmes meeting. His letter concluded by warning that there was a plan "by the parties of the Radical Right" to destabilise UKIP through infiltration and factionalism. The parties of the Radical Right believed that the time would come when the working classes would turn to them but that "middle class, middle England" would turn to UKIP. This they saw as the greatest threat to their "fascist progress" and they had therefore decided that UKIP should be destroyed. This was just a feverish fantasy on their part but one of them had been "positioned close to the centre of the party for some years now" and was about to be unmasked by the *Cook Report* that month. Sked hinted that this infiltrator was not alone and that his associates could include members who were at that very time "doing their very best to divide us and undermine the party leadership". He urged party members to have nothing to do with anyone who invited them to meetings not approved by Regent Street.

The exchange of letters by the two opposing camps, couched in barely diplomatic terms, was only the beginning of an increasingly vituperative conflict. On the 22nd May, Sked escalated the conflict by expelling Holmes from the party and shortly thereafter also expelling Lott and Farage. In his letter to Holmes, Sked accused him of trying to disrupt the party and even of trying to make it part of a new party. With bad publicity in the press, Sked said that he had "no alternative but to exercise the powers vested in me under the party constitution and to remove your name from the list of party members". Sked said that it was a matter of deep regret to him that "you could not work within the proper party framework".

Lott wrote to all party members again on the 28th May saying that, as a result of Sked's letter of the 19th, he felt obliged to offer an alternative view. It was obvious from the General Election result, he said, that if the party continued to look inwards it would never achieve its aims. Lott wanted to forge "a single umbrella establishment that will take organisation after organisation under its mantle to weld the whole together to achieve what we all desire". The first step had already been taken. Holmes had taken the initiative to organise a forum in Hampshire 'on behalf of the UKIP grass roots' to explore the future with former candidates and senior members of both UKIP and the Referendum Party.

In the media, the *Times* reported in early June that breakaway party members planned to form a national umbrella organisation that would bring together all anti-EU groups, including the Referendum Party. This summit of leading Eurosceptic figures would meet at Basingstoke to chart the way forward. On the same day, Bill Jamieson, who had stood as a candidate for UKIP in the General Election, reported on its troubles in the *Sunday Telegraph*. It had been "plunged into a civil war that could spell its doom after a disastrous election performance" and it was "riven with splits, defections and accusations of smears after a campaign in which it polled 106,000 votes".

Interestingly, the *Sunday Telegraph* reported later in June on an approach by Sked to Goldsmith. The article said that Goldsmith had been considering a return to politics despite his declaration shortly after the election that he would scale down the Referendum Party to a pressure group. It claimed that Goldsmith had agreed to hold talks with Sked with a view to forming an "antifederalist axis" with Goldsmith playing an active role.

What might have happened if that had gone ahead cannot be said because, although the article reported that Sir James was expected to be back in action after treatment for cancer, he died soon after on the 19th July. Sked issued a press release two days later:

> On behalf of the UK Independence Party may I express my condolences on the death of Sir James to all members of his family and to those who worked for him. He made a unique contribution to the struggle to regain this country's independence by his creation of the Referendum Party and fought a clean and determined campaign to achieve his aims. In the end he did persuade the ruling parties to concede a

> *referendum on a single currency, which was no small accom -*
> *plishment. He was a most admirable man and I much regret*
> *that I never had the opportunity to meet him.*

For UKIP activists a choice had to be made between loyalty to Sked and the official party organisation or whether to go with the Lott/Holmes/Farage initiative. I chose Lott.

The Basingstoke meeting of the 7th June was attended by about 80 people[†], including 40 UKIP 1997 candidates and 16 Referendum Movement members, most of whom had been 1997 Referendum Party candidates. Henrik Overgaard Nielsen and his wife, Sharon Bierer, of the Danish June Movement, described the experiences of the Danish antifederalist movement. After repeated failure to get MPs into the Danish Folketing, they changed their strategy and efforts were concentrated on informing the Danish electorate about EU matters. This effort was carried out through the June Movement, an umbrella organisation, and was part-financed by donations from sympathetic Danish MEPs. Both felt that fringe parties could win no seats under a first-past-the-post system.

The free-ranging discussions eventually concluded that both the educational and electoral approaches should be taken, although some at the meeting felt that the emphasis should be on fighting European Elections rather than elections to Westminster. Others countered that the almost million votes gained by UKIP and the Referendum Party in the 1997 General Election indicated that the Westminster route should still be pursued. A Steering Committee was formed to take the initiative, which had rather haphazardly taken the name "New Alliance", forward.

[†]Present at the meeting, among others, were Bill Jamieson; Christopher Booker; Richard North; Marc Glendening and Christopher Skeate from the Referendum Movement; David Wilkinson, now of the Referendum Movement; Campbell Poulter, John Whittaker, Ron Dickinson, Tony Gatling, Paul Sharp and George Franklin-Ryan from UKIP; Brian Mooney of the Campaign for an Independent Britain (CIB); the Overgaard-Nielsens from the June Movement; Chris Tame from the Libertarian Alliance; Andrew Fear from the Conservative Party; Norris McWhirter of the Freedom Association; Holmes, Lott and Farage.

After the main meeting, a private meeting of UKIP members assembled in an adjoining wood-panelled room. Explanations were given by Holmes and Lott of the situation and there was a tense discussion of events within the party. Holmes paced round the long oak table declaring hotly that he was going to sue Sked for libel.

David Wilkinson had re-emerged in Brussels as the founder-editor of *These Tides* magazine, a publication intended as a forum for antifederalist parties and organisations in all EU countries and beyond. This original and idiosyncratic magazine was to provide a focus for those groups over the coming years. The first edition appeared in June 1997. Wilkinson called it a "unique addition to the armoury of the anti-EU movement" and said that its appearance showed a "Europe-wide movement in cooperation with the people of different nations working together for freedom and democracy".

On the 11th June, Lott reported to UKIP members that the Basingstoke meeting had decided to go ahead with the attempt to create a "pan-antifederalist Alliance of organisations and parties" dedicated to advancing the antifederalist cause. Among its aims would be to fight any British referendum on the single currency.

Lott and Farage took legal advice as regards their positions on the NEC in the light of their expulsion as party members. It seems that the legal proceedings of the three succeeded since Sked wrote to Holmes on the 18th June to say that "after due reflection I have reached the conclusion that my letter to David Lott of the 15th May used intemperate language which I now sincerely regret...I also accept that you personally have never had any connection with the radical Right or any extreme political parties. I am happy to confirm that I do not believe you are an 'infiltrator' and I accept that in calling the meeting in Basingstoke it was not your intention to cause trouble within UKIP".

In a further letter of the 26th June, Sked told all party members that, at the time that he had expelled Holmes, Lott and Farage from the party, he had believed that they were intent on disrupting it. He now accepted that they had had no intention of doing this. He had therefore reinstated them to membership. Farage and Lott were to regain their positions on the NEC and Holmes's candidature to the Committee was likewise reinstated. In closing, Sked said "we have all agreed that this matter is closed. I very much hope that we will all move forward on a united front".

This did not turn out to be the case. Campbell Poulter, formerly National Agent, wrote an open letter to Sked on the 30th June calling on him to stand down as Leader. Chris Cooke, Regional Organiser for the West Midlands and a former activist in the Social Democratic Party, also called on Sked to resign and revealed that Sked's legal costs of £15,000 had been paid by the party, leaving only £6,000 in the party's account. Cooke also revealed that Paul Sharp, who had manned one of the Regent Street offices during the campaign, had been locked out of the offices and the locks changed. Gerald Roberts, NEC member in charge of Manifesto coordination for the General Election, though he had declined an invitation to the Basingstoke meeting, wrote to Sked in July saying that the best interests of the party would be served by his resignation.

In the middle of the internal dissent came the result of the Uxbridge by-election on the 31st July. We polled a miserable 39 votes and suffered a further blow to our morale. In the General Election the Referendum Party candidate polled 1,151 votes. It seemed that the Referendum voters had probably all been former Conservatives and had switched back to their old allegiance rather than vote for us.

Elections to the NEC were to be held on the 1st September. A number of letters to different groups of people recommended various candidates as against others, a reflection of the taking of sides that had occurred in the party. There was the danger that the new National Executive would divide into pro-and anti-Sked groups. Trouble re-erupted in August after Lott circulated branch chairmen and former candidates with a letter confirming Cooke's claim that Sked's £15,000 legal costs had been paid by the party. Lott said that he had assumed that Sked would pay his own legal costs but, now that he had found out that the party had paid them he was prepared to defy a National Executive decision to keep the matter secret. He was not prepared to allow the issue to be hushed up and he made no apologies for having broken the secrecy agreement.

The June issue of the party's Newsletter did not appear and, in a slimmed-down August issue, the final explosion occurred, leaving in its wake a silence that was to last until March the following year. In his regular editorial in the Newsletter, entitled *"Tirez Le Rideau"* for that edition, Sked resigned. His article lambasted his opponents, made clear who were his supporters, effectively urged party members to vote Conservative and hinted that he was considering starting another party. He revealed the true state of the party's affairs – that, in the year before the election, we had had a membership of about 3,000 and an annual disposable income after costs of around £8,000. We had a hard core of active members of at most two hundred. We hardly existed in Scotland and Wales. Despite this, Sked said, he had managed to trade on his personal academic reputation and personal contacts to present the party as worthy of media interest, although that reputation was "bitterly resented by the large anti-intellectual minority we undoubtedly have within the party". Going on to explain that the Conservative Party was now a changed animal, Sked said that he hoped to have talks with them soon but that he would not be conducting them as Leader of UKIP – "after six years of campaigning for an independent Britain at the head of a separate political party, I no longer have the time or the enthusiasm to do so". He went on to describe the final events that precipitated his decision. Apart from the bitter divisions within the leadership, abusive letters had since been sent to himself and colleagues. Admitting that he didn't mind leading what, in all honesty, was a fringe party, he had no wish to lead a lunatic fringe in which temporary divisions were fought to a bitter end. Finally:

> I should add that I am very proud that I founded UKIP and that for four years I was able to lead the only democratic, non-racist party in this country dedicated to full national independence. I remain eternally grateful to all of you for your hard work and support. We may not have achieved our aim, but, as I have already pointed out, we have shifted the parameters of national debate and can hold our heads high. Whatever happens, I pray that UKIP will remain true to its liberal principles and continue to be an explicitly anti-racist body with no prejudices against foreigners or lawful minorities.

Sked went on to recommend those who he saw as leading the

party in the future. A new Constitution was to be formulated and a leadership election would follow after the new Constitution had been agreed. Ron Dickinson, a close associate of Michael Holmes, was in charge of producing the new Constitution. Craig Mackinlay was appointed as acting party Leader and Tony Scholefield as acting party Secretary.

Sked's resignation and the state of the party was reported by the *Daily Telegraph* at the beginning of August. The resignation and the death of Sir James Goldsmith meant that both the main anti-EU parties had lost their leaders, the paper said. Sked's resignation followed the party's dismal performance in the Uxbridge by-election when the UKIP candidate had polled just 39 votes – ten times less than the Monster Raving Loony Party. Several other leading members of the party had resigned, it said, and there was doubt over whether the party could continue.

Whatever happened in the disagreements that led to his resignation, Sked's achievement cannot be faulted. He had the audacity and the will to start a new party and the political antennae to keep it together until it had roots throughout the country. Only we who have participated in such an endeavour know how difficult that is. It is a pity that, in subsequent elections, Sked turned so much against his own creation, seemingly embittered by his defeat in the bitter internal row.

Although severely weakened by internal dissension the party was able, eventually, to pick itself up off the floor and carry on.

Rebuilding The Party

The same August edition of the Newsletter contained news of other resignations. John Harvey handed over his position as the editor of the Newsletter. Jane Bellamy, who had been in charge of fund-raising during the General Election campaign, left the party. Bernadette Bullen resigned as party Secretary. George Fulford, Chairman of Sked's Romsey constituency, left the party. The Newsletter also carried the potted résumés of twenty five candidates for the NEC. The count was to be supervised by the Electoral Reform Society.

In a letter to former Regional Organisers on the 15th August, Lott described how the remains of the NEC saw the way forward:

Some of you will be wondering where the UKIP goes from here. Those of us on the NEC can assure you of a resolute determination to stabilise the UKIP with your support and help. Having done that and completed the election of new members to the NEC, and may we ask you to urge members to vote, then a new, vigorous and talented team can lead the party forward. They will meet for the first time on the 9th September. I shall propose that its first action will be to elect a Chairman and a Party Manager. The remains of the NEC (six of us, Nigel Farage, Craig Mackinlay, Gerald Roberts, Tony Scholefield, Ron Dickinson and me) met two days ago.

He set out a strategy for the party. We would, assuming members agreed, reorganise our structure around the constituencies of the upcoming 1999 European parliament elections. There was real hope that we could achieve representation at these elections because they would be fought under a proportional system. We would fight those elections and, if we won any seats, we would take them up: "If successful we recommend that our MEPs take their seats as part of the Europe Of Nations group (I-EDN group). I submitted UKIP's application to join TEAM yesterday".

The intention of taking up any seats won was a reversal of previous party policy and the opening towards TEAM, the European Anti-Maastricht Alliance, along with approaches to other groups in Britain, was a change from the more aloof attitude of the party previously. The first intention later caused some friction among those who saw it as a sell-out to the EU. Gerard Batten resigned on the issue. Even the reorganisation around the new European constituencies caused bitter resentment among a minority who saw it as the party bending to an EU-inspired plan.

In a letter circulated on the 18th August, Michael Holmes, in support of his candidacy to the NEC, set out his thoughts on the future of the party. "We need a new beginning", he declared – the NEC had to be reformed into a strong executive with experienced, able and honest members; the party's Constitution should be revamped; it needed a new Leader and a new full-time Chairman. Above all, the party had to decide "whether we are to remain an ineffectual fringe pressure group, or evolve into a mainstream political party strong enough to challenge the other three main parties at both local and national elections".

Holmes was a self-made businessman who had built up one of the largest free newspaper and promotions companies in England before retiring in 1987. He was 59 at the time of his election to the NEC. He had a very forceful character of great determination, sometimes abrasive, combative with those who opposed him, perhaps lacking in political skills, not naturally given to working in a team, and perhaps unable to adapt to the ethos of a party made of volunteers rather than a business owned and directed by himself. I saw this at first hand when he was the butt of a critical comment by a member at a meeting called to discuss organisation for the 1999 European election campaign. After the meeting had ended, Holmes stormed off after the member, rasping "I'm going to get that bastard!".

The New Alliance initiative progressed further on the 4th October when a meeting of around 400 people was held at the London School of Economics, bringing together representatives of a number of parties and groups. The meeting was chaired by David Wilkinson. David Lott, Richard North, Nigel Farage and Bill Jamieson were UKIP speakers. David Soutter reported on developments within the Referendum Party/Movement. John Boyd gave an analysis from the Left as a representative of the Campaign Against Eurofederalism. Mike Woodin spoke for the Green Party. Georges Berthu came from the Mouvement Pour La France, and Henrik Overgaard-Nielsen again represented JuniBevægelsen – the Danish June Movement.

On the 12th November, Holmes described the program of the New Alliance in a note to Chairmen and former candidates. The Alliance aimed to broker a single list of candidates for future elections to challenge the three main parties where their candidates failed to call for British withdrawal from the EU. "Never again must we repeat the mistakes of the 1st May, where multiple candidates split the vote, with disastrous consequences for the progress of the antifederalist movement".

In the same mailing to Chairmen and former candidates, Craig Mackinlay explained that a joint UKIP/Referendum Movement candidate had been selected to fight the Winchester by-election on the 20th November. The Referendum Party/Movement was, at that time, in a confused state, with some wanting to continue as a party and others content to become a pressure group. A local Referendum Party group wanted to put forward a candidate, there was a possible independent anti-EU candidate, and the New Britain party also wished to field a candidate. Negotiations allowed the joint UKIP/Referendum candidate to stand unopposed. In Beckenham, where a by-election was also due on the same day, UKIP stood aside to allow a joint Referendum/New Britain candidate.

The New Britain party was a smaller party led by Dennis Delderfield, a member of the Common Council of the City of London and a Deputy and Freeman of the City. In the European Elections of 1994 his party put up five candidates. Its philosophy seemed rooted in the Britain of the 1950s, concentrating on the Monarchy and the Commonwealth. Its September 1997 Newsletter, for example, carried articles on the Queen's visit to Canada ("A Successful Visit – Well Done Ma'am and Sir"), and an update on the party's campaign for a better deal for British Dependent Territories. After the General Election, twenty former Referendum Party candidates joined New Britain. These included Jeffrey Titford, who later became Leader of UKIP, and Mike Nattrass, later a Chairman of UKIP, who was a member of New Britain's National Executive and who had stood for the party in the Dudley West by-election of 1994. Nattrass stood as a candidate for the Referendum Party earlier that year despite being a New Britain member. New Britain, like UKIP, advocated withdrawal of the UK from the EU.

New Britain, like UKIP, has also been accused of being a racist party. Their September 1997 Newsletter did not contain any such articles and Mike Nattrass has always been steadfast in his rejection of racism, later actively encouraging ethnic minority supporters and candidates within UKIP.

At Winchester, Robin Page, the Referendum/UK Independence Alliance candidate received only 521 (1.0 per cent) votes, another disappointment. At Beckenham, the Referendum/New Britain candidate received 237 votes (0.8 per cent).

The New Alliance did not go on to become the national brokering organisation that it intended to be. The name carried on but only as a one- or two-man band under Brian Mooney, a former member of the Campaign for an Independent Britain (CIB).

The agreement as regards the candidate at Winchester was brokered by Lott who, notwithstanding Holmes's comments above, claimed that Holmes was bitterly opposed to the deal. Lott was also of the opinion that Holmes was responsible for the effective demise of the New Alliance. Nevertheless, the post-election discussions helped to bring new talent into UKIP.

On the 1st September, seven vacant places on the NEC were filled by election aided by the Electoral Reform Society. Holmes was one of the successful candidates. Lott announced his retirement from active politics. A new editor for the party's Newsletter was appointed and the October issue appeared as normal. Craig Mackinlay, as acting Leader, sought to draw the recent conflicts to a close: "In the last Newsletter Alan stated clearly his reasons for resigning as Leader. The good wishes of the party go with him as do our thanks for his energy, enthusiasm and foresight in forming our party when all around clung helplessly to the hope that the old parties could be changed from within".

Our new stance of forming links with other antifederalist groups was confirmed, especially links with the Referendum Movement and TEAM, with the CIB, and through the New Alliance. The intention to fight the 1999 European Elections, to take up any seats won, and to use MEPs' incomes to fund party affairs, had been confirmed unanimously by the NEC. Mackinlay restated the party's liberal principles saying that members could be sure that "the liberal founding principles of the party as a non-racist, moderate and democratic home for all voters who want Britain to leave the EU remain unchanged".

No proper national conference was held in 1997. Instead, a Constitutional Conference was held at the London School of Economics on the 13th December with the intention of approving the draft Constitution. The conference was attended by only around 100 members and achieved nothing except confused discussion. The Chairman of the meeting, Graham Booth, later complained bitterly about the confusion and the lack of progress. The NEC suffered a further four resignations during the NEC elections, leaving it with only eleven members out of the full complement of fifteen. A further three resigned subsequently, including Ron Dickinson, who had drawn up the draft Constitution. The three runners-up in the election were invited to join but one declined, leaving only ten.

Although some of the fallout from the recriminations and the resignation of Sked had been repaired, the NEC was weakened and the party Leader had only an acting capacity and was therefore unable to seriously take things forward. In January 1998, therefore, ordinary members had heard very little from the party for four months or more. Membership, by one estimate, had fallen by 1,500 out of 5,500 since the General Election. We could not progress until the question of the new Leader had been decided.

Activity in the extra-parliamentary and unofficial opposition to the EU increased slowly during 1998. There were protests, of sorts, on three occasions. The granting of the freedom of the City of London to Chancellor Kohl of Germany on the 5th February was accompanied by a demonstration of around two hundred people. German TV cameras were present and interviewed some of the protesters. A small contingent from the National Democrats, a splinter party on the far right, was crass enough to play a recording of a World War II siren and to swear aggressively at Dennis Delderfield, the organiser of the protest, when he objected. Delderfield, in full evening dress for the meal with Kohl, said "turn it off, for Heaven's sake". The National Democrat supporter leaned forward, expressionless, right up to Delderfield's face and said "F... Off Dennis!".

The demonstration had been called to protest at Kohl, a fervent supporter of the single currency and committed federalist, receiving the honour, not as an anti-German protest, a point explained by myself and others to the German television interviewers.

There were four candidates for the new Leader of the party. Craig Mackinlay sought full authority as an elected Leader. Michael Holmes put his name forward. Gerald Roberts was the oldest candidate. Bernard Collignon was a relatively unknown figure.

Collignon had been a member of the Social Democratic Party for fifteen years and had had a career in employee and industrial relations. His statement as prospective Leader emphasised the effects of EU regulations on business and put forward a program of nuts-and-bolts reform of the party.

Roberts said that the new Leader should provide the party with a sense of urgency, implored all to increase their efforts and proposed a moratorium on fighting by-elections for 18 months while the party built itself up in the North of England and Scotland, where we were much weaker.

Mackinlay, at 31 the youngest candidate, took a broader approach, discussing Britain's place in the world, highlighting the opportunities open to the party in the 1999 European Elections, offering cooperation with other groups, and proposing the development of policies for Britain post-EU.

Holmes proposed a four-year battle involving contesting local elections, the 1999 European Elections and the subsequent General Election. He wanted radical domestic policies for current problems and dismissed the establishment parties. He tentatively proposed changing the party's name.

The leadership election, due on the 6th March, was another period of friction, though less intense than the conflict of the year before. In a leaflet circulated during the election Holmes recounted further fighting in the NEC:

> *David Lott and Ron Dickinson resigned that night. A few weeks later Malcolm Turner, newly-elected, departed and has, I am told, joined the Tories. Fudged compromises notwithstanding, we have remained in acrimonious deadlock ever since. We are all to blame. Some seem to want Dr Sked to return, others would leave if he did. The new Leader may well have to cope with resignations in any case.*

Collignon, being relatively unknown, stood little chance of being elected. Roberts was more of a thinker than an inspiring Leader. He spoke slowly, thinking through his response, like a cautious academic. His physical appearance would not have worked in the media. Mackinlay was well-known in the party and would probably attempt to broker compromises and soothe conflict. Holmes was energetic and could be abrasive, always attempting to dominate conversation. The election of Holmes might spell future problems.

In the event, Holmes was elected and set out his goals for the party in the April Newsletter. Mackinlay, the runner-up, was appointed Deputy Leader. A committee was formed to prepare for the June 1999 European Elections and a relaunch of the party was planned for the 20th March in York, during a protest at the

ECOFIN (Economic and Finance Committee of the EU's Council of Ministers) meeting that weekend. An appeal to rejoin the party was made to members who had resigned because of the infighting. The NEC closed the matter: "It was agreed unanimously that we should respect the result of the election and give Michael every chance. It was also agreed that the infighting which has plagued us since last May must stop immediately".

This time, the agreement held. The fighting was over, we had s u rvived. All eff o rt was turned towards June 1999 in the knowledge that success was imperative. Failure then would most probably spell the end of our story.

Was it worth precipitating the conflict to achieve the stated aim – the forging of a pan-Eurosceptic alliance to fight the Eurosceptic cause? As I explained above, the sources of the conflict were several, but the 'official' story is that the desire to open up the party to other groups was the motivating factor. In this, it is fair to say that the initiative, when attempted, failed. We went on to fight the 1999 European Elections on our own, not as part of a broad alliance. The Greens fought separately, the supporters of the Referendum Party mostly melted back into the Conservative Party. Another strand in the conflict was frustration with Sked's attempts to keep the party in his hands. Yet Sked was not an autocrat and had allowed internal democracy to develop. With reasoned and persistent argument it is possible that he could have been persuaded to cede more power.

But the brew was too strong; disagreements on strategy became personal and the poison of supposed far-right infiltration and the suspicions that it provoked, caused the brew to overheat and overflow. It is a tragedy of human relations, and politics in particular, that reasonable and rational people may be able to successfully mediate their differences but may well get nowhere, while single-minded, stubborn and determined characters are required for success. Is it possible to combine the two traits? I doubt it.

The York ECOFIN meeting on Saturday the 21st March was held to discuss progress towards EMU. An intensive effort was made by Eric Wood of UKIP in York to bring together protesters from the 25 Eurosceptic and Eurorealist organisations. The main organisations involved were UKIP, the Referendum Movement, and the Campaign for an Independent Britain. Other organisations were the Green Party and, on the left, the Campaign Against Eurofederalism. Even the Socialist Workers Party (SWP) was invited, though without success. Wood told me that he had been thrown out of an SWP meeting, condemned as a fascist. The effort was part-coordinated through the Anti-Maastricht Alliance, an umbrella group of those 25 organisations. On the Friday the *Daily Telegraph* reported:

> A thousand Eurosceptics are expected in York this weekend to protest against the prospect of the abolition of the pound, targeted at European finance ministers meeting in the city to prepare for the Euro. An alliance of 28 anti-European groups has been formed, to produce the biggest show of strength against the single currency since the General Election...the rally was organised by the Anti-Maastricht Alliance, which includes the Campaign for an Independent Britain, the Referendum Movement, the United Kingdom Independence Party, the Labour Euro-Safeguards Campaign, the Green Party and the Bruges Group.

York was awash with banners and flags enthusiastically greeting the ECOFIN delegates and York Minster was flying the EU flag. The City Council had produced a booklet about events to mark the occasion. There were to be Prayers For Europe and events involving children. York was to be "put on the European map". The City Council, poor thing, was immensely honoured that York had been chosen for the summit.

Lords Stoddart, Tebbit and Shore, the three long-time Lords opponents of EMU and the EU, spoke at a public meeting on the Thursday evening. The relaunch of UKIP took place on the Friday evening, with Holmes and Mackinlay speaking. The *York Evening Press* carried an article "York Relaunch of Anti-Euro Party".

The protest at York did indeed involve up to 1,000 people, many of whom I could see had probably never been on a demonstration before – some of John Major's old maids "bicycling to holy communion through the morning mist" had transmuted into radical protesters. The demonstration began in the Museum Gardens, with many TV crews present, and proceeded through the town centre to the Assembly Rooms where the ECOFIN ministers were to meet at lunchtime. Crowd barriers had been erected along both sides of the route that the ministers were to take as they walked from their hotel to the Assembly Rooms and there was a substantial police presence. We lined the street on both sides of the cordoned-off area. A light aircraft, hired as part of the demonstration, patrolled the skies with a banner trailing behind. A Czech girl, joining the crowd out of curiosity, voiced the feeling of many at the time, in Britain and other European countries, that her country was too small to survive in the world without the European Union and its single currency. It has been said that fashion may be stupid but that it is folly to argue against it. Even politics – perhaps especially politics – has its fashions. We urged her not to be so defeatist.

Despite the intensity of the sentiments of the protesters, it was a peaceful and good-natured protest. A pony-tailed official strolling out of the meeting was greeted with a cry of "get yer 'air cut" causing laughter among protesters and police (and the official).

The ministers were perhaps reluctant to start their walk since they appeared much later than expected. When they finally appeared, the crowd erupted into chants of "No Euro, No Euro!", with Craig Mackinlay leading the chants through a megaphone. Paul Sykes, the self-made millionaire businessman who had contributed to the campaign finances of anti-EMU Conservative candidates in the General Election of the year before, appeared across the street and was interviewed by TV crews. The ECOFIN ministers walked the gauntlet with forced smiles. Mark Hill of the Green Party parodied the press release about the menu for the ministers' lunch. The faces of the ministers could occasionally be seen peering from their first floor dining room. Fabian Olins, a grizzled and normally laconic UKIP character, made vigorous hand gestures to the peering faces. They were not waves of welcome.

The York ECOFIN meeting was the last time that EU summits were held in relative proximity to the public. By the time the European Council visited Cardiff in June, it was impossible to get anywhere near the Heads of State. The whole University area had been sealed and entrance was by pass only. The perimeters were guarded by 900 police, ID cards punched through with twelve stars, I noticed. During the summit, safely within the sealed area, the Heads of State received a specially-arranged coachload of children waving EU flags. Cardiff City Council had, like York, decorated the streets with banners. Cardiff also was to 'arrive' as a European city.

An attempt was made, through the Anti-Maastricht Alliance, to organise a similar demonstration in Cardiff. It was not a success, probably because the organisers expended too little effort on bringing together all possible protesters. The Alliance seemed to be more involved with the parliamentary opposition in the form of allies in the House of Lords, rather than ordinary people of the wider movement. Whatever the reasons, a mere 200 people turned up on the 13th June for a meeting at which Lords Lamont, Tebbit, and Shore spoke. A demonstration had been planned but, in a casual aside to the meeting, one of the speakers suggested that the demonstration should be cancelled, as it had been raining earlier and the grass was wet! This produced heated opposition from the audience, many of whom were in a different frame of mind to the speakers from the House of Lords. They had come to demonstrate and they were not going to lose their chance, rain or no rain.

Confusion ensued. Many people drifted off to where the march had originally been scheduled to begin, in Bute Park. There was nothing there, but we discovered another demonstration gathering nearby. The Anti-Maastricht Alliance marchers therefore joined that demonstration, not realising that it was composed of around 1,000 members of the Socialist Workers Party and allied groups. Many of the antifederalist marchers were too naïve to understand that marching with Union Jacks and John Bull figures behind the SWP was hardly likely to be welcome to the hard left. There were cries of "fascists!" and physical conflict was only narrowly avoided, police keeping the two groups separated. The SWP march, with the AMA submarch behind, walked into the city centre and there almost collided with a UKIP march organised on the fly by Campbell Poulter.

Cardiff was a flop. Attendance from within the UK had been small and, although the event had been publicised in *These Tides* by David Wilkinson in the hope that Continental protesters would also come, there was a minimal contingent consisting of Wilkinson himself, there to report for *These Tides*, and a few Danish and Finnish Green Party members.

At the Cardiff meeting Michael Holmes was allowed a brief presentation in the afternoon. He reported later that his statement of UKIP's aims was warmly received by the audience but was met with stony silence from the platform. The Anti-Maastricht Alliance, with its links to Members of Parliament, was not in the same political arena as UKIP.

In 1998 two major organisations dedicated to keeping the pound were set up. Business For Sterling brought together leaders of major companies. Launched with 100 backers on the 11th June it had the support of over 200 two weeks later. Lord Marsh, a former Labour Cabinet minister, was Chairman. The *Daily Telegraph* reported that Marsh had criticised the insistence of the Confederation of British Industry (CBI) that British business backed monetary union. It is perhaps not surprising that the CBI, an association of major national and international companies, was so keen on EMU. Big business spawns bureaucracies and theories just like big government. Both generally follow the accepted line, the path of least resistance. In contrast, the Institute of Directors and the Federation of Small Businesses both supported Business for Sterling.

In September the Referendum Movement recovered itself after its post-General Election problems. Paul Sykes, the Sheffield businessman, offered up to £20million in support and the organisation changed its name to the Democracy Movement. The *Daily Telegraph* reported that the campaign had been launched "from the ashes of Sir James Goldsmith's Referendum Party".

The article mentioned the Democracy Days that the Movement planned to hold, in which campaigners would set up stalls in city centres and sign up single currency opponents in order to build up a database of supporters. The first Democracy Day took place on the 9th January. The Referendum Movement, in November 1998, had about 8,000 paid-up members. The Democracy Movement, with no subscription, had signed up around 40,000 people by March 1999 and, by May, had passed its target for the year of 100,000, ending the year with 130,000 supporters.

UKIP's third National Conference, given that the previous year's meeting was not a full national conference, took place at Methodist Central Hall on the 31st October. About 500 members attended. There was the possibility that, given the dissension within the party over the previous 18 months, conflict could re-emerge, but the conference passed without incident. The overall tone of the conference was one of satisfaction at the party's new-found direction and a motion put forward by Nigel Farage, Party Chairman since August, changing the party's refusenik position as regards sending successful candidates to the European parliament, a possible flashpoint, was passed with only around 20 dissenters. It was emphasised that former candidates of the Referendum Party who had joined UKIP, about 100 of them, were just as much UKIP members as those who had originally founded the party. Holmes had appointed Farage as Party Chairman with the specific brief to win over former Referendum Party candidates. Jeffrey Titford and Damian Hockney[†], the latter a 43 year-old owner of a series of fashion magazines, were two of the candidates that Farage brought on board.

Jeffrey Titford

Damian Hockney

Robert McCartney of the Northern Ireland UK Unionist Party was a guest speaker, marking a loose association between the two parties. Farage acknowledged the difficult time the party had come through and Holmes candidly admitted that he had been unsure at times whether the party would survive.

The 1999 European Elections

After Cardiff, we began our preparations for the June 1999 European Elections. Regional Committees were formed in each of the regions from which MEPs would be elected. The result of a by-election for the European parliament that took place in South Yorkshire on the 7th May 1998 had provided great encouragement. The campaign was run by David Lott, back from his political retirement, with help from local Democracy Movement members. "Keep the Pound" was the blunt message, Lott having been impressed by the power of the slogan at the ECOFIN demonstration in York. Lott's appeal for help to a large Democracy Movement meeting in Leeds just before the campaign resulted in most of Barnsley being leafletted by Democracy Movement helpers. The final campaign leaflet simply stated "Keep The Pound" on one side and "No Euro" on the other.

†The quality of the party's promotional literature increased dramatically through the skills and facilities of Damian Hockney. The purple and yellow party colours were chosen at this time, replacing the ragbag of styles used before then.

The result in the four-horse race was Labour 62,275, Liberal Democrats 22,051, Conservative 21,085 and UKIP 13,830 (11.6 per cent). Lott considered the result a watershed for the party: in his opinion, it encouraged a number of former high-profile Referendum Party candidates to join us, something which they had been reluctant to do up to that point because of the infighting which occurred in the period after the General Election. Lott told me later that the campaign and result served as the springboard for the 1999 European Election campaign.

A showing of 10-12 per cent in the European Elections, assuming they were fought under a proportional representation (PR) system, would almost certainly result in UKIP MEPs. It was not, however, certain that the elections would be fought under PR. That issue was only decided later by the events in Parliament of November to January when the Bill to establish PR for the elections resulted in a battle between the Commons and the Lords which was only resolved by the use of the Parliament Acts to force the Bill through. UKIP itself was generally not sympathetic to PR but, realistically, we knew that PR was the only way in which we had a chance of having candidates elected. There was no internal disagreement on this issue, this classic political contradiction, as it was viewed as a matter that would be settled outside the party. And, of course, the determination to gain elected candidates smoothed the way.

Holmes, Farage and Mackinlay formed the nucleus of the party's Central Campaign Committee, which included representatives from each region. Further efforts had gone into bringing former Referendum Party candidates into the party and Jeffrey Titford and others represented those former candidates on the Committee. George Franklin-Ryan was campaign advisor. Christopher Skeate, a former diplomat and number two on the South East list, was National Press Officer.

The London office would continue to be the public face of the party but Holmes would provide his Salisbury premises from September to deal with the election campaign itself. The London office would be freed from what would otherwise become an impossible workload.

From July 1998 the Regional Committees began the task of raising finances, interviewing possible candidates and drawing up a shortlist to be ranked by party members in the respective regions. Some regions held selection meetings, others used postal ballots, in order to rank the candidates in the lists. Each list had a few reserve candidates in case others dropped out. The top two positions in each list were reserved for the Central Campaign Committee to allocate. Each potential candidate was asked to pay £100 for his or her application. Each shortlisted candidate was required to pay £500 towards the election deposit of £5,000 in each region, returnable on request provided the deposit was saved. Candidates were further required to confirm that they had never had any involvement with political movements of the extreme left or extreme right.

It was not difficult to find good-calibre candidates. As we had put up 194 candidates in 1997 and around 100 former Referendum Party candidates had since joined, the 84 required for the lists, in all regions except Northern Ireland, could be found easily. A much more difficult problem was finance. A minimum of £500,000 was needed compared with the £100,000 that had been spent on the 1997 campaign.

On the 15th December the House of Lords voted for an unprecedented sixth time to reject the European Parliamentary Elections Bill, intended to introduce proportional representation for the June elections. The Lords were not objecting to PR itself but to the fact that the proposed form was the closed-list system in which voters vote for a party, not an individual candidate. Had the proposal been for open lists the Bill would probably have been passed. The government chose to present the situation as the undemocratic, hereditary Lords frustrating the will of the people. It was pointed out that Labour's 1997 election manifesto made no reference to closed lists. However, even though the Lords had again rejected the Bill, the government chose to use the Parliament Acts to ensure that the Bill was forced through.

The Labour government's commitment to PR, part of its "modernisation" agenda, was the saviour of UKIP. There would have been no UK Independence Party after June 1999 if this measure had not been passed: we desperately wanted real electoral success, in the form of elected candidates, after six years fighting, unheard, in the wilderness. Failure at those elections would probably have led to disillusionment and dissolution.

New Year 1999 marked a great triumph for the federalist side. A European single currency was finally born, ten years after it became a major part of the Maastricht Treaty, thirty years after the ideas in the Werner plan. In Brussels, the European Commissioner for Monetary Affairs, Yves Thibault de Silguy, and the first President of the European Central Bank, Wim Duisenberg, opened giant bottles of "euro champagne" and hundreds of balloons bearing the EU flag ascended into the night skies. Jacques Santer, then President of the European Commission, speaking more honestly than our own politicians, as was so often the case then, made plain the ultimate ambition of the federalists:

It is now up to us to see that we embark on the next stage leading to political unity, which I think is the consequence of economic unity.

The Italian Finance Minister, Carlo Azeglio Ciampi, confirmed it, saying:

It is a decisive step towards ever closer political and institutional union in Europe. Above all, it is political.

Those of us on the 'no' side, whether of the UKIP withdrawalist tendency or those who wanted to have their cake and eat it by staying in the European Union but not adopting the euro, could feel the battle coming closer. The *Times* said that a three year referendum campaign to decide the fate of the pound would now begin in earnest. Senior members in Business for Sterling warned in the paper that the euro could exacerbate European economic problems and said that Britain should stay out. Paul Sykes declared that anti-EU groups would give no quarter in their battle to keep Britain outside, because the euro would "fatally undermine the legitimacy of our domestic democratic institutions".

I watched the New Year arrive five thousand miles away in the mountains inland from Caracas, with fireworks marking the passing of midnight. For three weeks I was enveloped in an atmosphere of Spanish and salsa, parties and family gatherings. In early January I returned to Britain and, having landed at Heathrow, made my way to the flat I then rented in north London. Entering the flat I turned on the radio and a Mozart symphony filled the room. With great emotion I realised I was back in the Europe that I loved so much. But it was the Europe of Mahler and Mozart, Sartre and Céline that I loved, not that of Monnet and Delors.

By January 1999 our lists had been finalised, but the media seemed to be unaware of the state of the party. Early in the month the *Daily Telegraph*, in an article on the many groups campaigning against the single currency, reported our demise – "this arch-sceptic party never made a significant electoral impact and since the departure of its Leader, Alan Sked, it is seen as a broken force. But supporters will still be active in an anti-EMU referendum".

The growing forces on the anti-EMU side were illustrated by a listing of organisations, the principal ones being the Democracy Movement, Business For Sterling, the Campaign for an Independent Britain, the Global Britain think-tank, the Bruges Group, Bill Cash's European Foundation, the European Research Group, the Campaign Against Euro-Federalism and the Labour Euro-Safeguards Campaign.

On the 1st March the *Times* reported the launch of the New Europe group, led by Lord Owen, one of the "gang of four" who formed the Social Democratic Party in frustration at the direction of the Labour Party in the early eighties. New Europe, like Business for Sterling, believed in continued British membership of the European Union but were against British participation in the single currency. Those of us on the withdrawalist side thought their position illogical – no such choice was on offer in the long-term, we thought. As someone said at the time, it was like proclaiming oneself to be a devout Catholic but disagreeing with the Pope. Still, their existence would help in any referendum campaign because many who did not think as we did would be swayed by their less hardline stance.

The *Times* article, like the *Daily Telegraph* article, listed the various groups and said that UKIP was "widely seen as busted flush since departure of its Leader Alan Sked. Expected to reactivate for referendum".

The pace quickened with the announcement by Tony Blair of the grandly-named National Changeover Plan, mocked by William Hague as the "national handover plan" which would deliver the economic and political freedoms of the country into the hands of unelected politicians in Brussels.

I went to the third AGM of TEAM in Warsaw at the end of February as UKIP's representative and reported that we were hopeful of gaining six seats in the European Elections, a prediction that brought gasps of surprise, or perhaps disbelief, from those present.

It was a delight to be in Warsaw, that city formerly shrouded in a faintly threatening and exotic ambiance when it was under Soviet rule. Now it was rejoining the West. With similar feelings I had revisited Berlin after the fall of the Wall and took great pleasure in walking from the Alexanderplatz along the Unter den Linden and through the Brandenburg Gate back into what was previously West Berlin. On my previous visit to Berlin, ten or so years before, the Brandenburg Gate was the walled-up limit of the western sector. When the Wall came down, I never had doubts that Germany should be reunited. It was their country and the East Germans were their own people.

The *Daily Telegraph* noticed that, under PR, we had a realistic chance of winning seats. It reckoned that 8 to 10 per cent of the vote might be enough and that Farage, Whittaker and Titford were strong contenders in their respective regions.

But voters didn't seem too concerned about European issues. A Gallup poll, reported in the *Daily Telegraph* on the 5th February, rated 'Europe' as being a poor third in voters' concerns – health was top, with 29 per cent thinking it the most important issue, unemployment was second at 16 per cent, Europe/Common Market was at 9 per cent. In the standard question on voting intentions "others" bumped along at between 5 and 6 per cent.

Michael Holmes was top of the list in the South West region, Nigel Farage was top of the list in the South East, Jeffrey Titford topped the list in the Eastern region. Craig Mackinlay was number one in the London region. By March the party political broadcast was ready, organised and funded by Mike Nattrass. Nattrass was the founder of a firm of chartered surveyors and was now number one on the West Midlands list. The broadcast showed a burglar approaching 'UK House' at night and stealing a pair of scales (a reference to the "Metric Martyrs" affair), war medals, and cash from a safe. The video explained that, under the new PR system, there was a real possibility for the party to win seats – the "wasted vote" argument no longer applied. From

February, public meetings addressed by UKIP candidates were being held almost daily in many different places. Each region had a publicity vehicle of some sort, a 'battle bus', to lend support to particular constituencies and areas. It might be a fire engine or an actual bus, or just a car with posters attached.

By March, the party machine had been cranked up to around half strength. In a South East Regional Committee meeting chaired by Nigel Farage, which I attended with other county representatives, Farage admitted that, if we didn't achieve elected candidates this time, then the future for the party was bleak indeed.

The Conservative Party was clearly aware of the potential threat, not only from UKIP but also from the Pro-European Conservative Party, formed by two former Conservative MEPs, John Stevens and Brendan Donnelly, who resigned their positions in the Conservative Party in January 1999. The *Times* reported that Michael Ancram, Conservative chairman, speaking at a London conference, had accused them of mounting a "wrecking campaign". The Conservative Party would "treat with equal and determined hostility the wrecking campaigns of the UK Independence Party and of the pro-euro Conservatives".

We commissioned MORI to carry out private polling on whether people would vote for the party if we were the only party campaigning to keep the pound and to leave the European Union. The result, although the question was slightly contrived, was nevertheless encouraging. Published on the 25th March, the figures were Labour 43, UKIP 25, Conservative 17, Liberal Democrats 10 per cent. The *Daily Telegraph* carried a short article on the poll the following day, saying that the Conservatives risked being pushed into third place at the elections. The Conservatives said that the poll had no validity because the question was rigged.

A second poll in late May also found 25 per cent support in response to the same question. The eventual turnout in the European Elections was 23 per cent and the MORI poll question was no doubt different from the questions people asked themselves when they actually came to vote.

There were rumours that Alan Sked was planning to field a competing list of candidates as a spoiling operation against his own creation. It was not expected that he would be able to put forward a list in more than a few regions but the London region was a possibility. In the end, the threat never materialised.

In early May, David Lott returned from Australia to help Farage with the campaign in the South East. Michael Holmes had retreated to his South West region and Lott ended up as de facto National Campaign Organiser, alongside Farage. The party's campaign office for the South East region consisted of a few small rooms in the Redhill warehouse of a distribution business run by Ron Walters, a member of the party's South East Regional Committee.

The campaign was dogged by the problems and near disasters that always occur at such times. Events move fast, new developments break daily, problems in communications occur, returning officers raise problems, leaflets must be produced to strict deadlines and comply with electoral law, the attacks of the other parties need to be countered, adverse press criticism must be rebutted. What may look like an organised campaign to the outsider is, in reality, a central group of organisers working sixteen hour days in frenetic circumstances trying to keep the campaign on track.

Farage worked at national, regional and local level, mobile phone ringing constantly. Hockney, in London, was preparing a mailshot of over 40,000 letters to groups such as the Democracy Movement and Business for Sterling, and was difficult to contact as he also was so busy. Farage and Lott had to get the electoral address artwork to the printers by early May, ready for the production of 35 million copies. All this with Lott working in what he thought the other parties would use as a broom cupboard, and only two telephones. FAXes for the 40,000 mailshot went backwards and forwards to decide the final copy. Around £250 per day in donations was being raised and Lott knew it wasn't enough. The mailshot had to work because the money was desperately needed. There was friction between Holmes and Lott, the former worried that the latter was aiming to become Leader and also wary that he could get landed with campaign costs. Lott was worried that a plan to unveil Conservative defectors to the BBC, who were following a "Tory split" line, would alienate potential Labour supporters. Nothing to be done about it, he noted in his diary – TV coverage was vital.

On the day before the election address copy was due at the

printers there was a major panic – there were serious problems with the text and, in the South East, only four out of the eleven candidates had returned their nomination forms! The printers were demanding all the payment up front but the money hadn't come in yet. Gordon Rogers of the North West region heroically stood surety for the whole £190,000 cost. The bank refused to make a first payment of £14,000 because there were insufficient signatures on the cheque. Farage was in the thick of it with constant mobile phone calls. Whittaker was in bad odour for not having nailed down the contract with the printers. And it turned out that the same printers were also printing the Labour election address – was there a risk here? The 40,000 mailshot had been delayed because of the problems with the election address but it had to be out by the Monday because there would be problems with electoral law otherwise. There was a risk that the £11,000 mailshot would have to be pulped.

Farage was in a spin but in the end, with the chips down, he went into overdrive and pushed it through. On the last day for the delivery of the election address copy, frantic phone calls were needed to solve the crisis. Another crisis blew up on the same day. The returning officers in two regions had rejected candidate nomination papers and there had been a cock-up with the official emblem of the party – the £ sign. George Franklin-Ryan, his heart not in the best of health, had to drive all over the place to sort it out, remarking cavalierly that "I know my health isn't very good but, frankly, I don't care at the moment!".

By Saturday the 8th May, Lott was exhausted, but no rest was possible. More phone lines needed to be installed. Royal Mail was insisting that there were 700,000 more homes in the country than the party thought there were. The printing of the election address was to begin on the Monday. There were continuing problems with the party's logo on the ballot papers – there were different logos all over the country. On the Monday, a decision was taken to print the extra 700,000 copies of the electoral address. Then came a call from Gerry Kelly of the North West region, at the printers, saying that the copy about to be printed was different from the one Farage had approved. Frantic FAXing sorted that out and then, with minutes to go before the printing started, Royal Mail rang to say that the party's figures were right after all.

The 10th May brought, alternately, elation followed by panic, and neither for any good reason in the end. There was a whisper that the *Sun* newspaper was considering backing us in the election, a move that would have electrified the campaign and taken it to a whole new level. Conversely, there was panic when another rumour said that the BNP was going to use a £ logo similar to the UKIP one. Frantic enquiries revealed that it was only a rumour but, nevertheless, Farage asked the relevant people to let the party know if there was a last-minute attempt by the BNP to introduce such a logo.

The party's official campaign launch was on the 12th May at Methodist Central Hall and around 500 members attended. Speakers were Simon Heffer of the *Daily Mail*; Lis Jensen, a Danish MEP; Robert McCartney of the UKUP; Michael Holmes and Nigel Farage. No press representatives attended but the BBC carried a short clip on the Nine-O-Clock news, next to a similarly short feature about the Natural Law Party.

Thursday the 13th May was another frenetic day in the campaign HQ. The new telephone system had been installed but teething troubles had to be sorted out. But £2,500 of donations came in. Farage went to Wales to make a speech. There were PR problems – Holmes had his own team and the party had another. A recipe for trouble, Lott knew.

Simon Heffer ("Irrepressible, Irascible, Irreverent") gave the party a vote of confidence in his column of the 15th May:

> *With the Euro-election campaign begun, Mr Blair and Mr Hague have set out divergent visions of Europe. Neither is likely to prevail. The EU is a juggernaut determined to do what a majority – excluding Britain – wants, such as creating a federal superstate, a common army, and making us bail out European pension funds with our taxes. Meanwhile, the UK Independence Party, which wants Britain to leave the EU, is registering about 12 per cent in some regions and is likely to win seats under proportional representation. If you've had enough of believing our politicians can change Europe for the better, you know what to do.*

The Manifesto launch was on the 18th May and was more successful, with most newspapers reporting it and the BBC, ITV and Channel 4 giving the event some attention in their news bulletins. The Conservative Manifesto "In Europe, Not Run By Europe" was published on the same day and the Labour Manifesto was published the following day. At a press conference in support of the Conservative Manifesto William Hague, said the *Times,* dismissed suggestions that the Conservatives could "fall through a hole between the Pro-Euro Conservative Party – backing the single currency – and the UK Independence Party, seeking withdrawal from the EU".

By the third week of May Farage was exhausted by the demands of the campaign and the South East committee virtually ordered him to rest, at least for a day. He went to a cricket match – but still took his mobile phone with him.

"All hell broke loose", Lott recorded, when the Home Office sent a leaflet to every home explaining the system of proportional representation. In a mock-up of the ballot paper, the three main parties were all listed along with two fictitious minor parties and a couple of independents. This caused immense confusion among the electorate with hundreds of people phoning the party in the belief that it was not contesting the election. George Franklin-Ryan took up the issue and Holmes attempted legal action to get the Home Office to print and distribute a new leaflet, but to no avail. Lott spoke to an official in the Home Office, only to get a brush-off. The official requested that his name should not be divulged to the public. The election office gave it to everyone who called. Lott considered the Home Office publication to be deeply damaging.

There were disagreements between Lott and Holmes on newspaper advertising, Lott thinking that Holmes's ideas were "quite bonkers". Farage and Holmes started to talk to each other again. Farage was depressed by the lack of press coverage but Lott, already innoculated against the caprices – and the bias, as he saw it – of the press, was unsurprised. In fact, Lott was fearful of a well-organised ambush by the establishment, for whom the party was doing, he thought, far too well. Christopher Skeate was trying to get the *Daily Mail* to run a story on the latest MORI poll for the party, still showing a potential 25 per cent support. At first the paper said they would run it, but it soon died.

Still, Lott was beginning to feel optimistic. By the end of May leaflets were going out at half a million a week, the office was receiving donations of £2,000 or more per day and, despite being frazzled and despite the chaotic working conditions the team was working in, he had no doubt that the campaign was knitting together.

And there were the welcome social interludes that election campaigns bring. Staying with Farage over the Bank Holiday weekend at the end of May, the two went to a pub and met some friends: one was very right wing, another was an ex-Communist. Both were hilariously drunk and argumentative. Farage's wife cooked a meal in the evening. Breakfast the next day involved discussions about the welfare state and minimal government. A bit later, Kim Rose, an ex-Scargill supporter, rang to give his ideas about the party becoming a welfare-friendly party. Lott wondered how on earth they would be able to fit these divergent views into a coherent General Election campaign. At lunchtime on the Bank Holiday Monday, the group cooked themselves a barbeque and ate off up-turned packing cases outside the warehouse. Wine and conversation flowed, morale was high.

Lott was almost certain that Farage's life was about to change forever. Amid the hurly-burly of his business affairs, Farage, Lott reflected, was standing in the wings facing fame in less than two weeks.

At the end of May the *Daily Telegraph* published an opinion article debating which of the three (supposed) Conservative parties "good Tories" should vote for: the official Conservative Party, the Pro-Euro Conservative Party, or UKIP. It concluded that "the hard choice for most of us in the Euro-elections will be between the Conservative Party and the UKIP, between pragmatism and principle".

After over a week of preparation and talking to the *Sun* a full-page advert was ready to go in the paper. Then Lott felt relations cooling. The paper wanted to see a copy of the party's Manifesto. Then they wanted to see an advert that was going in the *Daily Mail*. At the beginning of June, the paper declared that they weren't going to run the advertisement after all. Lott's attempts to speak to the editor and other senior staff were blocked. The establishment was closing ranks, Lott concluded.

On the same day the *Daily Telegraph* published an article by Alan Sked advising voters to vote Conservative and Sked also appeared on the BBC's main One-O-Clock and Nine-O-Clock news, with UKIP allowed little time to reply. Lott sensed that the main onslaught was about to hit them – and he was right.

As Lott and Franklin-Ryan drove into the entrance of the office and warehouse in Redhill the following day, they could see Farage in the car park looking worried. It turned out that Sked had contacted the *Times* and the newspaper was preparing to print an article including the Farage/Deavin photograph, portraying the party as being on the extreme right. For once, Farage's customary confidence and optimism was dented. He threatened to sue if he was in any way associated with the BNP. In the event, the photograph was not published but the text was far from welcome:

> *The United Kingdom Independence Party, which is expected to win at least one seat in the European Elections next week, was yesterday dangerously split over allegations of far-right infiltration. Michael Holmes, the wealthy Leader of UKIP, has rebuked Nigel Farage, the party's best hope of winning a seat, for being photographed meeting the head of the extreme British National Party.*

The paper explained that Lecomber also appeared in the photograph. Farage said that he had met Deavin but, as regards Lecomber:

> *I have no recollection of ever meeting Tony Lecomber. I do not know him. I have never met him. I am at a mystery to explain how he got in the photograph. I have been stitched up. He said that he met Deavin shortly before the Cook Report exposé. He told me about (the antisemitic pamphlet). I told him that he was making a grave error of judgment. I have never spoken to him since then.*

Sked played up the supposed far-right contacts:

> *Dr Alan Sked, who founded the party but left after the General Election because of clashes with Mr Farage and Mr Holmes, said "There should be a full-scale investigation into UKIP because it is not the party that I founded. Many of us who left did so because we feared it was infiltrated by the far-right". Dr Sked, who has urged his former supporters to*

> *vote Conservative rather than UKIP, said "The fact that the*
> *BNP praises UKIP is a real worry. It has split UKIP down*
> *the middle".*

The *News of the World* also looked as though it was going to run the story but, after more communications from solicitors, backed down. On the 8th June the *Times* returned to the attack with another article by Sked in which he repeated the allegations. Farage again threatened legal action. The *Daily Express* and the *Evening Standard* joined in the attack and Sked also appeared on *Talk Radio*. The intensity of the attack, said Lott, pushed Farage into himself and he became unapproachable. Despite this, Farage took the decision to fight the whole thing, tooth and nail.

Anonymous mailings containing the photograph and allegations of far-right sympathies were received by party activists. The text of the mailings contained a flimsy attempt to establish a case. A subsequent anonymous mailing contained a copy of an affidavit that Farage lodged in his case against the *Times* in which he rebutted all the claims of far-right sympathies. In July, after the election, the *Times* printed a retraction of the allegations made in the article.

But any damage had already been done, both to our vote in that election and for the future. This chimera of far-right links continued after the election and became caught up in subsequent events. Indeed, it is likely that the Farage/Deavin meeting will be dragged out just before every election. Perhaps that was its purpose.

Our campaign was fought with full-page advertisements in national and local newspapers, the standard election address, mailshots to small businesses and selected voters, 'battle-buses', light aircraft with trailing banners, opinion polls, rallies, media contacts, and posters by the side of major roads. The party's £ logo was adopted at this time and, for the election, the slogan was "Make June 10th UK Independence Day", adapting the title of a Hollywood film of the time. Particular emphasis was placed on making sure that electors knew that the "wasted vote" argument no longer applied and on attempting to bypass the relative absence of publicity in the media.

In a final effort just before reaching the end of the campaign, car parks were blitzed with leaflets urging a vote for the party and some activists, including myself, were distributing over 1,000 leaflets per day. In the South East alone, by the end of the campaign, 1,700,000 leaflets had been distributed. Nationally, the party spent £358,000 fighting the elections, in addition to local expenditure by party branches. The party political broadcast had been well-aimed and successful. Membership had risen from around 3,000 eighteen months before to almost 8,000.

Voting took place on Thursday 10th June but, in order not to prejudice the outcome in other EU countries, or perhaps to nudge the UK towards Sunday voting, the continental norm, the count was delayed until the following Sunday.

On the evening of Sunday the 13th June, Lott, Farage, and others in the campaign team, and their families, gathered in the Guildhall in Winchester to await the results. Winchester was the regional centre for the collation of the votes throughout the South East region. Farage and Lott were there in a dual capacity – as the regional campaign workers as well as the key national campaign players. The count was in the main hall, with a balcony circling around the ground floor. A large TV screen had been set up at one end of the hall. As the results began to come in, the UKIP vote hovered around 10 per cent. It was enough, just. News began to come in from the other regional centres. How was Holmes doing in the South West? Would Whittaker make it in the North West? Would London deliver? A dramatic result from the Torbay constituency, Booth's patch – 20 per cent. Good, but still it looked as though Holmes might not make it. In the South East, we were pushing Labour and the Liberal Democrats into third and fourth places in some constituencies. As our votes went past 100,000, party activists raised a huge cheer. But Whittaker had not made it in the North West and neither had Nattrass in the West Midlands. London was slack, too. Rodney Atkinson (co-author with Norris McWhirter of "Treason at Maastricht") had an impossible job in the North East as there were only four seats up for grabs. But around one-o-clock in the morning, the UKIP group in Winchester was electrified by the news that Holmes had made it in the South West. They let out a cheer to raise the roof. At last! We had our first-ever nationally elected representative. A little later, again to a massive cheer, Farage became the second, in the South East region, and shortly after that Jeffrey Titford became the third, in the Eastern region. Another 0.25 per cent in the

North West region would have given us a fourth MEP, another 0.5 per cent in Yorkshire and Humberside would have meant a fifth, and 2 per cent more in London would have given us a sixth. Quite close to my Warsaw prediction.

After celebrations in the bar of the hotel where they were staying, Lott collapsed into bed at 4am. Farage got to sleep around 5.45am only to be awakened half an hour later by phone calls and a media onslaught. Hasty plans were made for a press conference in London. After breakfast came the moment for goodbyes to be said. Lott, intending now to go to the United States to "follow the sun", thanked and said goodbye to the party campaigners present and then turned to Farage.

In his campaign diary Lott recorded that it was difficult for both of them, such was the close relationship of trust that had grown up between them, the two who perhaps more than any others in the party had driven the campaign forward. The two said their goodbyes and Farage left for London. Lott was not sure that he himself would ever return to Britain.

For myself, after my own, much smaller part in that campaign, Tuesday evening saw me on a train heading out from north London in a beautiful sunset, with the second movement of Beethoven's Opus 20 septet on my mind. There are times, very infrequent, when one feels that one is walking in step with the world.

Among the smaller parties, the Green party had begun the previous evening as the only party distinguished by name from "others". By the following day UKIP had established itself, with the Greens, as the other smaller party to have emerged from the pack as one now known by name, winning 696,057 votes (7.1 per cent). The Greens picked up two seats. The Socialist Labour Party gained none. The Pro-Euro Conservative Party, which had received extensive media coverage in the campaign, gained only 1.3 per cent of the vote and no seats.

During the evening of the count, the BBC covered the elections in a special program hosted by David Dimbleby. Some minutes before the declaration of the result in the South West the program reported the distribution of the votes; "others" stood at 23.4 per cent. The BBC finally had to refer to UKIP by name when investigating that 23.4 per cent more closely. In three individual constituencies in Devon, we came second to the Conservatives, pushing Labour into third place and the Liberal Democrats into fourth.

On the day after the count the *Daily Telegraph* reported the unexpected renaissance of the party and noted the importance of a strong grass-roots campaigning force, even under the more promising conditions for smaller parties of elections held under proportional representation. In this campaign, as in others to come, in an age when voters were becoming thoroughly disenchanted with the status quo of establishment politics, 'unofficial' groups with strong grass-roots support could punch far above their weight. It said that, two years after its political obituary had been written, the party had staged a remarkable revival – "the tiny party, funded largely from the pockets of its own members, claimed its first seat in the South West with the election of its Leader Michael Holmes". In the South West, many of its votes had come from the Liberal Democrats. With little public coverage the party had "fought a grassroots campaign aided by the obvious enthusiasm of their supporters" and strong backing in areas where fishing communities had been hit hard by the Common Fisheries Policy.

For the *Times,* UKIP was the "surprise winner" of the elections. Its elected candidates marked the first success for the six-year old party. Holmes was quoted as saying "We were elected because so many of the electorate trusted our strident message that Britain should never give up the pound. It shows what a huge support there is for a Eurosceptic vote in the country".

Our three seats were just a toe-hold but complete failure would have put the entire future of the party in doubt. Demoralisation might have set in and the party could well have withered away. Instead, for the first time in six years of struggle, we had our first nationally elected representatives. It was a make-or-break occasion, and we made it. Ordinary members devoted large amounts of their time and contributed large amounts of money to the cause.

With that electoral success, we now had the chance to expand substantially, building on the credibility achieved in the elections. The six long years of political obscurity had come to an end.

5

Internal Conflict and Recovery II
1999 to 2001

Breaking The Consensus

The 1999 European Elections marked the beginning of a period of increased activity in the wider antifederalist movement. It was not by design, it may have been a coincidence, but a number of grass-roots initiatives occurred over the next year or so. None of these initiatives were anything more than minor pin-pricks in the side of the establishment. They were, rather, like low-level guerrilla warfare conducted by unofficial, freelance groups behind the enemy's lines.

Aside from UKIP's fortunes, the effect of the result of the European Elections on the overall tone of political debate and the competition between the Conservatives, Labour and Liberal Democrats, and the wider confrontation between pro-EU and anti-EU forces, was marked. It was a result that could not be ignored, even though the turnout was a miserable 23 per cent. Some said that the record low turnout was a sign that the electorate was not interested in European issues. Some said that the low turnout was because people were anti-EU. Others said that PR had turned people off.

Stephen Dorrell, Conservative MP for Charnwood and a former Cabinet minister, wrote to his party Leader, William Hague, one week after the European Elections:

> *You have made clear our opposition to European federalism and you have set out a position on the euro which is sceptical rather than dogmatic. But you have also insisted that Britain must be 'In Europe...'. That is our key point of difference with the UK Independence Party. They favour withdrawal. They are wrong. If we are to win back the support we have*

lost to them we have to make the case for Britain's active engagement in Europe. We cannot afford to look 'semi-detached'. We shall simply look as though we agree with UKIP but don't have the guts to say so.

In the run-up to the party conference season, the *Times* reported that the Earl of Bradford was to join the party with others expected to follow. Bradford thought that Hague's stance on the single currency was too soft and he intended to announce his defection at the UKIP conference.

The issue of British withdrawal from the EU was a significant factor in the fringe meetings of the Conservative Party conference in October, the *Times* reporting new infighting between the Eurosceptic and Europhile wings of the party:

Leading Eurosceptics last night called for a fundamental renegotiation of key European Union treaties as the issue of Britain's future in Europe set alight the Conservative conference fringe. Bill Cash, the MP for Stone, said that both the Maastricht and Amsterdam treaties needed to be watered down. Large planks of EU economic, home affairs and foreign policy should be reviewed, he said: any other approach would be 'gravely irresponsible'...Mr Cash's speech last night won warm applause but he was questioned by Idris Francis, of the UK Independence Party, who said there was not the slightest chance of renegotiating Maastricht and the only answer was to tear up the treaty and start again.

But the more important issue of the time was the way in which the pro-EU, pro-euro side prosecuted their campaign, changing their tactics in response to the results of the European Elections. Perhaps for the first time the pro-EU establishment came out to fight openly for their cause, rather than continuing the policy of obfuscation and deception. Six weeks after the European Elections Blair came out fighting for the European cause. It was said that he was to take on the forces of 'anti-Europeanism' in Britain, having realised that, not only was there a battle to be won on the single currency, but that even the case for Britain's EU membership had to be re-established. The fightback against

Euroscepticism would begin in a speech made 'against the backdrop of what Downing Street sees as a gathering anti-EU sentiment in the Tory party, the press and some sections of the public as shown by the European Elections'.

The tactic of focussing on the UK's membership of the EU rather than possible entry to the single currency was accompanied by a campaign to paint opponents of the single currency as extremists who were bent on taking Britain out of the EU altogether. This was certainly true for some, but not all. The *Times* reported that Kenneth Clarke was to join Blair in a pro-single currency campaign and that Blair had promised in a speech at the London Business School to fight the "growing tide of extreme anti-Europeanism" which threatened "exit from Europe". Pro-Europeans, it was reported, had reacted with delight to the speech.

In October the Britain in Europe pressure group was formally launched six months after its actual formation. The original purpose of the group was to campaign for UK entry to the single currency but newspaper reports concentrated on the change in the group's agenda from single currency entry to cheerleader for EU membership as a whole. It was reported that this change in its agenda had been forced on it by the Prime Minister:

> *The launch follows extensive negotiations in recent months between the pro-European Tories and Downing Street which ministers believe has succeeded in putting the Britain in Europe campaign 'back on track'. A series of postponements to the launch date, as well as high-profile resignations and damaging leaks from inside the campaign, had put Mr Clarke and Mr Heseltine's participation in doubt. However, Mr Blair's agreement to take part along with a refocussing of the campaign's aims away from overt campaigning for Britain's entry into the single currency has steadied the ship.*

Britain in Europe later ran a campaign called "Out of Europe, Out of Work" which implied that 3 million jobs would be lost if Britain left the European Union. The figure was based on research carried out by the National Institute for Economic and Social Research (NIESR). Britain in Europe had earlier claimed that 8 million jobs could be at risk, but was excoriated for gross exaggeration, as the *Times* reported in February 2000. The director of the NIESR was quoted as saying that the claim by Britain in Europe was "pure Goebbels. In many years of academic research I cannot recall such a wilful distortion of the facts".

The *Financial Times* summarised the NIESR report the following day. Around 2.7 million jobs were directly related to the export of goods and services to the rest of the EU and a further 500,000 people worked for companies supplying those exporters. But, if interest rates were cut and the sterling exchange rate was allowed to fall, perhaps 50,000 jobs at most would be lost. There would be no long term impact on employment but real wages would fall. After 20 years outside the EU the volume of output would be 2 per cent lower than inside.

Election success allowed Farage a long article in the *Times* in October in which he attacked the illogicality of the Conservative position on the EU, as encapsulated by the slogan "in Europe, not run by Europe". Farage pointed out that the European Communities Act subordinated British law to EU law and that the focus on the single currency was too narrow. In focussing his party's European policy on the defence of the pound, William Hague was setting up a Maginot line. The EU was still pushing forward towards the 'single political unity' that Romano Prodi, President of the European Commission, had declared to be his central aim. The Conservatives would be outflanked in all directions. The coming weeks would see EU ministers discussing proposals for a uniform legal system, 'fundamental threat to the British tradition of Common Law', and plans for greater tax harmonisation. Hague's "line in the sand" would not stop the advance.

We had decided prior to the election that, if we had candidates elected, our most important action would be to use our increased media profile to inform electors at home about what was being done in their name in the councils of Brussels. We shared the view, widely-held in the antifederalist movement, that the establishment parties operated an unspoken agreement to avoid explaining European issues. Additionally, we would use, as far as the party legally could, the salaries and expenses of our MEPs to fund the political fight at home. An opinion article in the *Daily Telegraph* in August described these ideas. Farage said that in order for the British people to have a real choice about their future they had to know what they had got into. But there had been a conspiracy of silence on the part of successive British governments about what the EU was really about. The government, and the media, were always happy to tell the public about EU contributions to projects in Britain but were silent on the £1million per hour that the country paid to Brussels. Now the party could break open that conspiracy of silence and, crucially, to do that, they had had to get to Brussels – 'we had to get there in order to be heard here'. Travel expenses were 'another racket' that the party aimed to expose. The UKIP MEPs would claim only the travel costs that they actually incurred, would publish annual accounts, and would donate any surplus to the legal costs of people taking action against the EU.

The *Times*, reporting on the "surprise success" of the party, said that its MEPs would not vote for any EU legislation unless it would lead to a reduction in the powers of the European Commission. Farage said that he would fight any move to sign Britain up to the single currency and that he would campaign for a dignified withdrawal from the EU.

After the European Elections, a new grouping was formed in the European parliament. The Europe of Democracies and Diversities (EDD) group included the three UKIP MEPs. With them were six MEPs from the French CPNT group (Chasse, Pêche, Nature, Traditions), three Dutch Calvinists and four Danish antifederalists, including Jens-Peter Bonde of the June Movement. Heather Conyngham, formerly manager of UKIP's head office in Regent Street, moved to Brussels to provide secretarial support to the MEPs and Richard North became research assistant to the EDD.

Jens-Peter Bonde

In the aftermath of the election, Global Britain, a group founded by Lords Pearson, Stoddart, and Harris, accused the television media of systematic pro-European bias. A professional media-monitoring company had been hired before the election to monitor the news output of the television channels in the five weeks up to election day. Analysis of the coverage of the main parties showed that stories about the Conservatives concentrated on party splits but articles on the Labour Party made no mention of their own Eurosceptics. Among the smaller parties, the Pro-Euro Conservative Party was given far greater coverage than UKIP, despite the fact that, in the event, the former took just 1.3 per cent of the vote while UKIP took 7.1 per cent.

A by-election just a few months after the European Elections gave us hope that, at last, our fortunes in these elections might be improving. At Wigan on the 23rd September, John Whittaker took 834 votes, just enough (5.2 per cent) to ensure that the deposit was saved. Leeds Central, conversely, on the same day as the European Elections, had yielded 353 (2.7 per cent). Hamilton South on the same day as Wigan matched Uxbridge for humiliation – 61 votes (0.3 per cent) – but Scotland had always been extremely difficult. Damian Hockney received 450 (2.3 per cent) at Kensington and Chelsea on the 25th November. The good news was that he was 5th out of 18, the bad news was that John Stevens of the Pro-Euro Conservative Party was 4th.

The Second Fracture Of UKIP

In an NEC meeting in February 1999, Holmes had offered his resignation but rapidly retracted it. It was claimed in an email in an unofficial discussion group that Holmes had been in a high temper. The appearance of this news in the discussion group was part of Holmes' subsequent evidence that someone on the NEC was leaking information. Conflict between Holmes and most of the rest of the NEC had continued after the February meeting and throughout the election campaign. A circular from the NEC on the 18th October, after the row had broken, claimed that "NEC meetings were largely reduced to consideration of lengthy, unsubstantiated allegations about 'moles' and criticisms of NEC members". The circular described the circumstances that culminated in a vote of no confidence in Holmes by the NEC on the 3rd September:

> *The NEC meeting of 3rd September 1999 voted, in accordance with the Party's constitution (para 7.18), a 'no confidence motion' in the Party Leader. This followed the summary dismissal of the Deputy Leader and unfounded accusations made against the Party Secretary. Each of the nine who supported the motion considered it individually, not as a 'cabal' as has been suggested. These events plus the numerous events at preceding NEC meetings, catalysed the calling of this motion, including his on/off resignation in February 1999, his unfortunate maiden speech at the European parliament and the absurd and lengthy dispute regarding an unpaid dinner bill.*

The reference to Holmes's maiden speech at the European parliament concerned a call Holmes had made in the speech for the European parliament to have more power. The speech ended with the statement "I am calling for true democracy and for the elected representatives to have much more authority over the programme and policies of this institution". Given that increasing its power, especially relative to the European Commission, is something that the European parliament is very keen on, the speech earned the applause of the MEPs present and caused great embarrassment for the party in the weeks to come.

Holmes' gaffe could only have been due to naivete. His conference speeches, for example, all reflected the party's core ambition of British withdrawal from the EU. No other act of his, to my knowledge, suggested that he was a closet integrationist. I can only suppose that he had a false conception of what the European parliament was all about. It could only have been naivete that made him call for more powers for that most ferociously federalist institution of the European Union.

The no confidence motion was proposed by Tony Scholefield, party Secretary, after Holmes had given him a letter in which he accused him of "erratic", "irrational", "disruptive", and "irresponsible" activities.

An agreement was reached that, for the good of the party, Holmes would resign at the national conference in October. Holmes agreed but insisted that the whole NEC should also resign with him. The NEC reluctantly agreed to this arrangement, later termed the 'mutual suicide pact' (see below). The agreement was made in writing, signed by all present, and witnessed by Hugh Meechan, a barrister and the party's legal advisor. The NEC also required that Holmes should not put himself forward for re-election as party Leader. The agreement read:

> *In consideration of Michael Holmes MEP agreeing to announce at the party conference his intention to hand over leadership of the United Kingdom Independence Party to a new Leader to be elected in due course according to the Constitution, and agreeing not to stand again as Leader of the party, the NEC agrees to submit itself en masse for re-election, such decision to be announced at the party conference as soon as possible after an amended Constitution and a party rule book have been produced.*

The fourth National Conference of UKIP assembled in Birmingham on the 1st October 1999 to celebrate the party's success in the recent elections. The two-day conference, as opposed to the one-day conferences of previous years, was divided into a first day open to the media and a second day for private discussion. About 830 members attended on the first day, many of them probably attending their first party conference, perhaps even as new members. A 1,000 capacity hall at the National Motorcycle Museum was the main conference room and adjoining rooms provided space for various stalls of related organisations and party groups.

The highlight of the first day was the speech by the Earl of Bradford in which he announced his defection from the Conservative Party to UKIP. The speech earned a 40 second slot in the main BBC news of the evening. Holmes, in the leader's speech, summarised the new status of the party:

> *No longer are we perceived merely as a fringe protest group but as a real threat to the complacency and duplicity of the parliamentary parties. We should feel honoured. They have sought to deceive the electorate for 27 years since Prime Minister Heath so mischievously signed the European Communities Act in 1972. They now know their political deception is at their electoral peril. Might may not yet be on our side but right most certainly is. We must use the next year to build up our membership and our party structure to take up the challenge of contesting the next General Election on a scale never before attempted by a non-Westminster party.*

Holmes underlined the party's commitment to non-discrimination:

> *We shall seek to encourage into membership former supporters of all mainstream parties and of none. Membership is open to all our citizens who want the United Kingdom to be returned to the status of a democratic self-governing nation with our own Parliament at Westminster solely accountable to our own electorate and with no legal obligation to the politicians and the politics of the European*

Union. We offer this opportunity to all law-abiding citizens regardless of race, colour or creed.

The second day was a traumatic experience of bloodletting, recrimination, accusations and counter-accusations that reduced some members to tears. How many members had been lost by the end of that day one can only guess. Farage began the day by openly admitting that there were considerable and very difficult problems in the operation of the NEC with the Leader. He said it was likely to be a very difficult session but that the problems needed to be solved that day for the sake of the cause and the party. We could then move on and start our preparations for the General Election.

Only a few people knew of the conflict to come. Clearly, the central participants – the NEC and the party Leader – knew all the details. A slightly wider membership – those particularly active in the party and those who subscribed to an unofficial email discussion group were aware of the problems in outline. Rumours were circulating that Holmes was going to renege on the agreement of the 3rd September.

It was difficult for anyone who was not a direct participant to establish what had happened and which of the accusations and counter-accusations were true. The anti-Holmes faction of nine members on the NEC maintained that Holmes was forever harking back to the dissension surrounding Alan Sked's departure. They alleged that Holmes could never forget who had been against him at that time. However, a member of the NEC who was reputed to be neutral in the affair was rumoured to have said that, in fact, the issue and others were raised by the NEC nine as a means of goading Holmes.

The original plan for a 'controlled explosion' went wrong. Holmes had indeed changed his mind about his side of the agreement of the 3rd September.

Holmes addressed the meeting and described the events of the previous few months as he saw them. He complained that his leadership had been under attack from the beginning. He described how he had dismissed Mackinlay, the Deputy Leader, for incompetence, how this had led Scholefield to propose a vote of no confidence. Holmes went on to say that seven of the nine who had voted in favour of the no confidence motion had been named approvingly by Alan Sked when he resigned. Clearly, Holmes felt that the NEC nine were still fighting the old battle from two years before. Holmes then described the "mutual suicide pact" and said that he had changed his mind and had decided to leave it to the conference to make a decision.

As already mentioned, during the European Election campaign party activists had received anonymous mailings alleging far-right links on the part of Farage and Holmes. The implication was that they were building up UKIP only to turn it into a far-right party. It is likely that these mailings were entirely separate from the internal dissension between the NEC nine and Holmes. Many were of the opinion that the anonymous mailings, and the 5th June article in the *Times,* originated in rival parties. In putting his case, Holmes put great emphasis on these mailings, reading out the contents of two in their entirety. His implication seemed to be that one or more of the NEC nine were responsible. In a party Newsletter he said that the reception of these anonymous letters was what changed his mind as regards not standing for re-election. At the conference he said that he had signed the "mutual suicide" agreement under psychological duress.

The AGM was turned into an EGM by a show of hands. Hugh Meechan presided over the EGM with inflexible will. Two motions were submitted: a vote of no-confidence in the NEC and a vote of confidence in Holmes. Meechan allowed those who had been named by Holmes to defend themselves, then gave those NEC members who had voted against the 3rd September no-confidence motion the chance to put their point of view.

The outcome of the first vote was 273 for, 52 against, with 3 abstentions. The NEC had been sacked en masse. After lunch, an amendment to the vote of confidence in Holmes was proposed. It called on Holmes to step down "with honour and integrity intact and to stand for re-election".

The amendment was defeated by 182 to 113 with 33 abstentions and the main motion of confidence in the party Leader began. At times the meeting degenerated into a situation where very forceful commands were necessary. Meechan was obliged to continually remind people, in his deep voice and Scottish accent, and very loud when required, that "I will take ONLY points of order or points of information". "No, I will NOT accept that, speak to the motion, PLEASE". "PLEASE,

PLEASE, speak to the motion".

The NEC nine no doubt felt aggrieved that Holmes had reneged on the agreement and could see that events were slipping out of their hands. Scholefield, as the principal antagonist to Holmes, felt particularly strongly and was the object of the Chairman's most forceful comments. Scholefield insisted on standing and talking even when the Chairman had ordered him to stop several times and the audience was shouting in agreement – "Tony, you have had your say....you have had your say, sit down Tony, SIT DOWN TONY!".

The result was 236 in favour, 35 against, and 55 abstentions. Holmes's gamble had succeeded.

Farage, in the chair, commented on what a difficult session it had been and attempted to reassure new members that this was not the normal nature of the party. Meechan said afterwards that it was the most difficult meeting he had ever chaired. The meeting moved on to appoint the members of a disciplinary committee and the conference steering committee.

The situation had, apparently, been resolved. But, as the members returned to their constituencies after that difficult day, some wondered. The party Leader had won his confidence vote, but he had reneged on a signed agreement. It was likely that those members of the NEC who had fallen out with Holmes would stand for re-election, and that they would be re-elected. Then the same situation would occur. Had anything really been resolved? Events moved much faster than that.

Scholefield, around midnight of the same day, changed the locks of the party's offices in Regent Street, putting a notice on the door saying that he had taken the action using his powers as party Secretary and stating that he had informed the police of his action. He then FAXed Holmes and Farage telling them what he had done and asked them to immediately confirm that they would take no action to interfere in the running of the office.

Late on Sunday evening, the 3rd October, the same offices were forcibly entered. The NEC nine claimed in the circular of the 18th October that "In an extraordinary move, someone acting on the instructions of the Party Leader forced entry into the party's head office on Sunday the 3rd October and the party's computer database, correspondence and financial records were removed, including cheque books, with subsequent attempts made to alter banking mandates".

The NEC nine in turn received a legal warning that they were a caretaker body only and could not take any significant decisions. There followed a three month period when the party appeared to have two head offices, one in Salisbury and the official one in London. The Salisbury office was the party's South West regional office and the centre of Michael Holmes's activities, with Ron Dickinson in charge. Members were receiving communications from both offices, including requests for renewal of membership. Some, not surprisingly, grew suspicious of exactly what was going on, especially as regards money.

We were split into two very polarised groups, each with their own 'head' office. Each side sought legal advice over whether the decision to hold the EGM had been constitutional. Each side received the advice they wanted. The two sides at least promised that any legal costs would not be borne by the party.

The *Guardian* picked up on the news two weeks later, reporting that the party had been "plunged into turmoil after members passed a motion of no confidence in its ruling national executive. The entire 15 strong NEC, including the party secretary, was forced to step down after the vote by 350 UKIP members at a stormy party conference in Solihull".

The NEC nine did not accept the result of the EGM of the 2nd October. They disputed that the EGM had been validly convened and took legal advice on the issue. The minutes of an Emergency Meeting held on the 13th October recorded that "the purported EGM of the 2nd October has no legal validity. The NEC was not removed from office and the vote of confidence in Michael Holmes as Leader has no validity". The minutes went on to give the reasons for their opinion: "The decision by Hugh Meechan that the conference could vote itself into an EGM is judged by Jeffrey, Green, Russell to be wrong in law. They refer in their letter to common sense requiring notice to be given to all members of the party. They have said that 300 years of common law show that a reasonable term of notice for an EGM to all members is three weeks, which is the same in company law".

The NEC nine reaffirmed that the vote of no-confidence in the party Leader of the 3rd September stood and decided that a properly-constituted EGM should be organised to ratify or overturn that decision. Further decisions were taken on the status of the party Secretary, maintaining that only the NEC could appoint or dismiss the Secretary; reaffirming that the party's head office remained in London and requiring that all materials be returned from Salisbury; condemning the leaks that had occurred in the party's unofficial email discussion group and other communications, and disowning the latest edition of the party's Newsletter as being unauthorised. Conversely, lawyers acting for Holmes were of the opinion that the calling of the EGM had been valid.

In an email of the 25th October, Tony Bennett, Jeffrey Titford's political assistant in the Chelmsford office, explained that it seemed possible that an application could be made to the High Court to decide the issue. Reflecting the state of near despair of party activists at such a prospect, Bennett asked:

> *Thus, dear fellow UKIP members, we are on the brink of expensive litigation in the High Court brought by one 'side' or the other. Is there no-one more senior in the party who is capable of bringing the two sides together? A number of ONELIST postings have called, with varying degrees of urgency, for a compromise. Its not too late now. It may be in a few days time.*

To ordinary members and activists outside the circles of the party Leader and the NEC it seemed that the two groups did nothing but bicker with each other for three months. For this reason, two groups acting disinterestedly began initiatives to try and resolve the problem. It was plain that the two warring factions would not settle the problem themselves. These two mediating groups proposed a fresh EGM under an article in the Constitution that mandated such a meeting if so requested by at least 20 constituency associations. An agenda was proposed and hotly disputed by the warring factions, although they did at least agree in principle to a further EGM. The wider membership of the party was variously disappointed, despairing, or angry. There was a sense that the two factions were going to be ordered by the membership as a whole to settle their differences.

David Lott, again returned from abroad, having left to 'follow the sun' across America after June 1999, set out his ideas for a resolution of the dispute in a letter and document to senior party members on the 8th November. He appealed to the party's three MEPs to take the document seriously and to go along with its proposals, however painful that might be for them. His proposals were 'humbly submitted with the interests of the country and the party in mind'. Lott, voicing the frustration and sadness of ordinary party members, said that the party's grass roots would be eternally grateful if the MEPs could use their influence to set up a meeting of members to resolve the dispute. He thought that any such meeting should take place before Christmas so that the party could start the year 2000 with renewed confidence. In the accompanying document Lott summarised what was at stake:

> It has taken hundreds of thousands of hours of devoted toil by ordinary members to bring UKIP to the point that it commands the anti-EU army. Those involved in this dispute have brought the party to the very brink of success only to take it on to the brink of disaster, a heartbreaking prospect for those fine UKIP members whose hearts and souls and magnificent effort went into bringing us this far.

Further bickering occurred over what constituted a party association. The most that could be said for the two factions is that they exercised some form of self-restraint.

Two days later Lott and others[†] met and decided to write to party chairmen to ask them to indicate their support for an EGM, as proposed by Lott. The letter reflected the feeling that the two sides would not settle the dispute themselves: "we perceived that everyone in the party wants a swift resolution to our difficulties, but that no-one appears to be doing anything effective". The group had therefore decided to take the initiative and to appeal right over the heads of the party leadership to ordinary members who would resolve matters for them.

[†]Mike Phillips (Chairman in Milton Keynes), Tom Wise (Chairman of the Eastern Region), Derek Clark (Chairman of the East Midlands Region), and John Harvey (Vice-Chairman of the South East Region)

Farage had not been sympathetic to Lott's original proposals, which he felt would institutionalise division within the party – "you simply cannot have two leaders", he said. Lott's proposals were then revised and received the support of Farage, who said on the 18th November that "I have believed for some time now that a full and fair EGM is the only way out of this crisis. The alternative would be a costly, and probably lengthy, legal action that would be disastrous for the party". The revised proposals allowed for a final decision to be made about the disputed conclusions of the Birmingham meeting and didn't require any constitutional changes. "On behalf of Jeffrey Titford MEP and myself I confirm that this proposal has our wholehearted support. Time is of the essence!"

A second group consisting of Lawrie Boxall, Michael Harvey and Ron Walters, all members of the South East Regional Committee, also independently pursued the same approach. Holmes, meanwhile, had organised an informal ballot of the party membership with three questions relating to the position of the NEC and himself. The results were overwhelmingly in his favour but the NEC nine disputed that the ballot had any constitutional validity. On the 16th November Holmes wrote to all branch Chairmen and activists raising various objections to Lott's initiative. He thanked Lott and the others involved in the initiative for their efforts but hoped that they would support his ballot of members as the best way forward.

A meeting of the NEC nine on the 17th November discussed the failure of Holmes and Farage to provide the NEC with details of their surplus expenses. All candidates in the European Elections had signed a pledge to donate these expenses to the party for use by the NEC. The meeting noted that this pledge had been publicised in the party's election address and that there had been adverse press comment. Holmes's ballot was discussed and dismissed as unconstitutional.

The new draft party rulebook had been stolen in the raid on the Regent Street premises and the Disciplinary Committee had been unconstitutionally elected. It was agreed, however, to take the Lott initiative forward, the meeting noting that "The NEC is fully aware of the distress of the membership and the NEC will continue to investigate every possible way of resolving the current situation".

On the matter of the surplus expenses pledge the *Guardian* claimed to have found evidence that the charms of Brussels had turned the new MEPs' heads, saying: "The comforts of office are proving irresistible to the three new Euro-MPs from the United Kingdom Independence Party despite their solemn vows to spurn the Brussels gravy train. Fellow MEPs are watching in amusement as the patriotic trio spend their daily allowances down to the last euro on smart hotels and restaurants, leaving barely any money for their promised 'fighting fund' to take Britain out of Europe".

The article did at least go on to point out that the hotel had been booked by the European parliament and to quote Farage – "we are new boys", he said, "we will be looking for more reasonable accommodation so that money can be ploughed back into our campaign fund".

January saw the beginning of the party's involvement with the antimetrication campaign, an attempt to defeat the new law making the sale of loose goods such as meat, fruit, vegetables, and fish in pounds and ounces illegal. The campaign was started and funded by a few brave market traders, the party and the British Weights and Measures Association (BWMA). Tony Bennett made the party's commitment to providing funds clear in an email in early January:

> To date, three barristers have offered free legal representa-
> tion to anyone who may be prosecuted for an alleged breach
> of the relevant regulations – the Weights and Measures
> (Units of Measurements) Regulations 1994. UKIP will
> contribute to other legal expenses incurred by traders who
> may be prosecuted – using UKIP's special fund for victims of
> the European Union. UKIP will make a contribution to any
> fines handed down by Magistrates under these Regulations –
> again using its EU victims fund.

The BBC's *Spotlight Westminster* program of the 24th October reported on the party's internal disagreements and Holmes's maiden speech in the European parliament. It showed video coverage of Holmes sitting down to applause from federalist MEPs. The clear implication was that the party had suddenly changed its agenda and 'gone native'.

In late November each side sent, to all members of the party, long accounts of their sides of the story. In this extraordinary exchange of fire the whole membership finally learnt the messy details. Scholefield issued a seven-page document on behalf of the NEC nine. It recounted the fiasco of Holmes's maiden speech to the European parliament, explained that he had opened a separate bank account in Salisbury in June 1998 and that he had refused to provide details of transactions to the NEC, that he had tried to change the signatories to the party's main accounts and that, as a result, the banks had frozen the accounts. According to the Scholefield circular, Holmes had also argued with representatives of other Eurosceptic organisations. The circular emphasised that media attention was being directed at the events within the party: "It is important to realise that national journalists as well as MPs, MEPs, and others already have access to the facts and are simply not going to brush this under the carpet. The UKIP must clean itself up or be treated as a joke". In summing up, the NEC nine demanded that proper control of the party should be restored. It was essential that the party should return to "lawful and constitutional action" because the future of the party was vital to the future of Britain. The party had to retain the respect of national journalists and commentators and public comment about it should be about its policies and strategy, not about internal squabbles and constitutional disorder. Above all, party members had to have full confidence that the NEC was in full control of its political and financial affairs.

In the response from the Holmes side fourteen party members put their side of the argument in a circular published by Chris Cooke, Regional Organiser for the West Midlands. The circular concentrated heavily on claims that seven out of the NEC nine were supporters of Alan Sked in the previous dispute and that they resented the position of Holmes as party Leader: "Dr Sked's parting message to these members was to encourage them to support a number of people for the NEC elections which were being held. It was not unnatural, given this Newsletter, that Dr Sked's supporters were overwhelmingly voted onto the NEC and remain there to this day". Cooke claimed that Holmes, as a member of the NEC, had had to face some very unpleasant meetings, with "continual sniping and petty arguing".

They went on to say that Holmes's maiden speech had been a perfectly good speech, maintained that the conference EGM had been validly constituted, supported the action of the disciplinary committee in dismissing Scholefield as party Secretary due to his actions in changing the locks at the party's Head Office, and argued that the removal of the party's records to Salisbury had been necessary to protect them from the danger of interference. The letter ended with a statement from the fourteen signatories: "Given all that Michael Holmes has had to put up with from the old NEC we, the undersigned, feel that he has more than earned the trust UKIP members put in him when electing him Leader. We will not subscribe to the holier-than-thou 'plague on both your houses' fence-sitting some UKIP members have adopted. We don't think that is fair on Michael Holmes. We believe Michael has done more than enough to deserve the outright support of all UKIP members. He should complete his term in office with a newly elected NEC that will work with goodwill and with the Leader of the party for the good of the party".

It is perhaps noteworthy that, among the intense personal disagreements, particularly that between Scholefield and Holmes, the NEC nine emphasised the primacy of the Constitution and the NEC as the principal authority of the party as opposed to what they saw as 'one-man rule', while the Holmes side seemed to concentrate more on the personality of Holmes himself.

In early December Holmes issued a writ which sought the resignation of all NEC members and fresh elections for all positions. The writ was due to be heard on the 17th December. Meanwhile, the support of over 20 constituency chairmen for a new EGM had been received and Methodist Central Hall in Westminster had been booked for the 22nd January for that purpose. The two sides were at least funding their legal actions through their own pockets and not placing a charge on the party.

At the Birmingham conference, as described above, the NEC had been voted out in the no confidence motion and Holmes had been confirmed in his position as party Leader. But, by December, the mood of ordinary party members had become less trusting of Holmes and the sentiment of a "plague on both your houses", referred to in the circular from the Holmes side, had become more powerful.

Mike Phillips wrote again on the 10th December on the progress of his petitioners group in setting up an EGM. He reported that a similar group had taken the same action and had also collected the necessary support from 20 party associations. A composite motion had been drafted by Phillips's group which they hoped would be seen to be impartial by both sides of the dispute. The "plague on both your houses" sentiment was mentioned in the letter which said that the motion reflected the majority view of people who had spoken to the petitioners – that "they should **all** stand down, with immediate elections to be held for their posts to give the party a fresh start". The motion would cut the Gordian knot of the vicious circle that "they" had got themselves into. The proposed motion was "That the party Leader and all members of the NEC be relieved of their offices, and that this Conference appoints A.N. Other to immediately organise elections for the posts thus vacated, and to act as caretaker manager for the party in the interim".

By the middle of December, Holmes had lost the support of his two fellow MEPs. In a letter to party activists, Titford and Farage regretted that the party had not moved any further forward since the European Elections and that too much time, money and energy had been wasted in the dispute between the Leader and the NEC. They said that, in their opinion, the two parties had now driven themselves into a legal cul-de-sac from which "we cannot see a solution that can be settled for several months". They had decided to withdraw their support from Holmes on account of the fact that Holmes refused to communicate with them other than through solicitors: "What started as a personality clash has developed into a legal tangle where at the end no one party will be satisfied with the legal result. That is why we and other prominent UKIP supporters at the weekend asked Michael Holmes to resign as Leader".

If only Holmes were to stand down, Titford and Farage said, the party could have a new NEC by the end of January and a leadership contest could be completed by the end of February. This course of action would avoid an unnecessary and acrimonious EGM. The party had "lost so much ground and missed opportunities to promote our Euro-realist cause. Now is the time to seek to work together with like-minded members resolved to put country before self".

More letters passed between the central participants in the following few days and Rodney Atkinson, later to stand in the leadership contest, circulated party members with his own pro-

Holmes comments. On the 5th January the NEC nine, now joined by Farage and Titford, issued a statement that they would "abide unreservedly" with the decisions reached at the 22nd January EGM, whatever they might be.

The High Court case brought by Holmes on the 6th December was finally heard on the 13th January. Tony Bennett, Titford's political assistant, who had had a part in the case, reported that the decisions of the Court explicitly recognised that the NEC nine were the legitimate NEC of the party and that all Holmes's applications had been withdrawn and that they could never be resuscitated.

Three days later, Holmes contradicted Bennett's claims in an email, saying "Although Mr Bennett's outpouring may still be within the letter of the law, as per the agreement reached on Thursday the 13th January, it certainly breached the spirit of that agreement. Regarding his 'explanatory notes' members who read these lists should be under no illusions that the permanent suspension of these legal cases DOES NOT IN ANY WAY ENDORSE the view that Tony Scholefield and the old NEC are still 'in existence'. The simple truth is that it has not been possible to test the constitutional validity of the meeting of the 2nd October in a full hearing before a judge in the High Court".

On New Year's Eve the two petitioners groups, representing 56 party associations, met and, with the aid of "extraordinarily fine diplomacy" according to one participant, agreed a common agenda for the EGM. The agenda was a complicated set of motions designed to cover all eventualities. The first motion, that both the party Leader and the NEC should be *asked* to stand down and that fresh elections should be called, was to involve neither speakers nor debate. It gave the possibility of a quick end to the conflict providing both sides did as they were requested. If that did not happen, there would be motions of no confidence in one or both parties, depending on which side had refused to stand down.

The completed agenda was circulated to all members on the 12th January, with the combined petitioners group commenting: "It is to be hoped that the conference will concentrate on the issues and not personalities but, even if it turns out to be a stormy occasion, at least it will allow the members to resolve the problem once-and-for-all. **In the meantime, we have requested that the** protagonists and their respective supporters desist from distributing any more material about the dispute. Similarly, members are requested not to distribute any further literature relating to the dispute at the conference itself".

Alarming rumours began to circulate in the week before the EGM that Holmes was thinking of starting a new party, based on the South West membership of UKIP, the strongest region, should the votes go against him on the 22nd January. The ad hoc petitioners committee discussed this threat and considered ways of persuading Holmes to stay in the party. In the event that Holmes did try to form a breakaway party, the ad hoc committee had tentative plans to try and strangle the attempt at birth by organising meetings in the South West region to keep members there on board. Any breakaway group would most probably destroy both parties, enable the media and the political opponents of UKIP to trash the party comprehensively, and persuade the electorate that we had self-destructed.

However, on the 18th January, Lawrie Boxall of the ad hoc petitioners committee spoke to Holmes on the phone and said that they had begun to hear the rumours about a breakaway party. Holmes replied that there was no way that he would do that. If the votes went against him at the EGM he would remain as a party member and UKIP MEP. Boxall suggested to Holmes that, if he were to admit some mistakes, ask for the party's support and promise a new start, he would win any vote of no-confidence. Holmes replied "I hear what you say".

A final planning meeting was held at the Carlton Club in London, on the eve of the EGM. Holmes and the core members of the petitioners committee met to reach a final understanding on the conduct of the meeting. Holmes succeeded in making a change to the agenda: he wanted the first motion to include a debate.

It was agreed that the agenda would be rigidly adhered to. There was a risk that various groups of people would try to change it. In the interests of conducting the business in the time available, and also to prevent the meeting getting out of hand, and tempers fraying, the conference Chairman and organisers would only depart from the agenda if there were very substantial reasons for doing so. Anybody distributing partisan literature, stickers and so on, would be ejected from the meeting.

The meeting, with 900 attendees, opened civilly enough but soon degenerated into disorder, with large numbers of those present protesting at the decisions of the conference Chairman, Norris McWhirter, perhaps the only person brave enough to take on the task. McWhirter explained the small change to the agenda but many failed to understand. As a result, the audience became confused about what was being discussed. Frustration mounted and McWhirter began to lose control of the meeting amid a barrage of shouting. To compound it all, he had misunderstood the purpose of the first ballot paper and announced that it was to decide on whether there should be a debate on the first motion, whereas it was to decide on the motion itself. The platform became confused, with various participants approaching the chair and attempting to save the situation. Within fifteen minutes of the meeting opening, it seemed set to descend into chaos. The prospect of the meeting breaking up in complete disorder seemed only minutes away.

At the height of the confusion, with people now leaving the hall in disgust, Farage hurried down from the back, took the microphone and calmed the meeting. The misunderstanding on what was being debated was cleared and the meeting got back on track.

Farage told me later that he felt that not just the meeting, but the party itself, was minutes from disintegration in the hall that morning.

Motion 1 requested both the NEC and the party Leader to stand down. Speakers from the two factions were called to speak for and against the motion. Nominated speakers from the floor were called, other speakers from the floor were invited. After a while the mood of the meeting was manifested in cries of "vote!, vote!". The attendees clearly wanted to proceed to a vote with minimal discussion and the mood suggested that they wanted to vote in favour.

The vote for the motion was a secret ballot, the first time that such a procedure had been adopted at a party conference. Ballot boxes were passed around the hall and then taken back to a table just below the platform. The petitioners committee had made careful arrangements and full provision had been made for tellers and proper arrangements for the count. The meeting then adjourned for lunch and the attendees dispersed to find food and discuss the proceedings in nearby pubs.

At 1.15pm the conference reassembled and the results of the ballot were announced: 643 in favour, 245 against. The mood of the members was becoming clear. They were, quite simply, fed up with the antics of both sides and wanted to make a fresh start and reprimand all those involved in the dispute. But the motion was only advisory and both sides, the NEC and the party Leader, refused to stand down. In fact, thirteen of the fifteen NEC members had agreed to stand down but two refused. As the NEC was being treated as a corporate body, the refusal of only one was deemed to be the refusal of the NEC as a whole. The conference therefore moved on to debate the other motions: a vote of no confidence in the NEC and a vote of no confidence in the party Leader.

In the contributions of those speaking for and against the motion of no confidence in the NEC, the mood of the conference was overwhelming – the NEC should stand down. Chris Cooke, one of the two NEC members who had refused this, seemed to take a tactical position: he said that the other members of the NEC had wanted to stand down so that there would be no discussion. He, in fact, thought that all should stand down, but he was refusing this as he wanted the issues to be debated.

At about this time, a member in the front row of the conference collapsed with a heart attack. The meeting was suspended while medical assistance was sought and an ambulance called. The suspension lasted until after 2pm. The member, Tony Semper, subsequently died, two weeks later.

A vote was taken on a show of hands instead of in secret, due to the time lost during the suspension of the meeting. The result was overwhelmingly against the NEC. Only about half a dozen disagreed.

The debate on motion 3, no confidence in the party Leader, was even more intense. It was acrimonious, passions ran high. The Chairman reprimanded some for distributing partisan literature during the debate.

Vitriolic speeches were made from the platform by some members. References were made to the anonymous mailings with thinly-veiled accusations about who might have been involved. One speaker went well over the allotted five minutes, gesticulating wildly, and the microphone was cut off. Farage referred to accusations that a Holmes supporter had attempted to persuade the BBC that Holmes and not he should appear on the *Question Time* program. This first significant television appearance was lost when the BBC, because of the confusion, cancelled the invitation. Farage brought the entire hall to its feet in thunderous applause when he said, thumping the lectern, "if you think I am angry about these accusations, you are right – I am not just angry, I am DISGUSTED".

The result was 569 to 250 in favour. In the four months since the Birmingham AGM and probably also due to the debate on the day, Holmes had lost the support of the party membership.

The EGM had therefore sacked the entire party leadership. Many felt that this was a just verdict on their collective failures at leading and managing the party. A sentiment often voiced at that meeting was that the members were sovereign – it was their party, the party leadership were their servants, not their masters.

As the meeting concluded and the members left for home or gathered in local pubs to discuss the day's proceedings, there was a sense of relief that, hopefully, the dispute had been resolved. The Holmes camp was angry, some were furious. The joker in the pack was whether Holmes would attempt to set up a rival party or, if not that, try to continue the battle through the courts. Would they accept the sovereign decisions of the conference or would they try to wreck them?

Another way of seeing the fight for control of the party was that it was perhaps not so much between the Holmes faction and others but rather between a 'hothead' faction and a moderate faction, between those who like to fan the flames of conflict and those who seek consensus.

The Sunday newspapers carried no accounts of the meeting but the *Times* reported on the Monday that "the future of the United Kingdom Independence Party as a political force was in tatters last night after its members dismissed both the Leader and the national executive". Many of the 900 present had been left despairing for the prospects of the party, the paper said. "Amid noisy and chaotic scenes, peppered with booing and shouting, Mr Holmes initially tried to ignore the vote for him to stand down before bowing to the inevitable".

Private Eye referred to the aborted appearance of Farage on the BBC *Question Time* program. Farage, said the magazine, had led the attack on Holmes and had accused both Holmes and 'his sidekick Janet Girsman, an ex-Tory candidate' of leaking stories about him to the press. They were also alleged to have 'sabotaged' Farage's appearance on the *Question Time* program, to be broadcast from Brussels on the 3rd February, by demanding that Holmes appear instead – 'the show's producer, understandably losing patience with the UKIP squabblers, eventually decided to use neither of them'.

Our prospects were resting on a very precarious base. The major question was whether Holmes would attempt to set up an alternative party, a move which would have spelled disaster for the whole antifederalist movement. Holmes wrote to members a few days after the conference, suggesting that they had been denied their democratic rights because no postal or proxy arrangements had been made, but he added "I shall however accept the verdict of the meeting although I do believe that with a postal vote the result may well have been different. I have done my best to pull the Party together over the last two years. We have more than doubled the membership and run a highly effective campaign, which produced a stunning result on the 10th June. We now have three MEPs in the so-called European parliament". Under the subtitle "A New Beginning – A New NEC – A New Leader" Holmes finished with:

> There is no doubt that the party's progress has been slowed because some of the NEC and I found it difficult to work with each other. A new NEC must run the party for all the members...I have therefore decided not to stand for re-election. I hope that a candidate will come forward whom a significant group of the members and I can support wholeheartedly. In this connection I do not believe the length of party membership should be the main criteria. The most important factors should be their personal, political and business/work background, their previous achievements for the party and what attributes and commitment they can bring to the service of the members as Leader for the next four years.

A tense few days ensued, waiting to see what the major players would do. Holmes had, immediately after the conference, repeated his message from the week before that he would stay with the party and that he had no intention of setting up a rival group.

The internal email discussion group was a barometer of party opinion on these issues. There was much bitter and acrimonious comment but the majority opinion was that the meeting had been validly constituted and that the issue had been settled and should be laid to rest. The majority of correspondents said it was time to move on and to get back to work. Postings into the list on Tuesday reported a talk that Holmes had given the previous day and said that he had said nothing that would threaten the future of the party. A posting a few days later reported that Holmes had pledged to work constructively for the future of the cause. It seemed that we had weathered the crisis without splitting, at least for the moment.

There followed a period of five weeks during which the election of a new NEC went ahead. There were 59 candidates for the 15 positions. The fifteen elected on the 1st March included Farage, Atkinson, Titford, Lott, Cooke, Mackinlay, and Scholefield.

On the 4th March the list of candidates for the leadership elections was published. They were: Rodney Atkinson, Bernard Collignon, Ian Gillman, Harold Green, Michael Holmes, Damian Hockney, Craig Mackinlay, Michael Nattrass, Brian Smalley, and Jeffrey Titford. Given the letter from Holmes after the conference, his candidacy was a surprise.

Ian Gillman and Bernard Collignon were unlikely to succeed as they were little-known within the party. Harold Green was more well-known than Gillman and Collignon but also had little likelihood of being elected. He had been a vociferous supporter of Holmes during the dispute. Holmes, as recounted below, subsequently withdrew his candidacy. That left, as realistic contenders, Atkinson, Hockney, Mackinlay, Nattrass, Smalley and Titford.

Nattrass, in his election address said: "My religion is Church of England, my friends are from all faiths. Racists are unwelcome. Our crusade has nothing to do with intolerance but with independence, freedom of speech, inventiveness, aspirations for peace and Churchillian philosophy".

Hockney, although of the moderate tendency and someone

who had performed great services for the party in improving its literature, and who had an excellent and appealing public face, was reputedly not very good in organisational skills. Titford was widely respected in the party. He had not participated significantly in the dispute and, indeed, when he spoke to the rowdy EGM of the 22nd January, his reflective speech was listened to in respectful and total silence.

Give and take a few minor criticisms here or there, the party might fare well under Mackinlay, Smalley, or Titford. Conversely, the party might fare badly under Atkinson as there was a section of opinion in the party which was strongly opposed to him. Atkinson had for some years been running his own campaign, the Campaign for UK Conservatism, which held two or three one-day conferences each year. This caused some, including myself, to wonder whether UKIP would be taken too close to the Conservative Party should Atkinson become Leader. I put this to him at a leadership hustings meeting. Atkinson responded to this worry in an email to members of the discussion group:

> *The Campaign for UK Conservatism has no connection with the Conservative Party. It was founded in opposition to virtually everything the Tory government was doing during the 1990s. It was the first credible Conservative organisation to campaign for withdrawal from the EU and it has as its supporters those who are in the Conservative Party, those who have left it, those who were never in it, former Liberals and even the occasional socialist and of course many UKIP members. Like Socialists and Liberals who are in UKIP I am also trying to convince the millions who are still inside the party I left to restore democracy, nation and constitution. As soon as one of the other political parties adopts UKIP's policy of withdrawal, we will ALL rejoice and UKIP will have proved the greatest success in British political history.*

However, Atkinson was quoted in the *Times* of the 26th February as saying "I am running to unite the party and fight the notion that UKIP can work as an alternative government, which some in our party believe we can do…We must not stand against friends in other parties".

As an aside, Rodney Atkinson is the brother of the comedian

Rowan Atkinson. The former often liked to say that his brother's profession was comedy while his own was tragedy. A good *bon mot*.

One of Atkinson's constant themes in his written work and talks was that the idea of European union originated in the Third Reich. While it is true that the Third Reich did indeed plan, for example, a single currency, many people felt that such a theme was mistaken and unhelpful to the cause in that it seemed to be suggesting an equivalence between the Third Reich and the European Union that even the latter's strongest opponents would mostly not subscribe to. Unease on this subject was expressed by Christopher Booker and Bill Jamieson, both *Sunday Telegraph* journalists and long-time supporters of the party, in a joint letter to NEC members on the 9th March. They said that they had to a certain extent staked their journalistic credibility on their support for the party and that they therefore felt that they wanted to express deeply-felt concerns about the leadership election. They lamented missed opportunities and media embarrassments for the party caused by the dispute, implied that Holmes would not be a good choice, and went on to say:

> *We regard it as equally vital that the Party should choose someone whose analysis of the nature and failings of the European Union is based on serious, up-to-date understanding of how and why the EU is developing in the way it is; and not some wider conspiracy theory which, however compelling to a minority of members, cannot be shared by the vast majority. We believe at least one of the candidates for the leadership falls into this latter category, Mr Rodney Atkinson. It is our personal concern that any Leader holding such views might try to take the Party in directions where it would be impossible for us to follow, as we would sadly have to make clear.*

The letter was circulated to UKIP members in general by a third party, causing Atkinson to counter-attack with accusations in another letter, thereby earning the censure of George Franklin-Ryan, Returning Officer for the election.

Antipathy to Atkinson was also based on other factors. First, for those who were concerned about factionalism, his alignment with the Holmes faction and his hard-line tendency. From Atkinson's comments it was clear that he would, if elected Leader, immediately indulge in factional fighting and divisive actions. Some felt that it was essential that Atkinson should not win the leadership election because his election as Leader would lead to the destruction of UKIP as a viable political force.

The NEC, conscious of the still delicate state of the party, stipulated that the candidates could issue a short election address only. No other mailing by either the candidates or their supporters, on paper or by email, was to be allowed. No derogatory statements would be allowed in the canvassing of support. A series of hustings meetings was organised in Winchester, London, Birmingham, Yorkshire and Paignton.

Holmes, in a final damaging act, withdrew his candidacy and resigned from the party in late March, thereby precipitating problems as regards who, if anyone, should become UKIP's MEP in his place. His statement to the NEC said:

I have today withdrawn my candidacy for the Leadership election and George Franklin-Ryan has confirmed his acceptance. Furthermore, after careful consideration, I have decided to resign from party membership as at 12 noon today, Monday the 20th March. This decision has not been taken without careful consideration. However, I remain implacable against our continuing membership of the European Union. I shall continue to campaign in any way appropriate for a dignified withdrawal from EU membership.

The previous Saturday Holmes had attended the Paignton hustings meeting and, according to Tony Bennett in the Chelmsford office – "Michael got a battering mostly from members in his own South West region, and was unable to answer embarrassing questions about why he had set up a separate bank account in Salisbury without NEC authority in 1998 and what he had done with his MEP allowances to date".

Despite the fact that the 1999 European Elections had been held under a party list system, in which voters voted for a party rather than individual candidates, Holmes remained as an independent MEP for the South West, thereby possibly damaging the party's standing among the voters of that region and affecting its vote in the 2004 European Elections. The *Times* reported, the day after Holmes's resignation, that the party had been "plunged into strife" and that it was now possible that a group of UKIP members would set up a rival Reform Party with Holmes as a prominent member. On the same day, Farage and Titford wrote to branch chairmen and activists:

> *The cause of national independence is far bigger than any individual and UKIP. Nevertheless, the UKIP is the only vehicle through which to achieve our independence, and the party will continue to prosper without Mr Holmes. We are relieved that the infighting is now at an end. The UKIP is conscious that our voters in the South West have been badly served and call upon Mr Holmes to resign as an MEP in order that our supporters are properly represented.*

The result of the leadership election on the 20th April was that Atkinson lost, by a very slender margin – 0.4 per cent – to Jeffrey Titford, after the other candidates had been eliminated under the single transferable vote system. Out of 7,869 eligible members, 4,107 voted. Titford issued a press release in which he congratulated Atkinson on the significant support he had gathered. He was also pleased, he said, to see Nattrass and Smalley showing up well in the leadership contest. He looked forward to all of them working together – "we've doubled our membership in less than a year; I believe we can redouble it within a further year".

Atkinson did not take up this offer but chose, instead, to resign from the party, alleging extremist infiltration, thereby providing more ammunition for our opponents in various quarters. The *Financial Times* reported that Atkinson "the businessman who mounted an unsuccessful legal challenge to Britain's decision to sign the Maastricht Treaty...alleged that the party had been 'infiltrated by extremists'".

Atkinson's failure in the leadership election was followed, a few days later, by a prominent article in the *Times* reporting in detail on the departure of 200 or so party members who intended to set up a new group called Reform UK. The statements of the Reform group heavily cited the supposed takeover of the party by far-right elements. The *Times* article even claimed that the party had "split amid accusations that it is dominated by far-right extremists". The paper said that more than 200 leading members had announced their resignation and, in a joint statement which party members would be receiving at the weekend, the departing members claimed that the party had been "condemned to the far right". The paper thought that "the decision leaves a huge question mark over UKIP's future, and its original aim of forging a mainstream anti-European party appears to be on the brink of collapse".

People inside the party dismissed the article. They said that the suggestion of a split was an exaggeration, that the 200 leaving were far from being all leading members and that the claim that the party was veering to the far right was completely false. It was unclear at the time whether the new group intended to field candidates and whether Holmes would be joining them. The *Times* article quoted the Reform group, saying that "those leaving, who include members of the party's national executive, Regional Organisers and candidates, said that Mr Titford would be a front for other political forces".

The sentiment among those leaving was probably based around the now old story of the meeting between Farage and Deavin, a story which had been repeatedly brought up in the national press, and also the fact that Titford had come from the Referendum Party via, briefly, the New Britain Party and that the latter was accused of having hard-line policies on immigration. The subsequent leadership of UKIP by Titford does not support that sentiment. It may be that the Reform group members, like Alan Sked in the previous fracture, conflated the intense disagreements between the two sides in the battle for control of the party with the accusations of far right sympathies that had been aired in anonymous letters. Perhaps they used these accusations as a pretext to justify their departure, a departure based on disappointment at having lost the argument. The *Times* article continued by reporting that those resigning thought that other members would soon have to decide whether "UKIP's disease is any longer worth the fight". But staying with the party "tars us with an extremist brush. We must move on". Those leaving included Chris Cooke, Ron Dickinson, and Janet Girsman.

Cooke subsequently said that the members of the Reform group were not the people that he thought they were. Girsman was widely thought to be a particularly difficult person to work with. Ron Dickinson, Holmes's close associate, was certainly a great loss to us on account of his determination and energy in fighting the party's cause.

The recurrent theme of Tory defectors surfaced again on the 4th January. The *Guardian* reported that Teresa Gorman was again on the point of defecting to UKIP, along with others. Farage was quoted as saying "I think things will happen over the next couple of weeks. I think that because there is a large element now in the Conservative Party who are very unhappy with Hague's policy of being in Europe and not run by Europe. They realise that that is not coherent, that the simple choice is that we are either in the European Union and we make the best we can of it, or we come out".

The *Daily Telegraph* on the same day reported that Rupert Allason was also a possible defector. He was said to be at the top of the party's list of potential defectors. Allason was quoted as saying that "I would never say never, because I'm rapidly coming to the conclusion that Britain's interests do not lie in being governed by foreigners".

A couple of days later, the *Independent*, pursuing the theme of Tory splits on Europe, reported the formation of an "intergroup" in the European parliament. It declared that William Hague's struggle to unite the Conservative Party's warring factions had suffered a new setback. Six Conservative MEPs had linked up with the UKIP MEPs in a group called SOS Democracy which was discussing plans for an 'anti-European' publicity campaign. Jeffrey Titford said in the article that "we are pleased that Conservatives, UKIP members and groups from the rest of Europe are binding together, conscious that democracy is being eroded".

The rather inflated claims of the *Independent* report were set in context by Roger Helmer, Conservative MEP for the East Midlands, in a letter to the paper the following day explaining that an intergroup was a loose cross-party, transnational group focussed on a particular issue – "the SOS Democracy intergroup includes Greens, Socialists, Gaullists and MEPs from many parties and countries".

The *Daily Mail* reported on the SOS Democracy intergroup and quoted Christopher Heaton-Harris, one of the Conservative members. Heaton-Harris, attempting to deflate the claim, said that just because one or two members of UKIP sat in the meetings hardly meant that they controlled them – "UKIP have been absolutely hopeless in the European parliament. We share no common ground with them".

The potential for illiberalism based on the drive to the utopia of a secular religion was demonstrated in the European parliament on the 2nd February. Titford, speaking in a debate about the formation of the new government in Austria which included the right-wing Freedom Party led by Jörg Haider, said:

> *We cannot, and we do not, support in any way the sentiments and politics of Herr Haider and we deplore his references to the Third Reich. We also, however, deplore the fact that your parliament should consider interfering in the policies of an elected government of any country, especially one which is part of the European Union. My party at home are certainly not racists, but we do not accept the rule or interference of the European Union very well. Are you going to interfere with Great Britain's Parliament if we were elected?*

Labour MEPs shouted: "Yes, we would".

A psychological threshold was passed later in the month when the *Daily Telegraph* published an editorial article on the launch of a poster campaign by Britain in Europe. The article said that, after several delays, Britain in Europe had launched its campaign and that it would focus, not on the single currency, but on the central issue of Britain's EU membership. It thought that this was 'clever politics' because the federalists knew that two thirds of the public were against the single currency but only around 40 per cent wanted to leave the EU. Rather than calling directly for the abolition of the pound, Britain in Europe wanted to play on the "inchoate sense that adopting the euro is somehow necessary to be 'in Europe' ". In conclusion, the article echoed the opinion so often voiced by ordinary voters:

Most voters, although they do not always put it in these terms, hanker after a kind of country membership of the EU: 'We voted for a common market, not a European superstate'. Yet it is precisely this option which pro-Europeans are ruling out. Given the choice between complete federalism and complete independence, people will choose independence. Paradoxically, Britain in Europe is driving Britain out of Europe.

The article was entitled "UKIP's Unwitting Allies". It contained no reference to the party. Our existence and our central policy were assumed to be known to all.

William Hague, Conservative Leader, had embarked on an anti-single currency campaign, speaking in town centres throughout Britain, and promoting the Conservatives' "In Europe, Not Run by Europe" slogan. Local UKIP members organised counter demonstrations. In Woking on the 23rd February Hague faced particular barracking from UKIP demonstrators with battle-bus in attendance.

Charges of bias in the broadcast media were raised again in January, this time by a Labour supporter, Lord Shore. The *Daily Telegraph* reported that Labour Eurosceptics had accused the BBC of "outrageous bias" in its coverage of the European issue and that they had complained that broadcasters were ignoring their point of view, being obsessed with stories of Conservative splits over the single currency. Shore, the paper said, as Chairman of the Labour Euro-Safeguards Campaign, had accused Downing Street and "Labour's Millbank tendency" of falling over themselves to suppress the views of Labour Party Eurosceptics. Shore complained that the BBC and other broadcasters had failed to interview a single Labour Eurosceptic in 600 hours of coverage of the European Election campaign. This was a symptom of a "broader and longer problem" of bias in the coverage of Europe on television and radio.

UKIP's list of candidates for the London Assembly elections and London Mayor were finalised on the 29th January. Damian Hockney was the candidate in the Mayoral election but the result was very disappointing, with Hockney coming tenth out of eleven candidates.

The fourth AGM of TEAM was held in London in early April.

By that time, TEAM grouped together 35 Eurosceptic organisations from 12 European countries, within or outside the EU. Most of these organisations were small but a few were of some influence in their own countries, most notably the British and Scandinavian groups.

UKIP sent Jeffrey Titford as a speaker. Other British organisations with representatives at the meeting were the Democracy Movement, the Bruges Group, the Campaign for an Independent Britain, the Labour Euro-Safeguards Campaign, the Campaign Against Euro Federalism, and the Anti-Maastricht Alliance. Also present was Jens-Peter Bonde, Chairman of the EDD group in the European parliament, the group to which UKIP's MEPs belonged.

At that AGM I spoke to Kristian Groth of the Danish June Movement and Lave Broch of the People's Movement Against the EU and passed on details of British journalists sympathetic to their cause who could help them with fundraising in the UK. The date of the Danish referendum on entry to the single currency had already been set for the 28th September.

Back home, by-elections continued to be disappointing for us. It seemed that nothing would improve our prospects in by-elections. Where the candidate was already a relatively well-known figure the results could be slightly better but were still disappointing. The average by-election result was usually around 300-600 votes. The best that could be said was that we usually came fourth, though Scotland was an electoral desert for us.

The by-election in Ceredigion on the 4th February, with John Bufton as the candidate, put the party fifth with 487 votes. The presence of Plaid Cymru and local Welsh political loyalties made our job particularly difficult. Our main emphasis in the mostly rural seat was the damage caused by the Common Agricultural Policy and the fact that EU Objective 1 grants – regional handouts from Brussels which supposedly help the poorer regions of the EU – were highly likely to disappear when the EU was expanded to the Eastern European countries.

That Scotland was almost impossible for us was shown on the 16th March in the Ayr Scottish Parliament by-election, where Alistair McConnachie came eighth with a mere 113 votes. The by-election was fought on the central policy of EU withdrawal but also on a platform of abolition of the Scottish Parliament, the

Welsh Assembly and the Northern Ireland Assembly, and the restoration of Westminster as the UK's sole legislature. A difficult platform in view of the Scottish vote in September 1997 for a Scottish Parliament and Scottish opinion for a degree of home rule.

In the Romsey by-election on the 4th May our candidate was Garry Rankin-Moore, a Liberal Democrat councillor who had resigned his national party membership but remained, at least at the start of the campaign, in the Liberal Democrat group on Test Valley council. This gave Labour the opportunity for a little light ridicule of the Liberal Democrats, with Hilary Armstrong, local government minister, asking "when is a Liberal Democrat not a Liberal Democrat? When they are a UKIP candidate. Its like some bizarre joke".

The fact that the candidate was already relatively well-known probably helped in the eventual result of 901 votes, a relatively good result in absolute terms but still only 2.3 per cent, and the result was not the decisive breakthrough that the party had been hoping for. Tottenham, on the 22nd June, with Ashwin Tanna as the candidate in a constituency with a high percentage of ethnic minority voters, only returned 136 votes (0.8 per cent).

We had never ascribed particular importance to local elections but, in May 2000, there were 41 UKIP candidates in the local elections, most having decided to stand on their own initiative rather than because of any organised party campaign. We had always felt that our message about the European Union would be too difficult to connect to voters at local level. But the results were very encouraging. One candidate was elected as a district councillor with 54 per cent of the vote, another gained 44 per cent. A third gained 19 per cent, a handful gained 10-12 per cent. Overall, our share of the vote was 8.3 per cent. It was in contrast to a natural supposition that the party's share of the vote would decrease as the election went from European Election to General Election to Westminster by-election and then local election.

Roger Knapman, the former Conservative MP for Stroud and a whip in a previous Conservative government, joined UKIP in May. Knapman had been a Bruges Group supporter in 1990, as described in an earlier chapter. The *Daily Telegraph* quoted Knapman as saying that it was impossible for Britain to be "in Europe but not run by Europe", as the Conservative Party was saying – "thirty five years ago people thought they were going into a Common Market and a lot of people still think they are". But, since then, there had been the Single European Act, "when Lady Thatcher said she was hoodwinked", the Maastricht Treaty, the Amsterdam Treaty, and now the country was set to sign up to the Nice Treaty. This would be the "final nail in the coffin" for Westminster and would lead to a United States of Europe.

Preparing For The 2001 General Election

With the internal party conflict resolved, organisation began for the 2001 General Election campaign. The regional structure of the party adopted for the European Elections was retained and it was agreed that regional committees would be able to interview potential candidates. Candidate applications were solicited from April 2000 onwards.

Mike Nattrass became Party Chairman and Bryan Smalley became party Secretary. A number of subcommittees were formed to handle party affairs: Manifesto, election and campaigns, membership, Constitution, General Election candidates, and others. It was recognised that the party Constitution and rule book required overhaul and also that attention was required to the IT side of the party's structure. The infighting had revealed weaknesses in the Constitution which prevented rapid solution of disputes and the circulation of letters by various factions had revealed how easily the central membership lists could be obtained. An IT/Internet subcommittee was charged with revamping the membership database, making it secure while still allowing appropriate people access, and generally increasing the use of IT within the party. The goal was electronic communication from London to the individual regions and party associations.

Michael Holmes still held on as a South West region independent MEP. The party attempted to regain the seat by negotiation with Holmes but was unsuccessful. Two attempts were made to persuade the Home Office that the seat should revert to the party but these also were unsuccessful. By November it was decided that it would not be practical to take the issue to court and that the situation would be left as it was. Membership growth in the South West region indicated that any damage had been slight. In the months after the January EGM Holmes suffered a mild stroke.

National membership was now at 7,500 and the party seemed to be heading towards a position where we might hope to make the 'little man' and small businesses our natural constituency. Farming and fishing had been hit hard by the EU's Common Agricultural Policy and Common Fisheries Policy. Small traders and companies were falling foul of EU regulations.

The imposition of metric measures in markets had generated "metric martyrs" who decided, as a matter of principle, and because their customers preferred British measures, to resist the new law. Steve Thoburn became the most famous of this band as the legal system pursued them assiduously for the crime of selling their goods in pounds and ounces. It politicised Neil Herron, Thoburn's friend and fellow market trader, thereby creating a great enemy for the system in the future, as this account will show. It created legal precedent as, desperate to avoid the conclusion that the Maastricht Treaty had been impliedly repealed, the judge in the case discovered a new hierarchy of statutes, hitherto unknown to the legal profession. Steve Thoburn died aged 39, four years later.

Steve Thoburn, John Dove, Peter Collins, Neil Herron and Colin Hunt on the steps of the court. *The Sunday Telegraph* 25th November 2001, picture by Justin Sutcliffe

Our fifth national conference was held on the 29th and 30th September, dates chosen to be immediately after the result of the Danish referendum on the single currency. The gamble was successful – the Danes had rejected the currency. On the first day about 500-600 members gathered in Methodist Central Hall and, at about midday, Ole Krarup, the Leader of the Danish People's Movement Against the EU, just arrived from Denmark, was welcomed into the hall to rapturous applause. The *Times* reported the following day that "Mr Kararup (sic) received a hero's welcome when he addressed the annual conference of the United Kingdom Independence Party in Westminster. After flying in from Copenhagen yesterday, he said that the lesson for the British was that they should never be cowed by the apparent might of the opposition".

Those in favour of the single currency in Denmark had consisted of 80 per cent of Danish MPs, 46 out of 48 newspapers, and the business and trade union establishment. British Eurosceptics helped in the campaign in at least two ways – repeated appeals for campaign funds were published in the Newsletters of Eurosceptic groups, so that ordinary members could send donations, and Paul Sykes also provided around £500,000 to fund 150 full-page advertisements in the Danish newspapers in the last days of the campaign. Daniel Hannan, a Conservative MEP who was closely involved on the British side, received considerable donations from "ordinary" members of the public, as he recounted in the *Sunday Telegraph* at the beginning of October:

> *I had a particular interest in the result, having organised a public appeal in Britain to help the cash-starved Danish No campaign. And here, too, I have bad news for Mr Blair. Our tiny operation – the donations were received at my flat and counted by my wife – raised more than £150,000, with most contributions coming in denominations of £20 or less. If this is how much people care about Danish freedom, it isn't hard to imagine how they would react in the event of a British referendum.*

The result of the Danish referendum showed us that we could win, even against all the odds. If the result had been 'yes' then, no doubt, our morale would have dropped. But now we knew it could be done and we knew we had like-minded friends in other countries.

The conference also heard speeches from Jeffrey Titford and Nigel Farage, from Christopher Booker and the Earl of Bradford, from Roger Knapman, and others. Perhaps the best presentation of the day came from Neil Herron, who gave an account of his and Steve Thoburn's dealings with trading standards officers in their part of the country. A significant change was signalled by the appearance of Marc Glendening as a speaker at the conference. Paul Sykes, the Yorkshire businessman who had funded the Democracy Movement, announced in the Movement's bulletin for June/July that he was rejoining the Conservative Party, convinced by William Hague's stronger opposition to the single currency. As someone with a declared party allegiance, both he and the Movement – an all-party organisation – recognised that he could no longer hold his position as Chairman of the Movement. Accordingly, Sykes stepped down. The appearance of Glendening at the conference signalled a move towards possible closer relations between UKIP and the Movement, perhaps eased by the departure of Sykes.

In turn, Nigel Farage was one of the speakers at a demonstration organised by the Democracy Movement on the 28th October. Other speakers included John Redwood; Peter Shore; Patricia McKenna, Irish Green Party MEP; Anthony Coughlan of the TEAM board; Jens-Peter Bonde; and Mike Woodin of the Green Party. About 8,000 to 10,000 people went on the "Stop the Eurostate" demonstration from Hyde Park to Trafalgar Square, many of them UKIP members, there being considerable overlap between the active members in both groups. There was virtually no media coverage of the event.

There were three by-elections on the 23rd November, in Preston, West Bromwich West, and Glasgow Anniesland. The latter also included a by-election for the Scottish Parliament. For UKIP, which fielded candidates in the two English constituencies, the by-election trend continued. In Preston, the party gained 458 votes (2.1 per cent), at West Bromwich West 246 (1.3 per cent). Anniesland was not contested by the party.

On that same Thursday, Farage finally appeared on *Question Time*. The audience appeared to be uniformly hostile but

Question Time audiences always were hostile to anything which they perceived as being on the right. Farage suggested that low turn-outs were because voters knew that Westminster was increasingly powerless. This earned him some booing from the audience.

The three by-elections of the 23rd November had all been Labour wins. The Conservatives' warnings of a superstate EU seemed to have had little effect. UKIP had done miserably. Opinion polls showed that a little under half the electorate had no particular qualms about British soldiers participating in the European Rapid Reaction Force, thus perhaps vindicating the government's claims that the electorate was nowhere near as Eurosceptic as some of the press.

The 2001 General Election

By 2000 we had long progressed from seeing ourselves as a home for disaffected Conservative Party members. We now understood that many voters for other parties held similar views to our own and that political success could only come from appealing to that wider cross-party sentiment. Accordingly, we decided to target Labour and Liberal Democrat supporters in our strategy for the 2001 General Election. The *Daily Telegraph*, reporting on this strategy in early December, quoted Farage: "At the last election we were out to kick the Tories. This time round, we want to put the fear of God into Labour and the Liberal Democrats".

Our intention was to damage the Liberal Democrats in the South West in particular, where they were relatively strong, and thereby to force a rethink on the European issue within their party. Scotland, it was accepted, would be a write-off and Wales would be little better. Scotland seemed to be intent on the SNP chimera of "independence within Europe" and Wales was still attached to EU handouts.

Realists within the party were inclined to discount claims of winning seats as being for public consumption and, instead, adopted a more realistic goal of greatly increasing the party's number of votes, in absolute and percentage terms. A million votes was the unofficial target. Nevertheless, it was important that we did much better than in 1997 to avoid calls for the party to abandon national elections and to concentrate only on

European Elections, such as had happened in the case of the June Movement and the People's Movement in Denmark. Such a development would mark the end of our ambition of becoming a serious national force.

The search for candidates began about nine months before the General Election. All candidates were required to make a formal, written application and to undergo an interview. In the months before the election a dedicated candidate support office was established, run by Heather Conyngham, seconded from her position with the EDD in Brussels for the purpose, and working with Kirsten Farage. In the later stages of the campaign, despite extra lines being installed to cope with the volume of communications, the office was barely coping with the demand from the eventual 429 candidates.

The party's efforts to financially help victims of EU legislation came under threat at the end of the year when the European parliament said that it would take legal action as regards the use of the expenses claimed by UKIP's MEPs. The *Times* reported in January 2001 that Farage and Titford had been compelled, by the European parliament's own rules, to accept £11,500 more in travel expenses than they had actually spent since their election in 1999 and said that "they have openly used this money to support a British shopkeeper who refuses to use the metric system; a butcher who has defied the EU by selling beef on the bone; and commercial fishermen facing EU restrictions".

"Blackmail" was the word the Conservative Party used to describe a possible deal between some Eurosceptic Conservative MPs and UKIP, a story which broke in late January. A meeting in early September between Lord Neidpath, a UKIP member, and Lord Pearson, a Conservative but one passionately opposed to the EU, resulted in the idea of offering us between £1million and £2million if we would refrain from putting up candidates against particular strongly Eurosceptic Conservative MPs in seats where the UKIP vote might lose them the election. The idea was floated by Pearson and went via Neidpath to Nigel Farage. A list of some 30 MPs was apparently drawn up but the idea was leaked and the Conservative Party leadership stamped on the idea. Farage was apparently sympathetic to the proposal, being reported as saying:

'They want us to call the dogs off' Mr Farage said. 'They

believe that in many marginal seats the UKIP could cost them their seats. There is only one way that a deal with the Conservative Party can work. For the UKIP to convince its constituency associations and candidates to stand down will only be possible if there is something in it for us. £1million would be a good start'.

The idea was to use the finance to help candidates in the North of England, where the party was weaker, and also to target Labour and Liberal Democrat candidates. It is quite possible, however, that, if the plan had gone ahead, some UKIP associations would have vigorously protested.

As in 1999, so in 2001, the smear tactics began again. The *Spectator* published a long article by Alan Sked in February in which the worst possible interpretation was placed on a string of issues and the old business of the photograph was again raked over. Sked lamented the supposed changes that had taken place within his creation – "in the beginning it was very different. When I founded the party it had clear principles. It would have no truck with racism and xenophobia and, because it refused to acknowledge the legitimacy of the EU claims to run this country, it would send no members to the European parliament". But, even more importantly, he said, he had intended that the party should not be a one-issue party. He intended it to have policies on a wide range of issues – health, education, devolution, economic policy – but, today, all those principles had been abandoned. "The party never publishes proposals on mainstream issues, and even on the EU it has concentrated its major effort simply on metrication. It now takes its money from Brussels but does nothing in return for it."

In judging the accuracy of these claims it should be noted that our election Manifesto for the 2001 General Election contained the familiar and long-standing statement of the party's principle of non-discrimination, that we were a non-racist, non-sectarian party that included people "of all backgrounds who value individual freedom, tolerance and our right to govern ourselves". Additionally, our Manifesto set out policies on the economy, health, social security, pensions, education, transport and the environment, home affairs, agriculture and fisheries, defence and foreign affairs, and the British Constitution.

A more principled attack was undertaken by Lord Tebbit who argued, as many did, that UKIP candidates would split the Eurosceptic vote and so allow the election of Labour and Liberal Democrat pro-Europeans. In his regular *Daily Mail* column Tebbit took up the theme of a previous article: "Readers should not get me wrong about UKIP. I was delighted when both Mr Farage and Mr Titford were elected to the European parliament, where they speak for the third of the British people who want to escape from the European Union now. But helping (even by accident) the Government to win power to bind us even more tightly into the Euro state with its own police, army, courts and laws – and powerful enough to ignore our own Parliament or elections – is a different matter".

Conversely, the *Guardian* published a special feature about Farage and Titford, describing their experiences in the "belly of the beast" in Strasbourg. Laced with a few mildly derogatory descriptions, it was nevertheless not something that UKIP could particularly object to. Chris Huhne MEP, a fervently Europhile Liberal Democrat was quoted as saying that "they're not fascists, they're not corrupt and they're not morons. Some of their members are headbangers, though".

The issue of the attendance of MEPs in the chamber and also of UKIP MEPs in committees was discussed. The article said that it was accepted that the debating chamber of the European parliament was a waste of time. Except for votes – MEPs had to vote to get paid – the room was empty. Huhne said that "the place where you change minds is in committee. You can actually alter legislation quite effectively there, and that's where UKIP doesn't play a part. They're a waste of space". Richard North, described as a "UKIP staffer", retorted laconically "Yes, its true, if you're very, very good, and work very, very hard, you can get to change a couple of words. Wow!". The original reason for sending UKIP MEPs to the European parliament was restated by Farage: "There's no point in going. We send a staff member to observe instead. We haven't come here to do a Billy Graham bit and convert everybody. We haven't come to change Europe. We've come to find out how it works and what it costs, and take that message back to the British people".

The paper's description of North as a "UKIP staffer" masked

another UKIP-style ruction. North had resigned from the party on the 9th February (for the second time, the first being after the Wirral South by-election in early 1997). Tony Bennett, Jeffrey Titford's PA in the Chelmsford office, was drawn into the argument as was Nikki Sinclair in the London HQ. Bennett was sacked by his boss, North rejoined the party. One newspaper gossip column referred to the party as a "nest of vipers" and a "Punch and Judy show". There was also trouble in the Yorkshire and Humberside region of the party. Then Sinclair, having been elected onto the NEC but disqualified for not relinquishing her paid job as HQ office manager, as the rules were thought to require, began legal action against the party which was still running two years later. There was embarrassment for us in Scotland where Alistair McConnachie, the Scottish organiser, had apparently made remarks doubting the scale of the holocaust. The NEC initially expelled McConnachie from the party but then reduced that to a one year suspension of membership.

The desirability, according to the Conservative Party, of UKIP candidates giving Conservative Eurosceptics a free run was again raised in a gossip column article in the *Daily Telegraph* at the end of March:

> *Among the Tories to feel the UKIP's clammy hand on his shoulder is David Heathcoat-Amory, industry spokesman. 'It makes no sense at all for the UKIP to stand for Eurosceptic Tory seats; it's insane,' he says, sweating on a majority of 528. 'It just makes it more likely for federal-minded Liberal Democrats to get in. The only conclusion I can draw is that the UKIP is an uncontrolled, disorganised rabble'.*

To which Farage subsequently retorted: "David Heathcoat-Amory recently called us a rabble...We are proud to be a rabble! We include viscounts and earls, fishermen, nurses and doctors among our candidates". The *Daily Mail* commentator Andrew Alexander urged the "amateurs" to stand down in favour of the Conservatives:

> *The trouble with amateurs in politics is that they tend to behave, well, like amateurs. The point is alarmingly well*

made by the United Kingdom Independence Party, dedicated to getting Britain out of the EU. Polls suggest a majority of voters would support our departure. But only the Tories can be expected to achieve that...My advice to UKIP supporters and party workers is to leave the party, withdraw any financial support they have been giving and abandon their voluntary assistance. The UKIP is bent on making an ass of itself.

But we continued to attract high-profile members and supporters. Sir Jack Hayward, the owner of Wolverhampton Wanderers football club, joined the party and donated a five figure sum, leading Farage to say that "with a month to go we are on course to spend £1m at the General Election which for little old us is not bad going".

In Bexhill and Battle, where Farage was standing as the UKIP candidate, the outgoing MP, Charles Wardle, a former Conservative immigration minister, declared his support for Farage and said that he would be campaigning on his behalf.

This is going to be fun': Nigel Farage, the UK
Independence Party candidate, who has the
support of rebel Tories
The Daily Telegraph 9th May 2001, picture by Ian Jones

The Manifesto was released on the 14th May. The primary contributors were Aidan Rankin, David Rowlands and John Whittaker, with further input coming from Tony Bennett, Craig Mackinlay, and Tony Scholefield. Rankin, an academic at the London School of Economics, brought a more liberal influence into the Manifesto discussions, especially on social policy, Whittaker provided input on economic policy and Rowlands provided input on agricultural policy. Rankin's aim was to position the party as "a party that stands for individual freedom and tolerance, and so rejects prejudice and political correctness". As mentioned above, the sixteen pages of the document covered all important policy areas, albeit in a broadbrush way, the party having as a whole long-recognised that a single-issue stance was less credible to voters and, in any case, as a party aiming to be long-term and more than a pressure group, it had a responsibility to explain where it stood on other issues.

The core of the Manifesto, "Better Off Out", was, as in 1997, the £20billion projected savings which would accrue from EU withdrawal, this time summarised in the slogan "The Independence Dividend". The party's election ambitions were summarised by the *Guardian* in an article of mid-May. With 401 candidates already lined up, the target was a million votes and three seats and emergence as a real political force. But there were more pragmatic assessments on the part of the party's leadership – "privately, the UKIP's leadership concedes the party is unlikely to take seats at Westminster next month, though it argues it can use the General Election as a step to greater success at the next European Elections".

Two stories gained us blanket media coverage during the election. The first was the news that Paul Sykes had decided to give the party very considerable financial help. Clearly, it was of immense benefit to have such financial backing and, as regards the media, it was exactly the kind of story they liked, especially given the parallels with Sir James Goldsmith and the Referendum Party. In a way, the overshadowed UKIP of 1997 was now in the same position that the Referendum Party had been in that election.

Sykes paid for the printing and distribution of the electoral addresses of every candidate – something like 65,000 high-quality leaflets for 429 candidates, as well as providing similarly high-quality posters and a further 10,000 leaflets for each candidate in the closing stages of the campaign, and full-page advertisements in several national newspapers. The total contribution of Sykes amounted to about £817,000.

The party election broadcast went out on the 18th May. It again featured the burglar in 'UK House' of the 1999 broadcast, but also carried short clips of Farage and Titford in order to emphasis to viewers that the party now had elected representatives.

The second story to gain blanket media coverage was the allegation by Lord Tebbit that the party had been infiltrated by members of the intelligence services in order to ensure that it damaged the Conservatives so much that, post-election, the Conservative leadership would go to a pro-European. This would then help to ensure a victory in any single currency referendum.

The claim backfired spectacularly. On the 23rd May the BBC Ten-O-Clock news devoted four minutes to the story as the second item and we received extensive publicity in the national newspapers the following day. Campaign activists, who had received an email around 8pm that evening telling them that a major story was about to break, tuned in to watch afraid that some truly damaging story was about to come out. Instead, some of us found ourselves cheering Tebbit for the immense favour he had done us. Some of us even wondered whether it was designed to do just that. Tebbit also made his claims in the *Spectator* magazine, in which he said:

> If I am right, UKIP's intervention will be immensely damaging to the Tories, and will give their Europhiles the platform to overturn a Eurosceptic leadership; Lord Brittan fired the first shots in that campaign in The Times *earlier this week. Nigel Farage – who left the Tories at the time of Maastricht – is confident that I am mistaken. If he is wrong, however, UKIP will have played into the hands of Blair and Brussels. A badly battered Tory party plunged into a leadership crisis would offer Blair the perfect opportunity to bounce Britain into the euro before the sceptics could be rallied to organise a 'No' campaign.*

Tebbit admitted that the people in question (probably Heather

Conyngham and Christopher Skeate) were only former, and not active, members of an intelligence service (thought to be MI6) and said that there were former intelligence agents in both Houses of Parliament, as one might expect. There didn't really seem to be much of a story, in fact.

Down in the South West there was evidence that the departure of Michael Holmes had not seriously damaged our vote. An article in the *Daily Mail* on the 25th May reported that we had registered 25 per cent in a recent poll. The article was about the plight of the fishing industry and it reported specifically on the trip of skipper Mick Mahon in his trawler from Penzance to the Scilly Isles to help the local UKIP candidate, Mick Faulkner:

> *Skipper Mick Mahon, a great Captain Haddock of a man, pushed a 'b******s to Brussels' cap to the back of his weather-beaten head and declared his contempt for the political establishment. A few teeth were lodged in his gums, like pieces of Stonehenge, and he lit another roll-up filled with dark baccy. From Europhile Lib-Dems and Labour to the more sceptical Tories, a sea-dog's cuss on all their houses. Britain's fishermen have been filleted and gutted by Europe, said the two Micks. It was time we got out. I have flown with Tony Blair in his election jet and have crossed the country with Charles Kennedy, but I cannot tell you how refreshing it was to escape the spin doctors and get a taste of politics in the raw, with real people who have real experiences of the red tape and meddling of Brussels officialdom.*

That "politics in the raw", the bloody-mindedness, the "8,000 members with 9,000 egos", the "rabble", was described later in the article:

> *Mick Faulkner, who recently broke up his own fishing boat because the money no longer made sense, described the doughty resolve, the glorious, stubborn bloody-mindedness of the great British fishermen and his ilk. Down in these parts, Europe is hated like an occupying power. There is little more love for the collaborators of Whitehall. UKIP appeals to the rebel in a man, the bit of him that snaps when asked*

*to fill in yet another ruddy quota form, yet another piece of
bureaucratic paper. A recent poll gave the party 25 per cent
of the West Country vote. They can't all be MI6 agents.*

There was more good news for the party on the same day, and
mild embarrassment for the Prime Minister, when the *Evening
Standard* reported that:

*Tony Blair may be riding high in the national opinion polls
but it would appear that his children are being educated in a
hotbed of Euroscepticism. The mock election at the London
Oratory has resulted in a landslide victory for the UK
Independence Party. The news will come as a fillip to UKIP,
which is currently reeling from claims by former Tory
chairman Lord Tebbit that they have been infiltrated by the
security services as part of an establishment plot to
encourage them to stand against right-wing Tories and thus
split the Eurosceptic vote.*

The vote at the school was UKIP 18, Liberal Democrats 13,
Labour 6, Conservatives 3. The party was said to be "tickled
pink".

In mock elections in other schools, an initiative of the Federal
Trust, the party also came first. According to Hockney, who
helped to coordinate with the schools, the first two results were
wins for the party. The first result came from Gloucester while, at
a school in Handsworth, Gurshuran Ghuman and Zeenat
Hassam won the poll for UKIP. Hockney alleged that the Federal
Trust told schools that anti-EU parties would not be standing and
that there was therefore no point in having UKIP candidates. The
Trust, he alleged, refused to cooperate with the party and, when
the first two wins for the party came through, attempted to
suppress further results.

Meanwhile, in the other parties, the Prime Minister spoke in
Edinburgh on the European issue. He presented what he claimed
was a modernised version of patriotism, a 21st century
patriotism, centred on Britain's alliance with the EU. Britain was
a nation that had ancient European roots dating as far back as the
Roman invasion and the mission of St Augustine, he said,
equating somewhat different relationships. He claimed, with

reason, that William Hague's pledge that he would not ratify the Nice Treaty unless all extensions of qualified majority voting were removed would leave Hague with two choices "the first would be a humiliating climbdown in the face of a united front from the other member states. Or the Conservatives would have to start the process of negotiating Britain's exit from the EU".

UKIP held a pre-election rally, also on the 25th, at which Paul Sykes appeared and, in a quiet speech in his Yorkshire accent told the audience not to worry about the money, he would take care of that, but they should get out and deliver the leaflets. Seven television cameras filmed him during his short speech and the *Daily Telegraph* reported his offer the following day – "Paul Sykes, the Eurosceptic millionaire, says he will spend £100,000 a day until the General Election on June 7th financing the campaign by the UK Independence Party...including posters in newspapers and 20 million leaflets".

A final flurry of full-page newspaper advertisements on the 6th June closed our campaign by exhorting voters to "Make Tomorrow UK Independence Day". It was all but over, the biggest campaign we had ever run – 429 candidates, something like £2million of expenditure, battle buses, battle fire engines, battle boats, thousands of miles walked delivering leaflets, talking to voters, fourteen hour days, interviews, newspaper articles, television programs, then the hours at the count and, for the grass-roots activists, back home to watch the election specials throughout the night.

The eventual result was below the goals we had set ourselves. At the same time, there were aspects which could be claimed as advances. So some felt that the party had failed and others felt that the party, although not attaining its goals, had advanced. Opinion was divided. On the one hand, the party had fielded 429 candidates and succeeded in attracting 390,000 votes, an achievement unique for many decades. Those 390,000 votes ranked us as fifth in terms of the number of votes cast among all the parties registered under the new rules of the Political Parties, Elections, and Referendums Act. If the SNP, as a regional party, were excluded, UKIP was fourth. And yet we had failed to win any seats and had fallen considerably short of our goal of one million votes. The highest percentage of votes gained in any constituency was that of Farage in Bexhill and Battle where he gained 3,474 votes (7.8 per cent). The overall result was, however, sufficient to keep the party together, as regards our morale and the avoidance of damaging splits.

'Europe' failed to galvanise the voters. The election was won on the issue of public services – how to improve them and how to fund those improvements. The Conservatives made the EU and the single currency the centrepiece of their campaign for a week or more but the opinion polls didn't move. In fact, they may even have shown a slight decline in Conservative support. William Hague's claim that voters would be taken into a "foreign land" by Labour was misunderstood or, quite possibly, deliberately misrepresented. Opponents took the word 'foreign' in a literal sense rather than in its metaphorical sense.

6

General Election to European Election – 2001 to 2004

A Long Preparation

After the election the Conservative Party went through the acrimonious process of choosing a new Leader. William Hague resigned on the day after the election, acknowledging that he had failed to persuade the electorate and that it was time for someone else to take on that task. The Europhile wing of the Conservative Party had their candidate in Kenneth Clarke. Michael Portillo, so long looked to as the Leader-in-waiting and supposedly a strong Eurosceptic, imploded in a badly-directed campaign concentrating, according to the media at least, on cannabis and homosexuality, or 'inclusivity' more generally. Iain Duncan Smith, a rebel at the time of Major and Maastricht, came in as a strong contender about mid-way through the campaign and eventually took the leadership. Many, in both UKIP and the Conservative Party, thought that he would lead the party in an explicitly withdrawalist direction, perhaps to the extent that we would be outflanked. Though Duncan-Smith did pronounce himself against the single currency in principle, and permanently, he promptly ordered the Conservative Party to stop talking about "Europe", a silence which continued for 18 months.

For ourselves, the three years leading up to the European election of 2004 began down at pavement level, with the party embarking on a strategy of expanding its presence in local elections. From the top came policy change that would fundamentally alter the party's policy stance when the European Elections came. Outside, it was clear that European issues were reaching a critical phase: a government decision on UK membership of the single currency was likely within two years and the Convention on the Future of Europe, formulating an EU

Constitution, would deliver its report in the run-up to the European election.

People And Places

The sixth party conference was held at the National Motorcycle Museum in Birmingham on the 5th and 6th October. A humourous comment from the platform expressed the most significant aspect of the party's 2001 post-election conference: it was almost the first post-election conference in our history that had not resulted in a major division and split. The hope, clearly, was that we had reached some kind of stability after the rancorous arguments of earlier years. Membership of the party had reached 10,000 and so it might have been expected that attendance at the conference would similarly increase. However, although there was a respectable showing of around 500-600 members, it was not a record event breaking the 1,000 barrier that might have been expected.

From abroad, Richard Matrenza from the Maltese Campaign for National Independence and Jens-Peter Bonde MEP addressed the first, public day of the meeting. Neil Herron, making another appearance on a UKIP conference platform, described the latest developments in the continuing "Metric Martyrs" campaign, beginning with a knock-about series of jokes in his heavy North East accent but ending with an emotive appeal for support. Robin Page began similarly, though with rather more risqué jokes and also ended with an emotive account, this time of the plight of farmers. Nigel Farage brought the day to a close with a typically powerful speech, ending it with his customary last line, now known by heart by many of the activists present:

> *We seek an amicable divorce from a political European Union and its replacement by a genuine free trade agreement which is what we thought we signed up to in the first place!*

The second day of the conference was private and was concerned with strategy, a review of the structure of the party, and motions for debate. One motion expressed disappointment with the fact that, late in the General Election campaign, the party's stance had shifted to a "Let the People Decide" call for a referendum. It was felt, and admitted by the party leadership, that this late change of policy had come about because of the funding and consequent influence of Paul Sykes. The motion was carried by a large majority, causing some to say that Sykes had received an unjustified rebuff from the party which he had so generously helped. The second day was also notable for the developing policy of increasing the party's involvement in local elections. Damian Hockney and David Lott both emphasised the success achieved by the Liberal Democrats and the Scottish National Party through dedicating themselves to local elections. It was felt, furthermore, that given the limited sizes of the electorates in local polls, and the low turn-outs, UKIP could capitalise on what we felt was the greater determination of our activists compared to those in the main parties.

Just after the party conference we were peripherally pulled into the Conservative leadership campaign when it was revealed that Edgar Griffin, one of Duncan-Smith's prominent Welsh supporters, was the father of Nick Griffin, the Leader of the British National Party, and that it seemed that he had considerable political sympathy with his son's party. The Conservative Party said that they would expel Griffin senior and, while the latter was waiting for the formal decision, he told the media that, if expelled, he would join either the BNP or UKIP. This statement was prominently reported in many newspapers and UKIP and the BNP were mentioned in the same sentence.

The party acted quickly to dispel the implication that it and the BNP were in the same political stable. The Leader of UKIP in Wales stated clearly that Mr Griffin would not be welcome and a letter to the *Times* from Nigel Farage told Griffin that he should save the cost of the stamp.

The Treaty of Nice passed its Third Reading in the House of Commons on the 17th October 2001. MPs' interest in the issue was so feeble that, between 7pm and 8pm of that day, there were only around 25 MPs present in the Chamber. Conversely, some 2,000 members of the Democracy Movement, many of whom would have been UKIP members, queued up outside the House of Commons to lobby their MPs on the treaty. They queued for up to four hours to try and get across to their MPs their concerns over the treaty, but to no avail.

Our support for the "Metric Martyrs" continued when their

appeal case was heard on the 20th November at the Royal Courts of Justice in the Strand. Titford and Farage, along with other party members, mounted a demonstration outside the courts, the *Daily Telegraph* reporting that "dozens of supporters gathered outside waving banners, flags and placards reading 'Keep Our lb', and 'No to Euro-Fascism'. Members of the UK Independence Party set up a fruit and vegetable stall selling in imperial quantities". In a previous letter to party members Titford and Farage had appealed for donations to the Metric Martyrs Defence Fund, saying:

> *The country was angered and outraged that these men were given criminal records and that one lost his trading licence for doing no more than serving his customers in a system of measurement that is part of our culture and history. We believe they are fighting for freedom, liberty and justice and should not be subjected to the political programme of stealth and deception which is being used to implement compulsory metrication.*

Preparation for the European Elections of 2004 began in February 2002, with the establishment of a European Elections Committee, chaired by Nigel Farage. The aim was to have the candidate lists finalised by May 2003 in order to give the successful candidates an effective year-long campaign leading up to June 2004. Candidates were warned that they would be asked to make a big commitment.

A new tabloid-style publicity leaflet was produced at the same time and during 2002 around 2.5 million copies were distributed by local associations. Another strand of this grass-roots campaigning was the production of a video "Britain and the EU – The Facts" aimed at by-passing the effective media blackout of the party. The video, unveiled at a Guildford rally in February, simply set out the facts about the EU without any mention of UKIP other than a listing of parties and their EU policies at the end. It was produced by the group Subjects Against the Nice Treaty (SANITY) which included Trevor Coleman and Ashley Mote as founder members, the latter becoming an MEP in 2004. Though SANITY was a separate organisation, set up to campaign on constitutional objections to the Nice Treaty (presenting a petition to the Queen under article 61 of Magna Carta and signed by 65 peers), there was considerable overlap in people. Around 15,000 copies of the video were sold in the months following the rally. A second video a few months later also sold around 15,000 copies.

The Countryside March of September was another chance to spread the party's message, as many countryside issues are directly or indirectly determined by the EU through its Common Agricultural Policy and environmental policies. At the huge march in central London around 100,000 specially-produced leaflets were distributed to the marchers.

The head offices were relocated in June from the Regent Street premises to Broadwick Street in Soho. With the issue of regional-isation rising up the agenda, at least of politicians if not the public, the party wrote in May to every local councillor, about 20,000, asking for their views on the regionalisation issue and, in particular, whether they felt that the policy was being driven by the need to fall in with the EU's policy of regionalisation. From the same premises a small telesales experiment began work in November and was turned into a paid project early the following year.

With the party at peace with itself and with Titford wishing to avoid a leadership election in early 2004 when the European Election campaign would be in full swing, Titford announced in June that he wished to stand down as Leader. The infighting that had hampered the party's progress for many years had come to an end, he said, and the party was now a much more united force for change in British politics – "my major objectives in taking on the leadership were to heal the wounds of previous internal battles and to generate a sense of unity in the party. I would like to think that I have achieved both".

Whereas Sked and Holmes had been uniquely single-minded, even egotistical, in their characters and leadership, Titford had been quiet and conciliatory. This had undoubtedly helped the party to avoid more internal wrangling. In August, candidates for the leadership, to be decided by a vote of all party members, were invited to put their names forward. Roger Knapman and Damian Hockney, both NEC members, were the only two candidates at the close of nominations but Hockney later withdrew his candidacy after having decided that Knapman had ambitions for the party similar to his own. In a statement after becoming Leader-elect Knapman paid tribute to Titford, saying that 'there will be a proper time and place to thank Jeffrey Titford for all that he has done to stabilise and strengthen the party. He took over at a time of dissension and retires as Leader having promoted a party with much greater determination and discipline'. Knapman also took the opportunity to emphasise the party's conception of itself as a distinct force, not an offshoot of the Conservative Party:

> *I arrived at the UK Independence Party from the Conservative Party but some others have migrated from the Liberal or Labour parties and many others from Britain's biggest party – the 'stay at home' party. It will be a sign of maturity when we do not think of ourselves as former anything, but purely and simply as UKIP members. UKIP was formed to get Britain out of the EU; to restore its independence and retain its currency as a matter of principle. There is nothing right-wing or xenophobic about these aspirations.*

Roger Knapman

The party conference of 2002 was at the Spa Centre in Scarborough, with the intention of making it easier for members in the North to attend. Speakers from abroad included Henrik Dahlsson from TEAM; once again, Neil Herron of the Metric Martyrs campaign; Mick Mahon, the fisherman featured in the 2001 campaign, and Bill Jamieson, now editor of the *Scotsman* newspaper. Knapman was approved overwhelmingly as the new party Leader and set out the party's ambition for 2004 under the slogan "80 weeks, 10 MEPs". David Lott and Nigel Farage were both contenders for the position of Party Chairman and Knapman appointed Lott to that position at the next NEC meeting[†].

Lott felt that his now extensive experience in leading campaigns was best drawn on in the role of Party Chairman. He had by then been intimately involved in two General Election campaigns, the South Yorkshire by-election for the European parliament and numerous Westminster by-elections and felt that he could play a powerful part in the European Election campaign of 2004. Lott, Knapman, and Farage agreed that the party should concentrate on building the membership base over the next year, based on the observation that one party member seemed to equate to 1,000 votes in national elections. They decided to introduce call centres into the party's repertoire, considering this vital in the job of expanding the membership. When, later, in May 2003, the issue of the EU Constitution became the subject of huge media attention and the party had initiated a street-stall petition collecting signatures against the Constitution, the call centres used the signatures to further leverage the party's efforts. Lott remained Chairman until shortly after the 2004 European Election campaign, playing a key role as national campaign manager.

The build-up to war in Iraq in late 2002 placed us in a quandary. We were broadly pro-American but also committed to the sovereignty not only of Britain but, by extension, other countries, even if they might have tyrannical regimes. The policy adopted at an NEC meeting in November stated that:

†Mike Nattrass became Deputy Leader. Graham Booth, Damian Hockney, and Craig Mackinlay became Vice-Chairmen. Derek Clark remained as party Secretary, John de Roeck as Treasurer, and Michael Harvey as General Secretary.

The UK Independence Party would support an allied invasion of Iraq, including the deployment of British armed forces, if this was sanctioned by a United Nations resolution. UKIP support for such a UN resolution would be conditional upon an invasion being in the UK national interest and on a clear and unambiguous statement of the aims of an invasion from the outset. UKIP considers our national interest to include security of our borders; safety of British subjects overseas; protection of British economic interests, including the promotion of free and fair international trade; and the upholding of international law. UKIP would not normally sanction interference in the internal affairs of another sovereign state unless these principles are at stake.

In late November the last episode of the UKIP and Michael Holmes story came to an end. Holmes retired through ill health from his position in the European parliament and Graham Booth, who had been second on the party list in the South West region in the 1999 European parliament elections, regained the seat for UKIP. Knapman commented: "Despite past differences, it was with great sadness that I heard of Mr Holmes' medical problems. He was a pioneer in the Eurosceptic movement and has worked tirelessly towards British withdrawal from the European Union. Graham is looking forward to following the example set by Mr Holmes and both he and I wish Mr Holmes a long and healthy retirement".

Another minor scuffle between UKIP and the Conservative Party occurred in February 2003 when several newspapers reported that the new Chief Executive of the Conservatives had almost defected to UKIP just before the 2001 General Election. Of more importance as an issue was the question of new proposals from the European Commission on the funding and statutes of European political parties. Only pan-European parties would be eligible for funding and they would also be under an obligation effectively to conform to politically correct European social democracy. The three UKIP MEPs, together with Jens-Peter Bonde, declared the proposal "illegal and certainly immoral" while Robin Cook, Chairman of the Party of European Socialists (PES), showed a unique understanding of democratic legitimacy by saying that the decision was a "boost for democracy at EU level". The MEPs later joined with 19 other MEPs from the SOS Democracy intergroup, including the rebel Conservative MEPs Daniel Hannan and Roger Helmer, in launching a court case against the funding proposals.

Strongly-held opinions again lead to frictions within the party. There was considerable disruption in the North East and the Yorkshire and Humberside regional organisations over the selection of candidates for the 2004 European Elections in those regions. There was visceral disagreement between Damian Hockney and most of the rest of the NEC[†] over what the former thought was a subtle change in the party's core policy of EU withdrawal and over the move of the party's HQ from London to premises in Birmingham owned by the Deputy Leader, Mike Nattrass. Hockney complained that the party appeared to be backing away from its policy of outright withdrawal, that it was essential that a national party should have a base in London and that it was highly questionable that the party's HQ should be in premises owned by one of its senior members, because of the dependency that created. Expenditure on the Scottish Parliament and Welsh Assembly campaigns earlier in the year led to a dispute between the party leadership and John de Roeck, later resolved. There were wrangles over the operation of the London and Ashford call centres. Richard North left his position as EDD Research Director after disagreements with Farage. Though disappointing, these were much further down the Richter scale of internal rows than the two bitter, almost terminal, disputes of earlier years.

[†]The February 2003 elections to the NEC produced the team that would be in place for the crucial coming year and the battle for a breakthrough in the 2004 European Election. Nigel Farage and David Lott were probably the best known; Mike Nattrass, Graham Booth, Damian Hockney, Craig Mackinlay, Derek Clark and Tony Scholefield were also leading members. The line-up was completed by Judith Longman, Lesley Brown, Tony Stone, Andrew Moore, Gerard Batten, George Stride and Ian Gillman. Roger Knapman and John de Roeck were ex officio members.

By mid-May 2003 the regional lists of candidates for the European Elections had been decided. Early July saw the formal launch of our campaign, with Dick Morris, the campaign manager who took President Clinton from Arkansas to the White House, on board. A chance encounter between Knapman and Morris, while on holiday, had lead to discussions with the party in late May and Morris was brought in to advise the party on political campaigning at least up to the European Elections.

At a South East regional meeting in Guildford on the Sunday after the campaign launch, Morris explained the genesis and the reasons for the unusual pairing of a former Clinton adviser and a relatively small British political party: it was a "labour of love" he said, after a tongue-in-cheek speech giving all the reasons why Britain should really be a member of the EU. More seriously, he explained his core idea that voters were simply looking for a way to say 'no', whatever their particular reasons for doing so might be. The broad strategy was simply to make UKIP and 'no' synonymous. Mick Mahon explained how he would sail his boat, the J-Ann, from Cornwall along the South coast, calling in at ports on the way, to arrive at Traitor's Gate at the Tower of London with effigies of Sir Edward Heath, John Major and Tony Blair at the climax of the 2004 campaign.

Membership was 12,000 in July, 14,000 by September, after the opening of a dedicated call centre in Ashford to carry out telesales and, at the end of November, it had gone beyond 16,000.

The 2003 party conference was held in London on the 10th and 11th October with a speaker line-up including Chris Woodhead, ex-Chief Inspector of Schools; Frank Maloney, the former boxing promoter, now UKIP's candidate for London Mayor in 2004; Robin Page, again in thoroughly un-PC mood and, a surprise for the conference, Tony Martin, the farmer jailed for murder in 1999 after yet another break-in at his isolated f a rmhouse, but now released. Martin was wonderfully off message, saying that he didn't really know anything about UKIP's policies and was really a non-voting Conservative and not really interested in Europe.

Moving Into Pavement Politics

Following the decision to start to enter local politics just over 160 candidates stood in the local government elections of May 2002, compared to just 41 in 2000. The highest percentage of the vote gained was 26 per cent and 16 candidates gained over 10 per cent, perhaps vindicating the tactic of relying on the determination of activists in small electorates with low turnouts. The results of the local elections the following year also seemed to bear this out.

In the May 2003 local elections there were 389 UKIP candidates in England, 41 candidates in the Scottish Parliament elections and 40 in the Welsh Assembly elections. This time, the concentration on local politics yielded results as 28 UKIP councillors were elected at various levels of local government and the general level of support, in percentage terms, was much higher than the year before.

Particular efforts were directed to the Scottish and Welsh regional elections. David Lott was, once again, assigned the lead role in these parallel campaigns, little-noticed by party members outside Scotland and Wales, but considered to be of great importance by Lott and Knapman. The Welsh regional committee of the party pressed the NEC for a vigorous campaign and the smaller membership in Scotland wanted the same. For Lott and Knapman, these elections were important for a number of reasons, not least because of the 'United Kingdom' in the party's name and the fact that Scotland and Wales were regions in the EU's overall regionalisation policy. They also felt that it was important to increase the party's visibility relative to the nationalist parties in the two regions. Thirdly, they would be useful dry-runs for the upcoming European Election campaign, enabling the party organisation to get to grips with the new Political Parties, Elections and Referendums Act (PPERA) and to again practise the process of party political broadcasts and the logistics of the distribution of millions of leaflets.

Some funds were raised by the Welsh and Scottish regional parties and the London call centre also contributed funds but much more was needed. In fact, the campaigns were considered important enough to raise money on the strength of projected future income from the call centre. The expenditure of £50,000 on the London Assembly elections of 2,000 was the benchmark. However, despite the importance accorded to the Welsh and Scottish elections, the NEC provided no budget for them.

Heather Conyngham, over from Brussels for the duration, was deputy to Lott in the Scottish Parliament elections and Jim Carver, Welsh Regional Organiser, was deputy for the Welsh Assembly elections. Lott coordinated both campaigns from his office at home.

In Wales the results were surprising. Lott had expected the party to pick up perhaps two seats in the so-called "top up" lists, where candidates were elected under a proportional representation system. In the event this did not happen but the party did surprisingly well in the first-past-the-post elections. In Gower, for example, we gained just over 10 per cent of the vote. In total, we polled over 50,000 votes in the Welsh elections, a result that Lott considered highly creditable. In Scotland, ever a weak area for us, no real campaign materialised.

Conversely, our results in parliamentary by-elections in the latter half of 2001 were even more dismal than usual. A by-election for the Welsh Assembly in Swansea East on the 27th September produced only 1.9 per cent of the vote. At the Ipswich by-election on the 22nd November the party gained only 1.0 per cent of the vote, coming fifth out of nine. At Brent East on the 29th September 2003, the party polled only 0.7 per cent.

Moving Onto Risky Ground

From May 2002 a series of policy reviews began. The first policy up for review – asylum and immigration – took us onto risky political ground. Asylum was certainly on the agenda of ordinary voters but, although Labour and even the Conservative Party might be able to discuss these policies, for us to step onto this ground was a perilous enterprise because of the view of many in the media that the party was positioned on the far right. There was a risk that the policy review – which was unlikely to produce a policy *more* in favour of asylum – would be taken as proof of this.

One of the first public manifestations of the change in the party's emphasis in the area of asylum and immigration was a speech by Ashley Mote at the Scarborough conference later in the year. Asylum and immigration seemed to be Mote's special area of personal concern, along with the issue of Britain's membership of the EU. By early the following year he had published "Overcrowded Britain", a book dealing with the immigration and asylum issue. He had also previously written "Vigilance – A Defence of British Liberty" dealing with the EU issue. His Scarborough speech, however, was a measured statement of what he saw as the problem. He emphasised that the issue was simply the numbers of people now arriving in the UK and that the principal problem was illegal asylum-seekers. The settled ethnic communities in the UK were not the subject of his speech and he emphasised the party's commitment to its non-racist principles. He attacked the culture of political correctness that prevented discussion of the problem and, to boot, recommended abolition of the Commission for Racial Equality, a statement that drew wild applause from the audience. I couldn't make out the reaction to this of the lone black woman at the conference.

In the Newsletter of December 2002, Knapman, as new Leader, said that it had rapidly become clear to him that the one other area of policy which many members felt needed to be beefed up was the issue of immigration – particularly, illegal immigration. Knapman acknowledged that this was a highly emotive area and that it should be approached with care. There would be no "compromise on our policy of treating all legally resident British citizens as equals" but, equally, he didn't see why political correctness should terrify the party from speaking out in this area.

By April 2003 the policy revision in this area produced a policy paper that considerably hardened the party's stance on the issue. The paper noted the large numbers of immigrants of one type or another involved and demanded immediate action, but stopped short of far-right rhetoric, concluding that:

> *The UK Independence Party wants Britain to uphold our tradition of treating asylum seekers fairly and humanely. But we are overwhelmed by the numbers. We have allowed ourselves to become the gullible loser in an appalling game of human pass-the-parcel. Britain deserves a government with the honesty to face this problem squarely, and the courage to take the necessary independent steps to solve it. There is nothing immoral about this. Every nation in the*

world maintains its right to decide which foreigners are allowed to join its population.

Goodbye Euro, Hello Constitution

At the end of 2002 the 'war' against subsumation into the EU was being fought on three fronts: the single currency, the proposed EU Constitution, and regionalisation. Ever since Labour's election to government in 1997, British membership of the single currency had been a constant personal aim of Tony Blair. The official, much-awaited government decision on UK membership, expected in June 2003, would be the culmination of a battle that had been in progress for at least six years, if not the ten years since Maastricht. Those years of campaigning by UKIP, the Referendum Party, the Democracy Movement, Business for Sterling, the No Campaign, the Campaign for an Independent Britain, and many other smaller groups on the anti side, and Britain in Europe, the European Movement, and the government on the pro side, were now coming to the point of decision. Those of us on the anti-euro side were preparing for a government decision in favour and the prospect of fighting an all-or-nothing referendum. The opinion polls were favourable, but there was no certainty that the referendum could be won. The precedent of 1975 was not encouraging, although it was argued that the circumstances in 2003 were entirely different.

By mid-2002 the anti-euro forces were finalising their referendum campaign arrangements. The most likely organisation to be designated by the Electoral Commission as the official 'no' campaign was (confusingly) the No Campaign, the fusion of Business for Sterling and David Owen's New Europe organisation. The Congress for Democracy, an umbrella group bringing together the great majority of organisations in the movement, had resolved at its 7th Congress in March 2002 not to pursue the option of being the official 'no' campaign. In an interview for the *Guardian* in July, Nigel Smith, the No Campaign Chairman, made clear that the campaign would distance itself from a still unpopular Conservative Party. The people that the campaign would have to put forward to win the referendum would have to be people with whom left-leaning voters could identify. He expected every one of the campaign's "assets" to "punch their political weight" .

But it was made clear by the No Campaign that UKIP would not be one of their assets. They were adamant that to mix the issue of EU membership with the issue of single currency membership could only be detrimental to the campaign. There was some justification for this decision, as some polls had shown that the electorate would rather accept the single currency than leave the EU, though later polls suggested the opposite. The danger was that the involvement of organisations such as UKIP would enable the pro-single currency side to turn any referendum campaign into the question of EU membership itself and to use the usual scare stories to terrify the electorate into accepting the currency. George Trefgarne, writing in the *Daily Telegraph* in September also rehearsed these points: "The No campaign must be seen as a broad coalition (which is why it is important that the Tories do not lead it, although they can play a part). Its theme is 'politicians versus the people'. The UK Independence Party and members of the take-to-the-hills tendency will have to keep quiet and stick to the issue on the ballot paper. Do you want to join the euro, or not?"

But we weren't content to stick to the issue on the ballot paper and as a result, Lott told me, we had been frozen out of any part in the official 'no' campaign. Instead, we approached other groups with a view to setting up a coalition to fight the referendum on political rather than economic grounds i.e bringing in the question of EU membership itself. A third contender was Paul Sykes who, even though he had contributed substantially to our General Election campaign, differed with us on how to fight the referendum. The *Guardian* claimed disarray within the anti-euro side and reported that UKIP now disagreed with its former benefactor and intended to set up a network of regional "Real No" campaigns.

The pro-euro side on the other hand seemed beleaguered and without any grass-roots support, a top-down organisation with plenty of money but no troops. Anecdote had it that Britain in Europe's membership had declined from 10,000 ten years previously to 2,000 by the time the decision on euro membership came. A month before the decision, Britain in Europe signalled that it would not survive if it was 'no', one board member saying "we will just turn off the lights, lock the door and get on with our lives...this organisation will collapse within a week of any decision to kick this issue into the next Parliament".

In the event, 9th June 2003 brought a serious setback to the federalist side. The Chancellor's decision was to say 'yes' in principle but, in practice, 'not yet'. There was much talk about annual reassessments being conducted to see if the British economy was 'fit' to join the eurozone in the years to come. In practice, in the months after the decision, it became clear that the whole project had been effectively shelved. A report in the *Daily Telegraph* in December said:

> *One of Mr Blair's biggest ambitions as Prime Minister was to lead Britain into the European single currency. But Government insiders say that 'little or no' work is now going on at No 10 on preparations for British entry into the euro. Ministers and Whitehall officials say there is widespread acceptance that there will probably be no referendum until around 2010 at the earliest.*

One of the three battles had been won, at least for the time being. But at the same time as that battle receded into memory, a greater one came along. In May the proposal for an EU Constitution was laid on the table, after over a year of deliberations by the EU in the shape of the Convention on the Future of Europe. A declaration attached to the Nice Treaty had called for ways to reconnect the EU with "its" citizens. The Convention had instead come up with a Constitution, a Constitution that was not only mind-bogglingly complex, difficult even for political obsessives to understand, but one that represented another huge power grab by the EU.

By the middle of 2003, the focus of the antifederalist movement had switched completely from the single currency to the Constitution. Britain in Europe, demoralised, losing money and staff, recognised in September that the ground had changed and said that it now accepted that it was very unlikely that a single currency referendum would take place before the next General Election. Since the June decision on euro entry there had been "renewed ferocity from the anti-European side that needs an answer". They intended, therefore, like their opponents, to focus on the EU Constitution.

For its part, UKIP launched a national petition campaign in June 2003 against the Constitution, with its three MEPs calling for "action this day" and reminding members that the party had been warning for years that the whole process was about constructing a centralised European state and that this construction had proceeded under cover of continuous lying by the political elites. The fact that those elites now wanted a Constitution removed any pretence that the Union was just about trade and cooperation. By the end of October, 100,000 signatures had been collected on the Constitution petition.

Regionalisation, the Government policy of introducing eight regional parliaments in the supposed eight regions of England outside London, was the third threat. Presented by the government as a means of devolving power downwards to the regions, a sort of English counterpart to Scottish and Welsh devolution, UKIP and the eurorealist movement in general were united in seeing the policy as simply implementing the greater EU policy of dividing the nation states of the EU into convenient, bite-sized chunks, the better to devour all in the process. Region would compete against region for the supposedly precious EU funds, thereby destroying the nation states.

Although considered a serious threat, events had necessarily kept the main focus of the eurorealist movement on the single currency and, now, the proposed EU Constitution. But it was known that the government planned referenda in late 2004 in the three regions of Northern England that they considered most likely to vote 'yes' thus generating, they hoped, a domino effect, just as with the referenda on accession to the EU of the Eastern European countries. With the single currency issue now at least temporarily fought off and with the date of the regional referenda coming closer, the issue of regionalisation climbed higher on the agenda of the movement. But higher still was the impending EU Constitution and the imperative need to defeat it.

The Opening Of The Second Battle

The single currency, the Constitution, regionalisation – these were the battlegrounds of the 'war'. By the end of 2003, one out of the three had been won. Then, unexpectedly, the Constitution agenda collapsed. Presented triumphantly by Valéry Giscard d'Estaing to a European Council in Greece in June, haggling continued in an Intergovernmental Conference (IGC) that began in October. Shortly before Christmas the project ran into the sands when another European Council, in Brussels, failed to reach agreement. Many commentators said that the Constitution was off the agenda for at least a year, possibly even till 2008. But others were less sure. Certainly, it would have suited the government not to have the Constitution as a live issue during the European Election campaign, but some on the eurorealist side suspected that the federalist desire for a Constitution was now so strong that it would overrule any considerations of electoral tactics – in any of the EU countries. They thought it would swiftly be back on the agenda.

And so it was. By March the project had been resurrected. A gift, the best gift that the Eurorealist side could desire, was handed to them; an EU Constitution on the agenda, likely to be signed at an IGC right up against the climax of the European Election campaign. The stage was set for the opening engagement in the second battle – the fight to stop the Constitution.

7

The 2004 European
Election Campaign

Crash

The campaign that culminated in near humiliation for the political establishment and the quadrupling of UKIP's votes and elected MEPs began as a whisper. Over the two years to the climax in June 2004 the middle-of-the-road campaign car became a lightly armoured vehicle and then turned into a battle tank. Through luck, planning, perspicacity, events, and the mistakes of the opposing side, the campaign accreted to itself just about every winning element.

Imagine 'political establishment house', the home of the offices of the main parties. By the end of the 2004 campaign, the UKIP battle tank had crashed at high speed into the front of the house. The Liberal Democrats had collapsed into the basement, the Conservative office was half falling through the ceiling, and Labour was gingerly walking around the holes in their floor while pointing to the damage to the Conservatives.

Three Outsiders

Three outsiders each played key roles in the 2004 campaign. Each nudged events in the right direction. Each entered the campaign at exactly the right time. Each raised the profile of the party and the heat of the campaign successively higher until the pot boiled over in the media frenzy of the last four weeks.

Dick Morris

With the May local elections of 2003 over, Roger Knapman and his wife joined a cruise ship to sail the Mediterranean, free from politics for a while. Not entirely free, however. Serendipity had arranged for the ship to also be hosting Dick Morris, one of the world's best-known political consultants, most known for his role in steering Bill Clinton from Arkansas to the White House and Clinton's stunning election comeback in 1996. Knapman approached Morris and, over two or three further meetings, was able to convince Morris to take on the party's cause. After returning home and after discussions between Morris and the NEC, Morris came on board for the duration of the campaign.

Dick Morris, on the left, shaking hands with David Lott

Famously dubbed "the most influential private citizen in America" by *Time* magazine, author of five books including a guide to modern politics entitled "The New Prince: Machiavelli Updated for the 21st Century", Morris had worked on the campaigns of more than 30 US Senators or Governors as well as presidential elections in Argentina, Mexico and Uruguay in 1999 and 2000. More recently he had advised opposition parties in Eastern Europe, in campaigns in Romania and the Ukraine, the latter of which later involved dramatic scenes of peaceful civil revolution. There could scarcely be a bigger fish in the political seas.

Despite the updating of Machiavelli, all the evidence suggests that Morris had a deep attachment to liberty and democracy.

Interviewed for *BBC Online* in early January, Morris said that he wasn't doing it for the money, for him it was a "labour of love" in his crusade for democracy in the place of bureaucracy. The tiny party had no realistic prospect of winning power but a vote for it would be a warning shot to the establishment – "the way people feel about Europe is a bit like volcanic emissions – if they don't find an outlet, it'll blow the top off the mountain".

In an article for the *Times* on the day after the top almost did blow off the mountain, Morris combined the theme of liberty and democracy with his other great belief, the partnership of the US and the UK:

> *Finally, it remains for me, as an American, to explain my commitment to British independence. In the Second World War and most recently in the War on terror, we in the United States have come to see how crucial it is for the world to have an independent Britain, able to stand up for freedom and democracy at our side. The traditions and the values of the British people are so deeply imbued with the love of freedom that they make the UK a reliable ally in the global battle for freedom in a way that many other nations – with their different national experiences – will likely never be. May there always be an England (and a United Kingdom, too).*

Max Clifford

The second outsider was Max Clifford, controversial publicist, avid supporter of Tony Blair, self-confessed socialist, who said that he couldn't remember where he was when Margaret Thatcher resigned but, wherever he was, he would have been celebrating. Early press officer to the Beatles, Jimi Hendrix, the Bee Gees and other groups of the seventies, Clifford now specialised in 'kiss-and-tell' stories for the tabloids. During the dying days of the Major government, Clifford was responsible for a string of stories about the bedroom antics of Conservative politicians, seriously denting the Conservative Party's reputation in the moral domain after Black Wednesday had destroyed them in the economic domain, and contributing to the collective sigh of relief that a rotten lot had finally gone when New Labour was elected in 1997.

Though still a supporter of Labour and Blair, Clifford did not share the fervent Europeanism of the latter. Speaking to the BBC in mid-January Clifford said that, when it came to Europe, it wasn't a question of left wing and right wing. It was the central question – who governed Britain? He and the party were in complete agreement that "the British people should be the masters of their own destiny through our parliament at Westminster, not subservient to Brussels". On joining UKIP as its publicist Clifford repeated that anyone who knew him knew that he had been a Labour supporter all his life. He was still a supporter of Tony Blair, but in the case of the European situation he simply disagreed with him. His simple view was that "the only people making laws and decisions about my country and therefore my future and that of my family are people that I have had the opportunity to vote for democratically". The authority to run Britain and decide its destiny should reside in Westminster, not Brussels.

Hypocrisy among politicians was also a motivator for Clifford who told Cambridge University's student website in March 2000 that there were a lot of politicians who were having affairs and who he could have exposed. But so long as those same politicians didn't lecture people on family values, he'd leave them alone. It was the hypocritical ones he didn't like.

Clifford's bill for the six months work that he took on as media networker and story placer for the party was £100,000, mostly paid for by Alan Bown, a retired bookmaker and a new, major donor to the party. The bill caused the occasional grumble from some party members. When asked how much work he did for the party, Clifford said "sometimes its as much as an hour a day. I don't want to sound arrogant but I can do more in an hour than other people can do in two or three months. That's the nature of the business".

Robert Kilroy-Silk

Robert Kilroy-Silk was recruited to UKIP in April during a lunch party with the Earl of Bradford at the latter's villa in the south of Spain. Bradford rang Farage to say that Kilroy-Silk was available and Farage then negotiated the details. Along the way, Farage took Kilroy-Silk to see Derek Clark, then in the party's number one position in the East Midlands where Kilroy-Silk eventually stood as a candidate. Clark agreed to step down into the number two position to give Kilroy-Silk the best opportunity. When Steve Harris, the party's Regional Organiser in the South East, phoned Clark, he congratulated him on his forthcoming success. Clark protested that he was now only number two on the list. Harris said not to worry – Kilroy-Silk would win it for him as well.

Robert Kilroy-Silk

The announcement of Kilroy-Silk's candidacy set off a firestorm of media interest that continued up to and after the election, such was his popularity as a long-term chat show host on BBC daytime television, the trenchancy and unpredictability of his views and the powerful personality behind them. Kilroy-Silk's entry into the contest took the party's profile into the political stratosphere and secured our domination of the campaign.

Kilroy-Silk, a graduate of the London School of Economics, was Labour MP for Ormskirk (later Knowsley North) from 1974 to 1986 and was a junior home affairs spokesman when Neil Kinnock was Leader of the Labour Party. Elected to the seat in the February 1974 General Election he declared that he wanted to be Prime Minister within fifteen years. In his later years in the seat he became embroiled in a vicious battle with the Militant Tendency which seemed to be the catalyst for his abrupt departure from politics. In an interview with the *Guardian* towards the end of the 2004 campaign, he recalled the "really nasty, acrimonious atmosphere" of that time. His constituency party had been disbanded and remained disbanded for ten years. It was difficult to be an MP because decent members were abused by the Militant few and were afraid to come to party meetings. Decent members were spat at, sworn at, or had their car tyres slashed. So only the Militant side turned up to meetings and they were opposed to official Labour Party policy.

Kilroy-Silk hosted his BBC show for 18 years until he was sacked for an article he wrote in the *Sunday Express* in December 2003. The article originally appeared in the newspaper in April of that year during the Iraq war. In very strong, some said inflammatory terms, he attacked Arabs for a litany of faults as he saw them, generating mountains of media comment as a result and complaints from ethnic minority leaders across a spectrum of groups. Kilroy-Silk later defended his article, which had apparently been republished without his knowledge, saying that he had been writing about Arab states and not the Arab peoples. Indeed, the first part of the article did refer to Arab states but the part that caused most offence and which was most quoted went:

> *We're told that the Arabs loathe us. Really? For liberating the Iraqis? For subsidising the lifestyles of people in Egypt and Jordan, to name but two, for giving them vast amounts of aid? For providing them with science, medicine, technology and all the other benefits of the West? They should go down on their knees and thank God for the*

munificence of the United States. What do they think we feel about them? That we adore them for the way they murdered more than 3,000 civilians on September 11 and then danced in the hot, dusty streets to celebrate the murders? That we admire them for the cold-blooded killings in Mombasa, Yemen and elsewhere? That we admire them for being suicide bombers, limb-amputators, women repressors? I don't think the Arab states should start a debate about what is really loathsome.

Strong language, but apparently not the first. According to a profile of Kilroy-Silk in the *Independent* on the 5th June, other remarks had been made in previous *Sunday Express* columns containing similarly pungent views on the Irish, Pakistanis, the French, the Germans, the Spanish and black British youth. And yet, was he really the xenophobe and racist that the articles seemed to suggest and that he was accused of being? In a *Sunday Express* article towards the end of the campaign, Kilroy-Silk addressed this charge. He said that one of the most remarkable features of his campaign was the way in which British nationality united everyone, whatever their ethnic origin, colour or creed. Every time he spoke to people in market squares, in town centres or in shopping malls, in Leicester or Lincoln, in Nottingham or Northampton, people agreed with his strong feeling that it was "important to get our country back from the remote, corrupt bureaucracy in Brussels and to govern ourselves". And when he argued that the people also had to get their country back from the "metropolitan, politically-correct elite" who wanted to make the British people ashamed of being British, it was the people of the various ethnic groups who shouted most enthusiastically "They have no problem about their identity. They are British, and proud to be so".

The metropolitan, politically-correct elite was a constant theme throughout the Kilroy-Silk campaign, alongside the central message of EU withdrawal. On joining the party and being given the lead position in the party's list in the East Midlands region, Kilroy-Silk told visitors to the party's website that he became an MP because he believed that British politics should be based on the principles of fairness, freedom and justice. In 1975 he had campaigned against Britain staying in the EEC but he was then, and remained, a believer in good trading relations with all countries in the world. Now, however, he regarded the EU threat as the single, most important issue facing the country. He intended to use his experience as a TV presenter and columnist to present a way forward for the UK – "outside the EU but on friendly terms with all the countries of Europe, whether they are in the EU or, like the wise and prosperous Swiss, Norwegians and Icelanders, outside the EU".

The campaigning style of Kilroy-Silk on the street was well summed up by an article in the *Scotsman* in late May:

> *Most politicians use the phrase 'pressing the flesh' with a certain disdain. Not Robert Kilroy-Silk. He doesn't just press flesh, he grabs it, holds it, clings to it as if for dear life. Everyone passing within 10ft of him is liable to be grabbed by the hand, patted on the arm, clapped on the back. Anyone directly in his path gets the full treatment: double hand clasps, bear hugs, cuddles, kisses on as many cheeks as are visible. Kilroy doesn't just invade your personal space, he sends in troops and tanks with air support, annexes it and proclaims it part of the Greater Kilroy Empire.*

This trio of outsiders and the now greatly experienced group in the leadership of UKIP, particularly Lott, Farage and Knapman, put together a more sophisticated campaign than any the party had run before. But we had another potent weapon – our grass-roots activists, an indispensable asset even in the age of spin doctors, publicists, and celebrities. In the campaign to come, ordinary party members were to hand-deliver nine million leaflets, taking the campaign managers by surprise with an unceasing demand for more, as fast as they could be printed. No wonder the party was described, in the thick of the campaign, as a "ferocious new predator".

Organisation For The Campaign

Morris outlined his strategy for the campaign in a video made during a stay in America. The core of his message was that the support was already there – it just had to be mobilised:

> *The grain is out there fully grown: we don't have to plant it, we don't have to plough it, we don't have to water it, we don't have to weed it, all we have to do is harvest it.*

Choosing a different analogy, more familiar in the United States, Morris said:

> *One match can start a forest fire but only if there is a vast amount of dry timber – tender, small saplings just waiting to be set on fire. And if there's that precondition, if there's that much dead wood, one little match can start a huge conflagration. There is that amount of dry timber...there is really a forest waiting to go up in flames – all that it requires is a match, and we in the UKIP must be that match.*

In early January, at a training and strategy weekend for candidates in Torbay, Morris spoke in person on his proposed strategy. Lott, speaking after the campaign, said that this weekend was crucial in getting the party to swing wholeheartedly behind the strategy, including a decision to pour money into billboard advertising. The regional organisations committed themselves to raising the large amounts of money required. Well over half a million pounds was raised from within the party.

Despite increased media reporting of the party since the election of our three MEPs in 1999 there were still many people who did not know of our existence. For example, of 8,000 respondents to an advertisement placed in the *Sun* newspaper near the beginning of the year, 70 per cent had not heard of us. Morris explained that the secret was to get people themselves to spread the word about the party. We just had to apply the match in the right way and the rest would happen. He also felt that there were many reasons why people might be anti-EU, but the campaign should be focussed around a core message that all those anti-EU objectors could respond to – "Say NO". This was not a time to try and convert people to the party's cause, it was a time to find our natural supporters. Morris urged those present to put everything into the campaign – "go for broke", "empty your treasuries". It was time to put "everything on the line", it was our "last, best chance". It was better to spend everything and be successful rather than hold back and meet failure. More, success would alter British politics and even European politics.

Accordingly, a huge billboard advertising campaign would be one of the centrepieces of the party's election push. Around 2,000 twenty feet by ten feet billboards were rented throughout the country, in two slots of two weeks each, for the last two weeks in April and the last two weeks of May. In addition, Alan Bown provided the very considerable sums of money needed for the nine million leaflets that were eventually distributed, something that Lott considered had a major impact on the eventual result. Campaign headquarters were set up in a modern office complex in Bramshott, in the heart of rural Hampshire, with Lott conducting day-to-day operations from there. Farage took on the job of talking to the media, networking, and reaching agreements, in particular with Paul Sykes and party sympathisers in the House of Lords. The media contacts of Max Clifford gave Farage access to the newspapers that we would probably not otherwise have had. Farage later said that editorials in the *Sun* in the last week of the campaign were especially helpful. Coverage of the party by the BBC improved considerably during the campaign and Farage had a hotline to the corporation's Chief Political Advisor.

Say No Poster

Activists on the ground were kept up-to-date with progress by email bulletins from Bramshott and daily website updates. Eight call centres were set up to handle calls from the public, using a single national telephone number routed through to the relevant call centre, and with a brief to go all out to sign up new members and solicit donations. Expenditure was centralised at the regional offices, with the branches being asked to transfer all their money into the regional accounts and to minimise their own expenditure. "Strip the branches" said Farage. Members were discreetly asked for the names of wealthy potential contributors. Farage approached the BBC to demand two party political broadcasts instead of the one that the BBC said we could have. Fundraising from wealthy donors and the party's income from membership subscriptions and donations meant that we would eventually spend over £2million on the campaign, more even than the Labour Party.

The Party's Policy Stance In The Campaign

The party's campaign leaflets for the 2004 election highlighted, as in past campaigns, the issue of Britain's EU membership but, as a strong secondary theme, they also gave space to the issue of asylum and immigration. Some would say, perhaps, in a not very sensitive way. Certainly, the issue of asylum and immigration was very high in the concerns of the public: in April immigration minister Beverley Hughes was forced to resign her position following a mounting scandal over the waving through of apparently fraudulent applications for visas from Eastern European countries. It was claimed that the applications were being hurriedly processed – and accepted – in advance of the accession of the eastern European countries to the EU so that the statistics on migration from the east, post-accession, would not look so bad.

Immigration, for long a concern of ordinary voters, but something that the main parties did not want to discuss, was almost certainly a vote-winner for the party in the political atmosphere of that election. Our political stance in the election, therefore, was, essentially, anti-EU primarily, but also anti-immigration, a stance perhaps uncomfortably close to the Front National of Jean-Marie Le Pen in France. Was the party about to move onto that ground and would it be successful in the medium to long term, rather than just gaining short-term, populist, support? To achieve long-lasting and solid support, would it not be necessary to gain the allegiance not only of working class voters but also of those in the middle range who would never dream of supporting a Le Pen-style party in Britain? It was very sensitive political ground. A comment article in the *Observer* summed up the approach:

> *Labour strategists are right to worry about a threat to some of their working-class supporters. A senior figure in UKIP – if that isn't a contradiction in terms – baldly describes their supporters as 'Cs and Ds'. You get a flavour of the waters in which UKIP is trawling for support from the headline points of the party's manifesto. 'The UK is already full up', it blares. 'We are bursting at the seams'. Its not fear of obesity they are playing to.*

In some ways our move into this area of politics seemed careful and planned. In other ways it seemed populist and crude. On the one hand, the party's 15-page brochure, produced especially for the campaign to give more detail on the party's stance – its European Manifesto, in effect – took great pains to submerge the issue of asylum and immigration under a section headline "Freedom From Overcrowding". But was it an honest attempt to take the race issue out of the question – "Space Not Race", as a past leaflet had put it – or was it just a thinly-disguised far-right policy?

The populist and crude part was our main election leaflet which featured, on the back, a cartoon beneath a large headline saying "IMMIGRATION SET TO SOAR" and, later, after the 10 new accession countries had joined on the 1st May, "IMMIGRATION SOARS". The cartoon showed the Channel Tunnel, as seen from the French side, renamed as the "channel funnel", with hordes of Eastern European immigrants flocking to enter, on their way to a life of benefits in "overcrowded" Britain.

Post-election reporting revealed that 91,000 people from the eight eastern European accession states had registered with the official government worker registration scheme in the first five months after accession. After a year, the figure was 232,000.

There may have been others who had not registered. Government estimates had been between 5,000 and 13,000 per year. Who was telling the truth?

UKIP, Immigration leaflet, 2004

A Pensioner Fires The Opening Shot

Eighty-three year old Elizabeth Winkfield, a pensioner from the seaside resort of Westward Ho in North Devon, effectively opened our campaign when, in late February, she hit the headlines with her refusal to pay part of her council tax. She proclaimed that she would go to jail rather than pay the full amount – even if she were a millionaire. Expecting a small local affair at the magistrates' court in Barnstaple she stepped into the full glare of national publicity, ending up on the *Breakfast with Frost* television program together with John Prescott, the pugilist Deputy Prime Minister.

Miss Winkfield was, in fact, a UKIP member as well as a member of the Devon Pensioners Action Forum, itself a part of a growing pensioner revolt against rising levels of council tax. Miss Winkfield, in addition to being concerned about the increase in council tax, also objected to the proportion of it being contributed to EU-related activities. Interviewed live on ITV she said "I am not paying because there is much waste in the councils and they are sending money to the South West Regional Assembly and to the EU without telling anyone. Our money is going to the French and others while we are told that there isn't enough money to do things here".

News of the stand by Miss Winkfield travelled up to Nigel Farage who then brought in Max Clifford to handle the publicity. Within a few days Miss Winkfield was interviewed by David Frost. In the Saturday interview, for broadcast on the Sunday, Miss Winkfield repeated her objections to money going to the South West Regional Assembly and the EU. When the interview was actually broadcast the next day, all references to the regional assembly and the EU had been removed and John Prescott was given a gentle ride, prompting one activist to complain that the program was a "John Prescott/David Frost/government/BBC stitched-up piece of propaganda using, as the example, an 83-year old pensioner who may well end up in prison for the sake of her principles".

Miss Winkfield's party allegiance remained unknown or unreported on at first but it took only a few days for the press to catch on to the UKIP angle and discover the hand of Clifford behind the scenes. Then the story of the story became the story, with the *Western Morning News* saying "UKIP Denies Its In a Spin" but Clifford telling the *Guardian*: "You don't have to be a brain surgeon, do you? It's a little old lady of 83, who's bright, and got principles, etc etc...I planted it. If it hadn't been on the front page of the *Mail*, it would have been on the front page of the *Sun* the next day. I knew it was a front page".

By mid-April the Bramshott national campaign HQ and the eight regional call centres were fully operational and the first set of billboard posters were going up. Membership was still climbing – it had reached 17,500 in late March and was now 19,000. Boxes of leaflets were leaving the distribution centres as fast as they were arriving, with Lott telling party activists in a campaign bulletin that he had never known such a hungry demand for leaflets – 3 million had been produced and another 5 million were being printed. It was possible that "our little old party" would deliver the best part of 8 million leaflets during the campaign, a "truly staggering number and we are all so immensely proud of you all". Two weeks later posters were available and these also were snapped up by the branches, to be hammered into place on makeshift structures in farmers' fields by the side of roads.

Into the campaign, on the 20th April, came the bombshell announcement that the Prime Minister had decided that a referendum on the proposed EU Constitution would be held after all. This came after three and a half years of denials, U turns, minimisation of the consequences, denigration of opponents, arrogance and deceit. The progress of the Constitution had followed at least the first two stages of the well-worn path of European proposals: first, the government said it wasn't going to happen; second, it was going to happen but it really wasn't anything very important. In November 2000, Keith Vaz, one of the first in a long line of Ministers for Europe, had told the House of Commons:

> ...the hon. Member for Ludlow said that the charter represented the beginning of a European Constitution. If a telephone directory were published in Brussels, the hon. Gentleman would believe that it was the forerunner of a European Constitution. We are not going to have such a Constitution, so I am happy to deny categorically his statement.

Tony Blair, in a keynote speech in Warsaw the previous month, had said that, in his opinion, the diversity and the complexity of the EU meant that its Constitution would remain, like the British one, scattered across a number of different laws and precedents. This had all changed by November 2002 when, in another key speech, in Cardiff, Blair declared that 'Europe' did indeed need a new Constitution. But it was made clear by Jack Straw at the same time that this was of no great significance because:

> All sorts of organisations which are not states have Constitutions – from golf clubs and political parties, to the UN. So I hope the debate on this issue will focus less on the label of a Constitution, and more on its substance.

One of the most important parts of the proposed EU Constitution was the Charter of Fundamental Rights. In his Cardiff speech the Prime Minister insisted that a legally-binding Charter extending EU competence over national law would be unacceptable. His Minister for Europe famously declared that the Charter would have no more significance than the *Beano* comic and later, in the House of Commons, in his usual patronising way, repeated that assurance:

> *Before the hon. Member for West Suffolk asks me about the Beano, I mentioned it because I know his usual reading material, and was trying to keep matters simple for him. The document will not be binding....it is not going to happen...it will not be legally enforceable...it could be a small pledge card or a larger document.*

In May 2003, the latest Minister for Europe, Peter Hain, in the face of an unprecedented referendum exercise by the *Daily Mail*, declared flatly that "those campaigning for a referendum might as well put away their placards and stop wasting their money, because we're not going to do it".

And now...they were going to do it. The announcement immediately took away a key plank of the Conservative campaign – the call for a referendum on the Constitution – and ensured that the issue of the Constitution was placed before the voters, something that almost certainly played to UKIP's advantage.

In London, our candidate for London Mayor, Frank Maloney, was at work putting into practice the party's aversion to political correctness. Interviewed in a local London newspaper, Maloney declared that he wouldn't be campaigning in Camden because "there are too many gays there". How times have changed, when it is possible for the reaction of the Gay Conservatives group to brand such a comment as the opinion of a "dangerous extremist [who should] resign or be sacked". The comment certainly did nothing to soften the assumption that UKIP was an anti-homosexual party. Later, post-election, claims said that there had been, in fact, around 25 homosexual UKIP candidates in the 2001 General Election. Still, it was not a branch of politics that we wanted to go down and Nigel Farage laughed off Maloney's comment – "Frank's not a career politician; he's the chirpy chap that he is. He's an honest bloke who doesn't try to put a spin on things".

Kilroy-Silk Brings Up The Heavy Artillery

The sensation of the election was the announcement of the candidacy of Robert Kilroy-Silk. It was the event that allowed us to grab hold of the agenda and to make our battleground the battleground of the campaign.

Trailed as a possibility for two days before the announcement, Kilroy-Silk was in Spain making no comment, but after the formal announcement by the party on Saturday the 8th May, Kilroy-Silk set out his stall in the *Sunday Express*:

> *I will be campaigning to ensure that Britain leaves this corrupt, bureaucratic, dictatorial regime in Brussels and to get our country back – not just from Brussels but from the lying politicians in Westminster who don't listen to what the people want and indeed to get our country back from the politically correct crowd from whom we have to ask permission what we think and what we say before we speak.*

The announcement generated a mountain of publicity, all of which referred to his comments about Arabs, and vitriol in the comment pages of the pro-EU media and among political opponents. Labour MEP Phillip Whitehead, for example, was scathing:

> *Robert Kilroy-Silk was once an MP and the self-styled next Prime Minister but three. He left that for the TV limelight until his crass views forced his removal from the screen. Now he is back, competing to be the most anti-European act in town on top of his other prejudices. The lights still flicker but no one is watching Kilroy now.*

On the Tuesday, Kilroy-Silk stepped out onto the campaign trail for the first time, visiting Leicester and Nottingham with party activists in tow handing out leaflets while he gave autographs, posed for photographs, shook hands and bear-hugged his way through the city centres, instantly recognised by teenagers and grandmothers alike who felt like well-known and favoured friends. The following day it was on to the party's official campaign launch to hammer out the message again. He said that, over the previous few days, as he had been campaigning on the streets, he had discovered that the people were fed up with being lied to. They were disenchanted, even hostile, to politicians. The metropolitan, political elite had lied to them for decades and they were still lying to them. Appealing for help on the party's website, he said that:

> *I don't want an EU Constitution, I don't want the euro and I don't want my grandchildren to live in a country called Europe. I want Britain to be governed by the British and more importantly, this is what I believe the people of this great nation want. It is what they are telling me when I am out on the streets campaigning.*

Our first election broadcast went out on the day of the campaign launch, the 12th May. It opened with a stereotypical Austrian dressed in lederhosen being slapped in the face by a British fisherman with a fish in a Pythonesque scene with a Benny Hill–type comedy theme tune as backing music, and went on to show furniture vans being loaded and unloaded in a parody of the regular movement of the European parliament between Brussels and Strasbourg. Not surprisingly, the first scene generated a few accusations of xenophobia. It was the kind of stereotype that probably plays well among some sections of the population but not to others, and certainly not to the metropolitan elite. Farage shrugged off the accusations, saying that at least the party still had a sense of humour. But times had changed since Manuel could be depicted as a numbskull Spaniard in Fawlty Towers.

Another salvo of sarcasm came from Gary Titley, Leader of Labour's MEPs, on the day after the campaign launch, probably with a reference to the election broadcast and the controversial asylum and immigration theme in the party's literature:

> *Nobody comes more metropolitan elite than a permatanned TV executive who used to be a politician. Mr Kilroy-Silk might offer some faded glamour to UKIP but no amount of glitz will blind us from the reality of UKIP's extremism and*

its crude attempts to stir up hatred.

Paul Sykes, the multi-millionaire businessman who had funded the party lavishly in the previous General Election, again came to the party's financial aid. Over the course of the campaign he contributed over £880,000 to our expenditure of £2million. Sykes announced his intentions in an article in the *Yorkshire Post* in mid-May in which he also set out his opposition to Regional Assemblies, which he said would pave the way for a centrally-governed Europe of the regions.

A couple of days later and down in the South West, Oliver Letwin, Shadow Chancellor, tried a more conciliatory line on those thinking of voting for UKIP. In an interview with the *Western Morning News* prior to a visit to North Devon to meet farmers and businesspeople, and with the paper commenting that UKIP had become a significant electoral force in the West country in recent years, Letwin appealed for a return to the fold, saying that there were serious choices to be made at the election and it was time to "stop playing politics and time to stop engaging in wild theorising". Peeping out here in the interstices of the sentence seems to be, yet again, the feeling that only votes for the main parties are valid – indeed, even that those votes *belong* to the old parties.

There were signs of possible conflict to come in the party, however – that the UKIP curse of fierce internal squabbles could return. A newspaper report claimed that Kilroy-Silk had "elbowed" Farage out of an appearance on *Question Time* on the 20th and that the former even had designs on the leadership, a claim that would rumble on after the election when Sykes threatened to withdraw financial support for the party if Kilroy-Silk was not the Leader and the latter signing himself as the "de facto Leader" of the party. The first claim seems unlikely, given the star media status of Kilroy-Silk, and Farage denied the charge, saying "I stood aside because I believed there would be a lot more people who would watch Kilroy on *Question Time* than myself. He appeals to lots of people who wouldn't necessarily vote UKIP".

The *Question Time* appearance was typical combative Kilroy-Silk and a later head-to-head with John Redwood on Channel 4 news pitted the energies of the former against the smooth reasonableness of the latter. Kilroy-Silk was a one-man roller-coaster campaign all by himself.

Party supporters in the audience heckled rival speakers during the *Any Questions* program on Radio 4 on the Friday before the *Question Time* program and a leaked email revealed that the party was trying to get its supporters into the *Question Time* audience. Cries of dirty tricks were raised.

A YouGov poll for the party in the same week did not look so good. The poll gave voting intentions as Conservative 27 per cent, Labour 27 per cent, Liberal Democrats 16 per cent, UKIP 10 per cent, SNP/PC 2 per cent, BNP 4 per cent, others 2 per cent, Respect 0 per cent. In a further question on EU membership, 48 per cent said that Britain should leave the EU, 39 per cent wanted to stay in, 13 per cent were undecided. The figure of 10 per cent was probably hiding large regional variations but the national figure in the previous European Elections was just below 8 per cent so, though the campaign felt good and we still had a strong grip on the agenda, the advance since 1999 seemed small. It would need more than 10 per cent to achieve those 10 MEPs and shake up the political establishment.

The Kilroy-Silk rollercoaster arrived in Lincoln later in the week. Bounding from his chauffeur-driven Jaguar, Kilroy-Silk descended on two white-haired ladies and demanded a kiss. "Its you isn't it?" one said. "Its me, my love" he purred. The *Times* continued:

> *He did not so much work the crowd as cuddle, stroke and squeeze it, as if trying to turn viewers to voters by the power of touch alone. Most of Lincoln was awed, and not just the ladies who came running from Clarks and Littlewoods to be embraced, pleading for him to sign the bronzed photo on his election flyers.*

May 23rd brought the rounds on the Sunday political programs. Farage appeared on the *Politics Show* on BBC1, Knapman was interviewed on Radio 4's *Westminster Hour*. Piers Merchant, a former Tory MP whose political career in the Conservatives had been brought to an end by, ironically, Max Clifford, discussed the nature of political protest on Radio 4's *Broadcasting House*. Merchant was appointed to the newly-created post of Chief Executive of UKIP after the election. Michael Howard was interviewed by David Frost.

"Our Time Has Come"

The next two days brought a surge in publicity as a new YouGov poll showed that we were likely to outperform the Liberal Democrats. Among those questioned who said they were very likely to vote, our share was 18 per cent while the Liberal Democrats had fallen behind to 15 per cent. In the *Daily Telegraph* there was speculation about just how big the party's success might be and about the scale of the threat to the three establishment parties: "Just as the Greens caused a sensation in the European parliament elections 15 years ago by finishing a strong third behind Labour and the Conservatives, so the United Kingdom Independence Party looks set to cause a similar sensation in a fortnight's time".

The paper's editorial bemoaned this irruption into the preserve of the big three and, speaking apparently for all of them rather than just the Conservatives, cast around for ways to discredit us. It said that, with just seventeen days to go, it was difficult to see what the mainstream parties could do about UKIP. It said that the party had "more than its fair share of freaks and obsessives". It was a single-issue movement with no hope of forming a government. It was "kooky, inept and hopelessly divided". But the voters didn't seem to care about all that and they weren't voting for the party because they wanted Kilroy-Silk in Downing Street but because "they wish to send a signal to all the parties about Brussels' interference in our national affairs".

Indeed they were, as I can confirm. Standing in glorious sunshine in the centres of Oxford, Banbury, Witney and other Oxfordshire towns, in that 2004 election and in others before, how many times had we heard it? "I voted yes in 1975 but if I had known then what I know now, I would have voted no". Or "we voted for a Common Market, not this Union business". Or, especially and uniquely in 2004: "they're not listening to us".

In the *Guardian*, Roy Hattersley fulminated for the Left. The Conservatives were either "devious or disingenous" because they should surely know that their policies, if ever put into practice, would lead to Britain being excluded from the EU or to a humiliating client status within the organisation, dependent on Europe but unable to influence the decisions that would shape the country's destiny. As for UKIP, it was "absurd but honest" in stating its policy of breaking free from "continental bondage".

On the same day, our membership went beyond 20,000.

The *Daily Mail* also commented on the YouGov poll and the heat now felt by the establishment parties. Its prediction for the number of seats that we might win went beyond even our ambition. Having moved past the Liberal Democrats into third place, there was the possibility of twelve seats in the European parliament. Pushing the Liberal Democrats into fourth place would provide an enormous psychological breakthrough for the party. In the light of this advance, all three mainstream parties were 'viewing UKIP's advance with alarm'.

On the same day, further celebrity endorsement came from Joan Collins, star of the *Dynasty* television series of the eighties. The media took great delight in the fact that Ms Collins spent much of her time in her villa in St Tropez, had never voted before, and that she occasionally constructed a less than perfect soundbite. Collins was introduced to the media at the Hilton hotel in Nottingham, as a new patron of the party, by Kilroy-Silk. This second celebrity endorsement was due to the enterprise of Bob Knockels, a Surrey party member who had stood outside the theatre in Guildford where Ms Collins was appearing, waiting until she emerged after the show, and who pushed a "Better Off Out" video in to her hands.

On the more controversial side of the party's campaign stance, the focus on asylum and immigration, a separate YouGov poll suggested that the focus, in simple electoral terms, was well-aimed. Home Office figures showed that 120,000 foreign nationals were granted UK citizenship in 2003 and a further 140,000 applications had been made in the same year. The *Daily Telegraph* concluded that voters had virtually lost faith with government policy on immigration – "people do not trust ministers either to give them the true picture or take their wishes into account". The poll even suggested that immigration was now seen as the most important issue facing the country, it said.

Jeffrey Titford, writing in the *Guardian* also on the same day declared that:

> *Our time has come: at this election we are going to shake*
> *British politics to its core....What does all this mean on the*
> *streets? Well, for one thing, I don't have to keep explaining*
> *who we are, as I did in 1999! People have actually heard of*
> *us and respond warmly whenever I greet them. I am picking*
> *up a strong sense that voters have not only had enough of*
> *seeing their country being pushed around by Brussels but,*
> *interestingly, they are just as disillusioned with the big three*
> *parties and want to use this election to raise a metaphorical*
> *two fingers at them.*

I know this was true for I also had felt that same disenchant-ment out in the streets campaigning. "They're not listening to us" pretty well summed up the feeling of many people.

The time had certainly arrived for the party to start receiving notice beyond the UK. Election reports in newspapers throughout the world began to mention our existence and our core policy. Not surprisingly, the continental media were particularly interested. *Le Monde*, against a background of increasing media attention on the party in France, commented:

> *Les conservateurs risquent de suffrir, sur leur droite, de la*
> *poussée antieuropéenne de formations plus radicales, aux*
> *militants plus motivés, comme l'independence Party (UKIP),*
> *favorisées par la représentation proportionnelle et*
> *l'absentéisme du plus grand nombre. Un récent sondage,*
> *qu'il faut toutefois accueillir avec prudence, attribuait à*
> *l'UKIP 18% des voix et sept mandats (contre 7% et trois*
> *sièges en 1999).*

> *[The Conservatives risk damage on their right from the surge*
> *of more radical organisations, with more motivated activists,*
> *such as the UK Independence Party (UKIP), which are*
> *favoured by proportional representation and a very low*
> *turn-out. A recent poll, which should nevertheless be read*
> *carefully, suggests that UKIP will gain 18 per cent of the vote*
> *and seven seats (against 7 per cent and three seats in 1999).]*

The *Financial Times Deutschland* reported from Romford market where Gerard Batten seemed to have met strong – and xenophobic – support:

'Wir werden ihnen gehörig in den Arsch treten', verspricht ein rothaariger Unterwäschehändler. Neben dem Sonderangebot von drei Schlüpfern zum Preis von 5 £ bietet er Meinungen feil wie: 'Diese Mist-Europäer. Ich will nicht nur gegen sie stimmen, sondern ihnen klar machen: F... off! Sie sind nur neidisch auf uns'. Dann klopft er den Wahlkämpfern der UK Independence Party (UKIP) auf die Schulter und sagt: 'Auf meine Stimme könnt ihr euch verlassen, Jungs!' Gerard Batten lächelt verbindlich und drückt dem Mann ein paar seiner Broschüren in die Hand, die auf dem Markt weggehen wie geschmiert: 'Sag Nein zur europäischen Verfassung, sag Nein zum Euro, sag Nein zur EU, sag Nein zur Mitgliedschaft, wir wollen unser Land selbst regieren' steht darin zu lesen und: 'Großbritannien steht kurz vor seiner Zerstörung als unabhängige Nation'.

[*'We will kick them in the ass' promises a red-haired underwear trader. Next to his special offer of three knickers for £5 he gives vent to his strong opinions: 'These rubbish Europeans – I not only want to vote against them, I want to tell them to f... off! They're just envious of us'. Then he claps the activist of the UK Independence Party (UKIP) on the shoulder and says: 'You can count on my vote, boys!'. Gerard Batten smiles obligingly and presses a couple of his pamphlets into the man's hands and leaves the market saying 'Say No to the European Constitution, say No to the Euro, say No to the EU, say No to membership, we want to govern ourselves' and 'Great Britain faces its destruction as an independent nation'.*]

In London, which yielded disappointing results for us in the 1999 European Elections, a YouGov poll put us on course to win a seat in both the European parliament and the London Assembly. Rising support for UKIP was thought likely to prevent the British National Party from gaining a seat in the Assembly. Damian Hockney was at the centre of the campaigns in the London area and was a candidate both for the London Assembly and for the European Elections. The *Evening Standard* said that

Hockney could be faced with having to choose which position to take up if he were to win both. Hockney said "when we drew up the lists, we never expected for a second that we would have this level of support. Now there is a real chance that I will have to choose between London and Brussels. I haven't yet worked out what I would do".

Of Cranks And Gadflies

As the campaign approached its climax, the gloves came off, at least on the Conservative side. Rattled by the YouGov poll of the 24th the Conservative Party issued a briefing document which took the old 'wasted vote' line, backed up by assertions of varying irrelevance, inspired at times by misunderstanding of what our strategy was. And, as in all elections since the acrimonious departure of Alan Sked, the latter weighed in during the thick of the campaign to place his piece on behalf of the Conservatives. Following the tone of the Tory briefing document, Sked opined that UKIP was a useless protest party. It was, he feared, "entirely unworthy of support". The party's candidates were often "intellectually low-calibre" who could achieve nothing at all. In fact, he wondered whether they were only in it for the money – all those European parliament salaries, pensions and expenses. Only Westminster could take Britain out of the EU and the only party which could do that was the Conservative Party "and I for one will be voting for it".

The Conservative briefing document made many claims about us but the phrase that hit the media headlines was "cranks and political gadflies". As seems to be increasingly the nature of politics, the document was immediately leaked. It was billed in the press as a savage attack on us. It may have been counterproductive. Many Conservative grass-roots supporters were thought to be in sympathy with our aims (one front-bench Conservative MP confided that he thought 20 per cent of his Constituency association would vote for us), so the put-down was taken as an insult to them as well as to UKIP.

The United Kingdom Independence Party claims to be a home for Eurosceptics but in reality it is full of cranks and political gadflies. Worryingly, some UKIP members have even had links with the Far Right. A UKIP vote isn't just a wasted vote: it is a dangerous vote for useless representatives who will do next to nothing for their constituents. A vote for UKIP is a vote for the Little Englanders. A vote for Labour or the Lib Dems is a vote for the Little Europeans. Only the Conservatives can offer a Britain that can be proud of itself, proud in Europe and proud in the world.

The Conservative Party was not alone in feeling the need for a rebuttal document. Labour also weighed in, though their rebuttal didn't even attempt to be a reasoned argument against our position. Instead, it took it for granted, or insinuated, that our position was extremist, the "Militant Tendency" of the Conservative Party, in Tony Blair's and Jack Straw's soundbite of the time. Having labelled us as extremists it then used guilt by association to present the Conservatives as also being extremist. The document, entitled "The UKIP Connection – How Michael Howard's Tory Party links to the Extreme Anti-Europeans", either through misunderstanding cause and effect, or deliberately in order to supposedly maximise damage to the Tories, put the cart before the horse:

Michael Howard's Tory Party is now in a panic about UKIP. Having created the Frankenstein monster of populist anti-Europeanism and given it respectability, the Conservatives now face being, if not destroyed, deeply damaged by their own creation.

It is true that the Conservative Party, mostly, helped to create the UK Independence Party – and myriad other groups – but not because they were engaged in some anti-European frenzy. This history has set out our true roots and explained that they lie, precisely, in the pro-European policies of the Conservative Party in the eighties and nineties and, indeed, in the decades before. And in no sense had the Conservatives tried to give respectability to those groups. The opposite had always been the case, with UKIP and the other groups always being *personae non gratae* with the Conservative Party since their inception. Labour was indulging in a good old exercise of spin and damage maximisation. Afforded the luxury of watching two rival parties slug it out among themselves, Labour was able to evade any criticism of their own policies, and to avoid the responsibility to explain to the electorate, as should be the case, in a mature democracy composed of individuals and parties willing to take the hit for their policies, just why their pro-Europeanism was the right direction for the country to take.

After the YouGov poll of the 24th the next YouGov poll on the 29th showed a further rise in our support. The 14 or 18 per cent support of the previous poll, depending upon which figure was taken, had risen to 20 per cent. Unprecedentedly, the support for "others" in a General Election was at 12 per cent:

> *With less than two weeks to polling day, the Conservative lead has dropped by five points. They are on 34 per cent, while Labour has lost two points to 33 per cent. But support for 'other parties', which includes UKIP, has almost doubled from seven to 12 per cent in the past month. Within that total, UKIP, which wants Britain to pull out of the EU, is on five per cent, and the extreme-Right British National Party is on two per cent. The Liberal Democrats, who are seeking to turn the elections into a vote on the Iraq war, have picked up two points and are on 21 per cent. But UKIP is emerging as a favourite for a mid-term protest against the Government and could win as much as 20 per cent of the vote on June 10th.*

The editorial in the same edition of the paper reflected a feeling that the campaigns of the main parties had been eclipsed by that of UKIP and that the political establishment was almost being sidelined. A "melancholy stasis" was affecting all the major parties and Labour and the Liberal Democrats had their "feet sunk in electoral concrete".

Through Farage's contacts with Lord Pearson, a long-term critic of BBC bias on the European issue, and also those of Lott with Vladimir Bukovsky, the former Soviet dissident who was also waging a campaign against BBC bias, approaches were made to peers in the House of Lords to come out in our support. An agreement was reached with twelve peers and it was decided to toss this grenade into the campaign. Five Conservative and seven independent and cross-bench peers agreed to put their names to an open letter which was issued as a press release by UKIP on the morning of the 29th:

> *As loyal Conservative, independent and cross-bench peers, we urge those who normally vote for one of the main political parties to lend their vote at the European Elections on June 10th to the UK Independence Party. Only thus will the main parties be persuaded that their policies toward the European Union are not in the national interest. It is to that national interest that we all owe our ultimate allegiance.*

Not surprisingly, the whip was withdrawn from the five Conservative peers, though one recanted, and the row went on for days. Lord Pearson, a longtime opponent of UK membership of the EU and a figure behind the scenes in several Eurosceptic groups, made it clear that his allegiance still lay with the Conservative Party but that he saw a large vote for UKIP as a means of pushing his party in the same direction. It was only a tactical move, not a full declaration of long-term support. The row generated by the open letter gave rise to articles such as one the following day in the *Observer* which claimed that Howard's sacking of the four Conservative peers marked the most serious internal crisis for his party since John Major withdrew the whip from the Maastricht rebels. But, although the Conservatives had been hardest hit by the rise of UKIP, the party posed a "threat to all mainstream parties, epitomising a backlash against professional politicians – and worrying levels of support for extreme policies on immigration".

Alan Sked returned to the fray on that same Sunday with a trenchant attack on the party he used to lead. Writing more in sorrow than in anger, he said, he attacked the decision to take up any seats won, claimed that the party had given up thinking about policies and that its activist base was shrinking. He brought up the naïve maiden speech of Holmes to the European parliament in which the latter had called for more powers for the parliament. Drawing on leaked internal emails he referred to the latest resignation from the party of Richard North, the party's Research Director in the EDD group, after disagreements with Farage on the nature of North's job:

I am not and was not prepared to be a bag-carrier. Nor would I fetch and carry for Farage, or write his letters, or be available to pour him into a taxi when he was so blind drunk that he could no longer stand, or cover for him when he failed to turn up for morning appointments because he had been out on the tiles all night long. I am almost old enough to be his father, but I am not in the business of being his nanny. I am a professional researcher and that, in my mind, was what I was employed to do.

Sked again brought up the supposed link with the BNP, mixing in a dubious claim by Nick Griffin, the BNP Leader, that an informal pact existed between the two parties and the acknowledged fact that there had been occasional infiltration of BNP members into UKIP. At least Sked did acknowledge that the party denied any pact with the BNP and that any members of that party discovered in UKIP were immediately expelled. He complained about our harder line on immigration but said that his most fundamental objection was that we had not done the hard work of policy formulation. Dismissing us as a lighweight party he ended with his now customary declaration for the Conservatives. They had changed course on Europe and were now saying 'no' to the euro and 'no' to the EU Constitution and were now even advocating the repatriation of some powers. That wasn't a policy of withdrawal, which Sked still believed in, but it was a policy that would radically alter the position of Britain in the EU – "and they are in a position to achieve this. So, for now, this UKIP founder will vote Tory on June 10th".

This hard-hitting salvo brought return fire the following week with Sked branded as "the Ted Heath of UKIP" in the letters column of the paper.

But more serious and potentially damaging was a report in the *Mail On Sunday* of that weekend before the election. According to Sked, interviewed by the paper, during a row between the two about the inclusion of a non-discrimination statement - around ten years previously - on membership application forms, Farage said that "we will never win the nigger vote, the nig-nogs will never vote for us". Farage later said the claim was rubbish, absolute lies, and that Sked was "demented".

Democracy, as understood by the Communication Workers

Union at any rate, included their right to refuse to deliver the leaflets of "extreme" parties. Their threat began with the BNP but then extended to ourselves and Operation Christian Vote, the latter campaigning against abortion, human embryo research and euthanasia. Opinions might differ on the BNP but it is difficult to conceive as Christians as extreme. The putative ban did not, apparently, apply to such parties as the far left Socialist Workers Party.

Finally, also during that penultimate weekend before the election, a Labour campaign strategist complained that we had no strategy and used, once again, the old slur:

> *They are not a political party, they have no co-ordinated programme, they have no ideas that will make a positive difference to the way people live…all they are concerned about – obsessed with, in fact – is saying 'no, no, no'…their appeal is founded on the basest of instincts, like xenophobia and Little Englandism and they are seeking to use that to exploit any hint of discontent with the government. That doesn't represent a political strategy to me.*

With the month of the election arrived, the Conservatives swivelled around their big guns and put us in the cross-hairs for the first time.

Coming To The Boil

After the "cranks and gadflies" insult, and with recriminations within the Conservative Party over UKIP's rise now intense, Howard decided to heap up the coals even more, taking us on directly in a major speech for the first time. At the beginning of June in a speech in Southampton calling for a "live and let live" Europe, he sought to present the Conservative Party as the moderate centre:

> *Here in Britain we face a clear choice. At one extreme there are the candidates from the UK Independence Party. They represent a party that wants to pull out of the European Union altogether. They have frequently failed to vote in the European Parliament on issues that are vital to Britain. At*

the other extreme are Labour and the Liberal Democrats –
who want to transfer even more from Britain to Brussels,
setting Europe on the path to a single European State. The
Conservative Party rejects both these extremes.

The speech echoed the speech made by Howard to the Konrad Adenauer Stiftung in Berlin in February. The problem for the Conservatives was that people, even many Conservatives, questioned whether it was remotely possible for a single Member State to bring about a major change in the direction and the nature of the European Union. What would a future Conservative government do if the other Member States simply said that they weren't interested? After all, none of them showed any signs of a similar desire. Howard replied that Margaret Thatcher had got what she wanted at Fontainebleau – the British rebate and a rejig of Community finances – and that he could do the same. But, came the reply, Thatcher had a key weapon to wield: the Community would run out of money if the negotiations were not concluded to her satisfaction. What weapons did Howard have? He had explicitly said that he would never take Britain out of the European Union. Indeed, in an interview on the *Today* program back in early November, Andrew Marr, the interviewer, asked Howard a blunt question:

Marr: *"Are you, Michael Howard, completely committed*
to Britain's membership of the European Union?"

Howard: *"Absolutely. I always have been, I've made it*
absolutely clear."

The Conservative campaign had a big problem, therefore. If push came to shove in future negotiations with the other Member States, Howard had already announced that he wouldn't play a key card. As Lord Pearson put it on the day before the election, the Common Agricultural Policy and the Common Fisheries Policy would never be renegotiated unless Michael Howard added "or else" to his negotiating stance. Kilroy-Silk also counter-attacked and asked for some honest speaking from the Tory MPs who agreed with UKIP's aim:

I could give you the names. I know them well. I say to those Tory MPs who share our views and our aspirations, and there are many of them, who Michael Howard has just called gadflies and extremists: that's what your party Leader thinks of you because you want Britain to be a sovereign independent state.

It was difficult for Howard to go too far down the road of invective against UKIP and its policies because many Conservative voters and grass-roots activists were sympathetic to the party and intended to vote for it on June 10th, perhaps helped along the way by our appeal to them to "lend" us their vote just for that election.

Meanwhile, in the other camp, the Labour Party was being given virtually a free ride by the inability of the media to treat the campaign as anything other than a sort of internal spat on the Right. Labour was able to sit out the campaign like a spectator in the front row of a boxing match egging on one side and then the other, and thoroughly enjoying the spectacle. The Liberal Democrats had presumably decided that their European policy was too unpopular to talk about and they would talk about Iraq instead. One of the leaders of the media left-liberal chattering classes at this point produced perhaps the best insult of the campaign, best because it showed the intense annoyance of the pro-European camp. Polly Toynbee seemed to be in particularly fine and angry form in the *Guardian* just after Howard's speech:

He could have made the UKIP look like the pathetic little rump of neo-fascist populist opportunists that they are. Joan Collins of St Tropez and tangerine man Kilroy-Silk?..But yesterday he took the low road, as most British politicians do over Europe. Steeped in sneering Europhobia, this was the speech of a Euro-wrecker, not a would-be reformer. Instead of denouncing the UKIP, he stood firmly on their platform: 'say no to the new Constitution' which sets us on a path to 'a fully fledged European state in the next 20 years..I do not want to be a part of a country called Europe..we don't want to be railroaded into handing yet more power to Brussels'. He took the UKIP's asylum theme too and stirred it together with anti-Europeanism into a poisonous anti-foreigner brew.

But we were on a roll, dominating the campaign, with the polls showing support steadily moving upwards. West Midlands regional organiser Denis Brookes, interviewed by the *Times* in early June said, in the Birmingham HQ, "we came in one day about three weeks ago and it just exploded – the phones never stopped ringing, we couldn't print posters fast enough, it was bedlam. We're just battling to keep up with it all, the exponential take-up".

In the southern counties, and the South West particularly, hundreds of smaller posters in farmers' fields supplemented the billboard posters, with Daniel Hannan, a Conservative MEP for the South East, saying "they are definitely winning the poster war. You think, my God this is everywhere. There's a great surge in it".

A bit of good, old-fashioned rhetoric from the opposite sides on a question felt by each of them to be fundamental is part of the knock-about of politics (unfortunately perhaps) and anyone engaged in the affair needs to learn to have a thick skin. But the *Daily Mirror* reached new depths of smear when it printed a particularly ugly picture of Kilroy-Silk next to a particularly ugly picture of Enoch Powell under the headline "Remind You of Anyone?".

A first indication of the level to which our vote might go in different regions was provided by a YouGov poll of early June on voting intentions in London. The poll found that we were now in second place to the Conservatives, registering 23 per cent support compared to the Conservatives' 32 per cent. Labour was at 21 per cent and the Liberal Democrats were trailing at 19 per cent.

My pessimism at the beginning of the campaign, when I wondered if we could retain *any* of our seats, was replaced with the question: "where is the ceiling?".

In the second election broadcast of the campaign, on the 2nd June, an immaculately dressed Kilroy-Silk strolled through a typical street of urban Britain and dropped into the local market, all the time exhorting viewers to the cause with expansive, inviting hand gestures and a soothing voice. To underline the party's continuing efforts to attract ethnic minority voters, a black and a Sikh voter were included. Farage spoke in his usual direct way, standing by the side of the Thames with the Houses of

Parliament on the opposite bank. Knapman was featured directly outside the House of Commons.

In the final week of the campaign there were signs that the establishment parties were becoming seriously ruffled by UKIP's threat. Some articles also pointed out that Labour's delight and fanning of the flames could backfire on them in the longer term if we were to gain a permanent foothold in British politics. What chances, then, for a 'yes' vote in an EU Constitution referendum? True to form, EU form anyway, where referenda are rerun until the correct result is obtained, the leaders of the Conservative and Labour MEPs in the European parliament began to muse whether perhaps there should be a change in the electoral system used for elections to the parliament. Gary Titley, for Labour, showed signs of panic, saying that, "after these elections there is going to have to be a complete rethink about the electoral system as part of the review of PR as a whole". Jonathan Evans, for the Conservatives, found it a rare occasion of cross-party agreement, though he did blame Labour for the change to PR – "the current structure has meant that MEPs are anonymous within the vast euro-constituencies that his Labour government has created".

This interesting conception of democracy in action was also demonstrated by Matthew d'Ancona in his *Sunday Telegraph* column when he, also commenting on the current PR system, said that it enabled minor parties to make "smash 'n' grab raids upon the democratic system". Presumably, what he really meant was "smash 'n' grab raids" on the established parties' votes. In a very good article, despite the sentiment above betraying his true concern, he did approach something close to the truth about UKIP:

> *The UKIP is merely the latest mutation of a persistent strain in Right-wing politics which has taken many forms since the fall of Margaret Thatcher in 1990, but has as its binding force the belief that the Conservative Party betrayed true Euro-scepticism when it ditched her, that the Maastricht Treaty was treasonable and that New Labour's infatuation with the EU has made withdrawal the only patriotic course.*

Ending his article, he said that those of us on that side of politics had chosen to fall asleep while the modern world passed us by and, in a really rather good invention, signed off with "to adapt the words of the Iron Lady: UKIP if you want to".

Another tendril of public opinion slowly moving in the political undergrowth, and probably an issue that we will have to confront at some stage, was the perception among some that we were dogmatically pro-American. Some on the left were able to work themselves up into their standard anti-American mode and make their bizzarre claim that there isn't really any democracy in Britain (partly true but, of course, I would say for different reasons) followed by the accusation that UKIP wanted Britain to become the 51st state of the Union. From where did this impression come? It is almost certain that the mere presence of Dick Morris in the campaign contributed to this sentiment, especially when, at the beginning of the campaign, he linked the cause so explicitly with the war in Iraq, not particularly flavour of the month, perhaps even among those who broadly supported it. A telling moment occurred when Morris appeared on *Question Time* and spoke about the dollars that Britain sent to the EU. Dimbleby, with a cross between a smile and annoyance, corrected Morris, saying "we use pounds here, Dick". Neil Clark, in the *New Statesman*, house journal of the soft intellectual Left, looked at the American dimension. He conceded that we were neither isolationist nor xenophobic but came up with yet another novel interpretation of our ethos. We were "free-market ideologues" who believed in the "divine right of big business to go anywhere in the world in search of profit – unencumbered by social chapters and other regulations – and in the economic and military supremacy of the superpower in whose interest such an ordering of the world is done".

A penultimate YouGov poll was conducted four days before the election. It showed us now in a clear third place, having widened our lead over the Liberal Democrats. Among voters who said they were very likely to vote in the election, 26 per cent backed the Conservatives, 24 per cent Labour, 21 per cent UKIP, and 13 per cent the Liberal Democrats. The poll did not, however, support our contention that we were taking votes equally from all three main parties. Only around 5 per cent of people who usually voted Labour or Liberal Democrat said they were considering changing their allegiance while 25 per cent of Conservative voters said they were considering switching, prompting the report in the

Daily Telegraph to say that:

> After being mauled by Labour over the past decade, it seems
> that the Conservative Party is about to fall victim to a
> ferocious new predator: the United Kingdom Independence
> Party.

A ripple of concern went through the party when reports
appeared that Kilroy-Silk claimed that he had been asked to
consider becoming party Leader, raising the prospect of another
damaging internal row. Party sources confirmed that the issue
would be on the agenda at a meeting later in the week and Kilroy-
Silk admitted on GMTV's *Sunday Programme*:

> You are right to ask those questions and I would be foolish
> and I would be lying if [I said] they have not been raised by
> people in the party, both at Westminster and in the
> leadership, and I have not given some thought to them. Of
> course I have, but it is really, honestly, one step at a time. We
> have to see what happens on June 10th and after that we will
> make decisions about the future.

The continuing feud between Damian Hockney and most of
the rest of the NEC surfaced again late in the campaign with the
Evening Standard reporting that Hockney had been barred from
standing in the NEC elections for a reason that the party would
not divulge. As so often, the threat of legal proceedings was in the
air.

These two strands were to come together after the election to
precipitate yet another damaging, internecine struggle in the
party, Kilroy-Silk ruthlessly promoting his candidacy for the
leadership with Hockney one of his key supporters. Many in the
party had begun to feel that perhaps we had reached a level of
stability after the two bitter earlier struggles. It was not to be. The
elation and euphoria that came with the result was soon replaced
with bitterness – and concern for the very survival of the party.

With just two days to go, the campaign team at the Bramshott
campaign centre exhorted members to a last effort as the party
moved 'into the straight':

In what may be the final pre-election bulletin, we would simply ask you to make that final push and keep hard at it right to the end. Those last few leaflets delivered late Wednesday night could just mean one more MEP than we would otherwise see elected. The campaign has surpassed our most optimistic expectations and the positive feedback we are now getting – from branch to campaign office level – is quite staggering. You have all done a fantastic job.

Newspaper adverts featuring a smiling Kilroy-Silk appealed to the electorate to consider that the £30billion that the party said went to Brussels would pay for 10,000 new hospital beds, 68,000 new policemen, 66,000 new teachers, 125,000 trainee nurses and even then would still be enough to give every pensioner a £34 per week rise in their pension.

On the day before voting, a YouGov poll for the *Evening Standard* put us equal second with the Conservatives, with Labour on 26 per cent, UKIP and the Conservatives on 22 per cent, the Liberal Democrats on 16 per cent and unspecified "others" on 13 per cent. For the London Assembly elections we were reported to have 10 per cent support. Just 5 per cent was enough for us to have a candidate elected.

Interviewed by an online politics website on the same day, Farage anticipated upwards of 20 per cent of the vote and underlined our detachment from any idea of reforming the system from within – "we are not going to Brussels and Strasbourg with any pretence that we are going to reform it and change it – we are not. The model is far too advanced and far too rotten as far as we are concerned to be reformed".

On the final day the *Times* again wheeled out the wasted vote line:

Many in Britain will be tempted to vote today for the UK Independence Party (UKIP). Such a vote, they think, would make them feel good and give a slap in the face to conventional politicians. Voting UKIP is a wasted vote...A UKIP vote will not improve the EU itself. And Mr Blair will be able to dismiss any surge in UKIP support as the visceral response of the disaffected.

The last leaflets were distributed, the battle buses finished their tours of the towns and villages, the anti-EU Constitution stalls were folded up in the shopping centres, the halls of the last public meetings were locked up. We, the activists, could now stand down and the candidates and party leadership ready themselves for the results to come. In the early afternoon of June 10th the Bramshott office sent the last communication of the campaign: "a BIG thank you all from David Lott and the Bramshott team for your energy, stamina, enthusiasm, loyalty, and everything else".

The campaign was over, the waiting began.

Champagne And Then To Wreck?

In the no-man's land that lies between the day of the election and the actual counting of the votes, at least in Britain and some other countries, party activists chewed their pencils and their fingernails, attempting to divine what the results would be from the sparse information coming through.

Local election results and the London Assembly elections were not subject to these restrictions. Early on the Friday, from London, a part of the country not hitherto good ground for the party, Damian Hockney emailed members with news of the results from his area: "Dear Fellow Member: It is well after midnight, and after several hours celebrating by Tower Bridge I am dropping you a quick line to share with you great news from UKIP in London. We have won 2 seats on the Greater London Assembly".

For the European Elections, Richard North, now running a blogspot dedicated to EU affairs, also early on Friday morning, reported evidence from South West constituencies putting UKIP at around 23 per cent. An AOL exit poll the previous evening gave a similar figure. By Saturday lunchtime, North was posting predictions of 23 per cent to 27 per cent, figures which, if true, would give us up to nineteen seats.

Knapman was touring the radio studios. On Radio 4's *The World At One* program, he said that it would be wrong to assume that UKIP would only take votes from the Conservatives, asserting that "it's the Labour vote that is particularly soft. Where we are really having good results are in places like Hull, Hartlepool, and Derby – which are not really Conservative hotspots". It was said that his remarks would alarm Labour strategists who hoped that Tony Blair's tactic of making the election a choice of "in or out" of Europe would only appeal to hardline Conservative Eurosceptics, not Labour supporters.

That the threat was not only to the Conservatives seemed to be acknowledged by Labour the following day in the leading article on the front page of the *Sunday Telegraph*. The paper predicted that Labour was on course for an even worse "kicking" than it had suffered in the local elections a few days before. Labour ministers had apparently conceded that Labour Eurosceptics had deserted the party and would be switching to UKIP.

With the count begun, by 11.30 pm we had our first two MEPs, Gerard Batten in London and Godfrey Bloom in Yorkshire and the Humber. Our share of the vote was still only at 13 per cent but those two regions were among our weakest. An hour later the tally was seven and an hour after that it had reached eleven.

With the results all in later in the morning for the eleven regions in England, Scotland, and Wales, the full tally was twelve. In Kilroy-Silk's East Midlands region, where he and Derek Clark had been elected, we came second in the contest, less than half a per cent behind the Conservatives, with both parties gaining 26 per cent of the vote. In the South West, we were also second to the Conservatives and just 9 per cent behind. We were also second to the Conservatives in the Eastern and South East regions. In the West Midlands we reached third place and in London, Wales, the North East, the North West, Yorkshire and the Humber, we were in fourth place. Our relative weakness in Scotland was shown by our sixth place position there.

Turnout had increased to 38 per cent from 24 per cent in 1999 and it is possible that the increase was due to the UKIP presence bringing out voters who would not otherwise have voted. Labour's share of the vote was down marginally, from 26.3 per cent to 22.6 per cent, but its representation in the European parliament dropped from 29 to 19. The Conservative share of the vote was down 7 per cent, from 33.5 per cent to 26.7 per cent, and their seats had dropped from 36 to 27. The Liberal Democrats had increased their vote share by 3 per cent and had increased their number of seats from 10 to 12, possibly due to their opposition to the Iraq war rather than support for their

European idealism. Between them, the two main parties failed to gain half the vote. Labour suffered its lowest share of the vote since before the First World War while the Conservatives had to look back to 1832 for a worse result. The *Times* reported "Parties Hit Panic Button As UKIP Drinks To Success" while the *Independent* saw "Tories and Labour crushed under the wheels of UKIP's bandwagon":

> *UKIP, which wants Britain to withdraw from the European Union, took votes from both main parties after dominating the campaign and sending shockwaves through the political establishment.*

Despite the paper's naked antipathy to the party, it at least praised the way in which our campaign had been run, conceding that we had mounted an attractive, modern and energetic campaign. None of the other parties "ran a campaign that came close to UKIP's in terms of directness, simplicity or glitz".

Lord Tebbit, feeling the Tory ship in a severe squall, acknowledged the possibility that we could do serious long-term damage to the Conservatives: "I think voting UKIP, for a lot of Conservative voters, is a way of firing a shot across the bows of the Conservative Party. The trouble is that if they are not careful they could fire it a bit close to the waterline". But the damage was not only to the Conservatives:

> *The results of the European Elections are every bit as damaging to the two main parties as had been predicted. By coming almost from nowhere to seize 17 per cent of the vote, the UK Independence Party, barely taken seriously until now, has engineered one of the greatest coups in modern electoral history.*

On a sunny Monday, one of the hottest days of the year in fact, the newly-elected UKIP contingent assembled on College Green outside the House of Commons for a photocall. Champagne bottles were opened and glasses raised to toast the victory, a beaming Kilroy-Silk pictured with glass raised in triumph. The team then proceeded to a nearby conference room for a victory press conference. Knapman, Farage, and Kilroy-Silk sat at a small table and the remaining eight lined up behind. After Farage had opened the press conference, Kilroy-Silk was asked what he intended to do in the European parliament. In typically forthright style, and to perhaps embarrassed laughter, he replied:

> *Wreck it.... Expose it for the waste and corruption and the way it is eroding our independence and our sovereignty. Our job is to go there and turn round and say 'this is what they do. This is how they waste your money. This is how they all go on the gravy train and spend their time in restaurants and all the rest of it'.*

It was a typical Kilroy rhetorical flourish, probably made in the euphoria of the moment, but it was taken up by the pro-European media to criticise us. At the beginning of the new session of the European parliament, however, Kilroy-Silk made clear that he would not be attempting to wreck the parliament, though he still insisted that he would spend as little time there as possible. He would spend most of his time in the UK, carrying forward the party's continuing campaign.

And, indeed, we were concerned to build upon the great success we had achieved. Later the same day, the party leadership and MEPs held a strategy meeting to plot the way forward. Farage had already declared the night before that "our aim and ambition is to turn the UK Independence Party into a mass movement".

We were also planning a role for the party in the third battle of the war, coming into clearer view now that the European Elections were over: the referenda planned in three Northern regions on the creation of elected Regional Assemblies. In addition, there was the referendum on the proposed EU Constitution to be considered. The *Times* reported that the party planned to "gatecrash" these referenda, elbowing aside the Conservative Party role in these campaigns and qualifying for state funding on the 'no' side. Upcoming by-elections were looked at for the chance to keep the momentum going though the party, uncharacteristically, stood aside from the first two a few months later. Dick Morris flew back to London to discuss the next phase of our advance into British politics – the drive to gain our first MPs at Westminster, our real goal, despite the fierceness of our

European election campaigns. Morris's advice was the opposite of his advice for the European Elections, David Lott told the *Times*: "Dick has said that it is going to be the programme we put before the public which will make or break us in terms of seats at Westminster... Broadening our manifesto is the next step and it will move along the lines of small government, in every walk of life".

As the electoral fireworks of that remarkable election died away, Michael Howard summoned his party's MPs to a "council of war" amid worries that party infighting over the EU would break out again, taking it back to the divisions under Major and Hague. Eurosceptic members were pressing for a hardening of policy to prevent further defections to UKIP. Indeed, some months after the election, Howard signalled a toughening of his party's stance on the EU by bringing John Redwood back into his shadow cabinet with a brief to focus on EU regulations, even, supposedly, single-market legislation. This was followed in short order by a significant hardening of the party's policies on asylum.

Tony Blair likewise convened his MPs and told them to concentrate on the domestic agenda while saying that he hoped the furore over Iraq would soon die down. A series of announcements on domestic policies was planned for the weeks ahead.

There was no word from the Prime Minister, but commentators pointed out that the UKIP share of the vote surely demonstrated that the chances of winning a referendum on the Constitution were low and could get lower if UKIP were to capitalise on its success and take the antifederalist message deeper into the electorate, talking about the issue as opposed to the establishment parties' attempts to keep things under wraps. Blair travelled to Brussels knowing that a sizeable part of the electorate wanted out altogether. We made sure that the message was driven home by hiring a poster lorry to drive around Whitehall and Westminster with the message "Don't sign the Constitution, Tony, Britain says No". Kilroy-Silk had already rammed home the message:

He has had seven years to persuade the British people that they need to be somewhere called the heart of Europe. If we get a significant vote, and I suspect we will, then clearly, the

British people don't want to be there with him. He'll be there by himself. This will be a tremendous snub to him. He cannot go ahead this week and sign up to the new Constitution if there is a significant number of people voting for UKIP. He would be treating the electorate with contempt.

Commenting in the *Independent*, Bruce Anderson was perhaps optimistic, from his point of view, about what the future held for the EU cause in the United Kingdom. Had thirty years of EU membership come to this? Was the cause dying?

Tony Blair thinks of himself as a devoted European. Indeed, he had expected to be the most pro-European premier since Ted Heath. He had intended to use his hold over British public opinion to persuade the voters that their destiny lay in Europe. So what happens, seven years into a Blair government? He fights a European election in which Europe is hardly mentioned. He doesn't try to persuade the voters to love Europe; he simply wants them to hate Michael Howard...Europe has never had less resonance with British public opinion...last week's elections have resolved nothing. They have confirmed the electoral death of the British Euro-federalist cause.

If the cause was dead, the Prime Minister seemed not to have noticed. Later in the same week Blair headed for Brussels and signed the draft EU Constitution.

Old stereotypes die hard.

The Guardian, 4th June 2004 cartoon by Les Gibbard.

8

European Election 2004 to General Election 2005

The End Of The Beginning

What delight it was to be a UKIP activist in the summer of that early year of the 21st century. For the first time, history and the party seemed to be walking together. The conference later that year was to be the "Celebration" conference; media interest in the party was higher than ever; the political establishment had been well and truly rattled in June, and there was a feeling that this might only be the beginning. But there were problems to come that would dent the euphoria. There were gaffes and embarrassments with some of the party's MEPs in the European parliament and, in consequence, at home, this time in the full glare of media attention. As Jeffrey Titford put it, the MEPs were not so much under a magnifying glass as under a microscope. And worse, far worse, we were heading for yet another outbreak of the disease from which we thought we had cured ourselves: vicious internal infighting.

Robert Kilroy-Silk had been the party's single greatest asset in the campaign of 2004. Now he was about to turn into our greatest liability, a possible mortal threat to the existence of the party and, by extension, to the cause of an independent Britain. Robert Kilroy-Silk was the proverbial double-edged sword. And both edges were extremely sharp.

Meanwhile, there was the battle against regionalisation to be won and, after that, the crucial battle against the proposed EU Constitution, both against the backdrop of the General Election of 2005.

European Elections, the fight against regionalisation, the EU Constitution referendum announced, internal dissension, preparations for the General Election. An intense period of activity, concertined together. Hard decisions, hard work, hard pounding.

The House On The Rhine

There is no smooth, fault-free ride for any party. There are always problems: problems of PR, problems with embarrassing candidates, problems where policies may not add up. We were no exception to this. Indeed, because of our nature as a relatively young party without the strict, centralised controls of the establishment parties, we were especially prone to these difficulties. These are the difficulties of any enterprise involving thousands of people – to coordinate the activities of the organisation as a whole and to make sure that it hangs together as a more or less coherent entity.

The gaffes began even as the cheering was subsiding after the end of the European Election campaign. Ashley Mote, in the number two position on the party's South East list and now elected as an MEP for the party, one of the party's prime motivators of the hardened stance on asylum and immigration, was accused of housing benefit fraud. The *Daily Telegraph* reported that Mote's case had recently come before the Crown Court and that he was facing nine charges of false accounting and one of making a false representation. Mote claimed that the charges, relating to events ten years before, were politically motivated. He was, he said, in dispute with his local authority and the matter dated back many years to a time when he was in financial difficulties after being made redundant and advised to claim benefit. He and his legal team were confident that the affair would not come to a trial and that the charges would be dropped – "there are people who are out to discredit me and they are seeking to damage my reputation", he said.

The accusation meant that the party had to distance itself from Mote, whether the charge was true or not, and Mote lost the party whip in the European parliament a month after the *Telegraph* article appeared. Thereafter, he worked in the non-aligned group.

Another gaffe followed on the day of the official opening of the new session of the European parliament in late July. Fiona Bruce, fronting the BBC Ten-O-Clock news on the occasion, reported on the comments of Godfrey Bloom, elected as a UKIP MEP in the Yorkshire and the Humber region. The report switched to Bloom in the European parliament, surrounded by a gaggle of reporters, making outspoken comments about the role of women in employment on the occasion of his candidacy for the women's rights committee of the parliament. Bloom said:

> No self-respecting small businessman with a brain in the right place would ever employ a lady of child-bearing age. That isn't politically correct, is it, but it's a fact of life. The more women's rights you have, its actually a bar to their employment...I quite simply feel that they don't clean behind the fridge. I represent Yorkshire women who always have dinner on the table when you get home. I am going to promote men's rights.

Howls of indignation greeted Bloom's remarks. They were "neanderthal", "outrageous", "absolutely unacceptable". The Leader of the Party of European Socialists in the parliament added somewhat ominously that "we will be following up Mr Bloom's remarks". Farage tried to limit the damage: "We believe that 60 per cent of our voters are women, and we don't want to see them discriminated against in the workplace in any way, but some of this EU legislation is counter-productive".

Bloom was a 54-year-old investment fund manager and a sponsor of Cambridge University women's rugby team. He was noted for his bowler hat which he seemed to wear on all occasions. A flamboyant character, he said that the rugby team were "a lot more badly-behaved than the men. These ladies are wicked. One of the girls had a pump-action shotgun full of beer – there was a lot of squirting... and no shortage of throwing up afterwards". He also said that he enjoyed visiting pubs and that he had "fallen out of more taxicabs drunk than you could shake a stick at". He later clarified his position on women at work, saying:

> It is my intention that there should be much better, simpler and more flexible employment legislation. In my opinion, the current situation clearly disadvantages working women and I want to do something to put that right. To that end, I

> *am working in co-operation with the Danes who sit on the Women's Rights Committee. I will be able to provide more detail on this at a later stage. The joke that I made about cleaning behind fridges was intended to give me a platform to comment on a serious issue. I do recognise that, initially, it had the unintended effect of burying my central point. However, the later media coverage has been more positive and brought out my argument with greater clarity.*

The newspapers had a great time depicting Bloom as the neanderthal representative of a neanderthal party. How many votes were lost as a result of this outburst is not known but there is no question that it was a serious gaffe for a party now under intense media attention.

Back in the European parliament, the machinery to decide the make-up of the new European Commission was grinding away. After a couple of months out came the result in the form of the proposed line-up of the new Commission. National nominees for Commissioners were handed their proposed portfolios by the President-elect and the day came for them to be unveiled before the European parliament for its approval. The parliament had the right to veto the putative President's overall choice of Commission members, but not the right to veto any individual. Confirmation hearings before the parliament began at the end of September. These proceedings brought forth two explosive confrontations, the second almost ending in the arrest of Farage.

Beginning as a storm in a Strasbourg teacup, a row over the opinions on homosexuality and (again!) the place of women in society of the Italian nominee for the Commission escalated into a full-blown confrontation between the parliament and the President-elect, José Manuel Barroso. Barroso, a former Portuguese Prime Minister had, so the media reported, made the somewhat unusual transition from Maoism to Thatcherism. Rocco Buttiglione was a traditional Catholic, even said to be a friend of the Pope, and didn't think too highly of the particular bedroom pursuit in question. He was up for the Justice, Freedom and Security portfolio but got caught in a welter of Orwellian-sounding terms and the traditional intolerance of the liberal Left. The Civil Liberties committee of the parliament voted him down. Barroso refused to budge. The parliament didn't like that and, when the vote came up on the 28th October, Barroso looked at the precipice and decided he wasn't going to jump. With even the 88-strong so-called Liberal group deserting him, he withdrew his proposed team. British media reports said that the climbdown took place in a packed parliament chamber with MEPs jeering and cheering and that the "stunning climbdown" had profoundly altered the character of the European Union. The Leader of the Liberal group proclaimed that the parliament had exerted its authority over the executive in a historic way:

> *Today, this house on the river Rhine grows in stature. Its will was tested – its will prevailed. At no time did we ask for anything more than was our right.*

But the second detonation in the confirmation hearings left the Buttiglione fiasco looking like a minor bust-up. Who lit the fuse? No prizes for guessing correctly.

Speaking as co-president of the Independence and Democracy in Europe group (IDE), the successor to the Europe of Democracies and Diversities group, Farage rose to speak when the revamped Commission came up for approval three weeks later in the postponed vote. With Barroso sitting at the centre of the hemicycle, Farage launched into a blistering attack on the proposed Commission. In trademark pinstriped suit, pound badge in his lapel, and pink tie, he called the new line-up a clique of "crooks, liars, Communist lackeys and political failures". Dropping a bombshell into the proceedings, he revealed that the proposed French Commissioner and Vice-President, Jacques Barrot, up for the transport portfolio, had in 2000 received an 8-month suspended sentence for embezzlement and had been banned from holding public office for two years. He reminded the parliament that Laszlo Kovacs, a former Hungarian Communist, would be Commissioner in charge of tax policy. Siim Kallas of Estonia was for twenty years a "Soviet party apparatchik until his newly-acquired taste for capitalism got him into some trouble". Farage was referring to the trial of Kallas in Estonia on charges of abuse and fraud in some shady dealings just after the time that Kallas had been President of the Bank of Estonia. Though acquitted of those charges, he was found guilty of providing false information. In mounting disgust, Farage noted that Kallas had to be approved in the anti-fraud post. With Barroso in an embarrassed smile, Farage said "I mean, you couldn't make it up!". Mike Nattrass, sitting behind Farage, burst into laughter. From the UK, Peter Mandelson, twice sacked from the government, was to take on trade policy. At least he was one of the more competent candidates, Farage said. From the Netherlands came Neelie Kroes who would take on the competition portfolio. She had been accused of lying to the parliament, said Farage, as Barroso sank into open laughter, though looking around in some embarrassment. "Ask yourself a question – would you buy a used car from this Commission?" Farage angrily asked as Nattrass collapsed into laughter behind him. "I mean, the answer simply must be no!" he said. Rounding up his speech, he said that even if the proposed Commission was competent – and he didn't think it was – the Independence and Democracy group would still vote no. The Commission was the motor of European integration, it was the Commission that was the government of Europe, accountable to nobody. Even though the EU Constitution was far from being ratified, twenty of the proposed Commissioners had stated during their parliamentary hearings that they would press ahead with implementing it. "In the face of such breathtaking arrogance, nobody in the Independence and Democracy group will vote for this Commission", Farage said as he sat down.

Even before he had finished, the roof began to fall on his head. One MEP, Jacques Toubon, a former French Minister for Justice, stormed down the aisle and, a mere ten yards to Farage's left, began to scream and shout at him, while demanding that the parliament's President should halt the proceedings. Farage later recounted that Toubon got more and more desperate and eventually resembled a man "running around a burning room looking for the door". A row developed in the chamber and leaders of the parliamentary groups attacked Farage and threatened him with legal action for defamation, even though he had immunity in the chamber. Josep Borrell, the President of the parliament, referred to "legal consequences". Farage almost wavered under the intensity of the threat but decided to soldier on, saying that he would only apologise if his assertions turned out to be wrong. Jacques Toubon had been involved in the same case as Barrot.

It was the Barrot revelations that were the real trigger of the explosion, and not surprisingly, because the French establishment had sought to cover up the whole affair of the Barrot trial. Under one of those special laws beloved of manipulative governments – everywhere, not just in France – Barrot had received a Presidential amnesty which meant that reporting of the trial was banned from the media. The blackout had been so successful that Barroso was completely unaware of the affair, his Commissioner having also omitted to enlighten him. Barroso was left swinging at a press conference the next morning, when he admitted that he had known nothing of the Barrot trial until Farage had dropped his bombshell in the parliament. UKIP issued a press release urging him to sack Barrot and suggesting for good measure that either Barroso was covering up or he was incompetent. For a while the fate of Barrot hung in the balance but MEPs, having swung round to recognise the gravity of Farage's revelations, nevertheless closed ranks and what *Libération* referred to as "la chasse au Barrot" fizzled away.

Steve Harris, Regional Organiser in the South East office of the party told me later that, after the affair, Farage had had to avoid France on his return from the parliament because he risked arrest if he crossed French territory.

Kill The Tories

Away from that "house on the river Rhine" the somewhat more prosaic town of Hartlepool was to become far more important to the average UKIP member and activist and likely to send a frisson of fear down the spines of Conservative and Labour alike. But before Hartlepool, the third by-election after the European Elections, there were by-elections in Birmingham and Leicester which the party, for some reason, sat out. There is little to suggest why it did this. Maybe it was just too broke after the millions spent up to June. Maybe it was just too tired. There is nothing to suggest a connection to the tumultuous row with Robert Kilroy-Silk which was already brewing behind the scenes. Indeed, Kilroy-Silk had said during June's victory press conference that he would not be the candidate for the Leicester by-election. At Birmingham Hodge Hill the party apparently squashed the desire of the local Chairman to stand as a UKIP candidate and, in the event, at

Leicester South, there was an 'independent UKIP' candidate.

When the time came for the party to look for a candidate for Hartlepool the situation wasn't so clear. Here began another bout of email discussion group comment, media speculation, and party denial. It was rumoured that the party leadership had sat on a Kilroy-Silk candidacy for Hartlepool because they feared that, if actually elected, the 'housewife's choice' would become unstoppable in his bid for the leadership. A party member was quoted as saying that "keeping Kilroy down has become more important than getting an MP". Well, we don't know who that party member was and, if he or she was a senior member, would the article not have said so? Richard North, now devoting his energies to his EUReferendum blog, declared that UKIP had "blown it" by not selecting Kilroy-Silk as the Hartlepool candidate. Given how desperate we were to get into Westminster this poking of sticks into our own wheels seems unlikely. And journalists, when it comes to political parties, love to use words like "disarray", "split", "meltdown". The party declared on its website that the rumours were all false and that the story in the *Times* was a hoax. Winning in Hartlepool would mean that Kilroy-Silk would have to leave the European parliament and probably have to fight the seat again in short order at a General Election the following year.

By the time the statement was posted, Stephen Allison had already been selected as our candidate for the by-election. A 44-year old management consultant and born in Hartlepool, Allison was formerly a member of the Labour Party but then had joined the Conservatives and had acted as agent to the Conservative candidate in Hartlepool in the 2001 General Election. He was a local independent councillor from 2002 and had only just joined UKIP in the August before the by-election.

It was a hard-fought by-election with fourteen candidates. Liberal Democrat activists arrived in the constituency by the coachload, hoping to clinch the seat. But their candidate suffered a bad case of 'foot-in-mouth' disease and made an apparently derogatory comment about local residents on her campaign website. She never heard the last of it – literally: Labour played and replayed the comment from mobile loudspeakers around the town and used it endlessly on their leaflets. Most probably it cost her the seat because, in the event, only 2000 votes separated her from the eventual Labour victor.

Unseen, mostly, in the national press, UKIP established an office in the constituency, headed by Steve Harris, and called in activists. Piers Merchant, the new Chief Executive of the party, came up for the duration. Robert Kilroy-Silk came, to be admired by the activists and the voters alike. Merchant got the party some publicity, certainly, when the *News of the World* photographed him with another young love.

But more seriously, when the count came and the votes were being dumped in bundles into their final trays, it became clear that we and the Conservatives, though far behind the piles of Labour and Liberal Democrat votes, were actually vying for third place. Harris told me that, close to the end, he had begun to accept that the Conservatives would just clinch the third place and that he had started to text Knapman with the news. As the last bundle of a hundred votes was dropped into place, however, Harris could see that we had just edged ahead. He cancelled the text.

UKIP 2004 Party Conference, Bristol

Two days later the party gathered in Bristol for its annual conference. A thousand members, not noticeably swelled by the success earlier in the year but in fine, fighting form, feeling the wind in their sails. Hartlepool was the icing on the cake and the dream event of every conference organiser. A last-minute change was made to the Saturday morning schedule to enable Allison to talk about the Hartlepool campaign. Petrina Holdsworth, appointed just after the European Elections as the new Party Chairman to take over from David Lott, formally opened the conference. Allison, the new star of the party, speaking in front of a giant yellow pound sign suspended from the ceiling behind him and standing in front of the purple lectern, described his success in Hartlepool. Then the party's batch of MEPs were paraded across the stage after being marched in by a bagpiper.

Farage was first up for the heavyweight speeches. Confident as ever, feeling that the years of struggle had finally borne fruit and that here, at this conference billed as the "celebration conference", at last some self-congratulation was fitting. "Good morning gadflies!" he began, to laughter and applause.

> *You know, its been a long road for many of us, because for years we were completely ignored. At the times that the media did look at us it was said that we were mad, or that we were bad – or that we were both.*

He said that the people in the hall knew that that week the party had really arrived in British politics. We were there and we were there to stay and we were bringing something new to British politics – the politics of conviction. "We say what we mean and we mean what we say!". Millions of people knew that for 30 years they had had nothing but lies and deceit from the big parties. To applause: "And that is why 2.7 million people rallied to the UKIP colours because they, like us, believe that the best people to govern Britain are the British people themselves".

Farage paid a generous and heartfelt tribute to David Lott. Speaking of the organisation for the European Election campaign, he said:

> *We set up a proper, professional campaign office down in Bramshott and indeed we were very privileged to have David Lott in there running the logistics of the campaign. There isn't a better bloke in this party – there probably isn't a better bloke in this country – than David.*

Going on to talk about the EU Constitution referendum, Farage said that it was vital that the party played a major role in the campaign to come. The party had to be ready to "throw everything we've got" at it. He didn't want to see just 51 per cent of the electorate saying 'no', he wanted to see a thumping 75 per cent vote 'no' – "leading us out of the Union". Emphasising again the party's internationalist outlook and repeating again that the party was not anti-European, Farage ended with the plea for an amicable divorce from the European Union that he customarily used to end his speeches. So well-known now that the audience said it with him.

Farage was followed by Alan Eastwood, a former Chairman of the Police Federation and Nils Lundgren of the Swedish Junilistan party which was formed only in 2003 but which had scored 14 per cent of the vote in Sweden in the European Elections, taking votes from all the established parties. Junilistan's three MEPs were now allied, in the Independence and Democracy group, with those of UKIP.

Later that morning it was the turn of Robert Kilroy-Silk, the superstar outshining all others. Around midday, Kilroy-Silk strode onto the stage for his speech, amid huge media interest and adulation from the audience. The tan, the silver hair, the patrician demeanour. A wave to the audience as he approached the lectern. Smart suit, purple tie. For twenty seven minutes he cajoled, he caressed, he inflamed, he whispered, to his audience. He flattered them, he took them into his confidence. He smiled, he was angry.

Leaning on the lectern he said with a wide smile "I've been *dying* to meet you!". After the laughter had subsided – "I've never known what a load of cranks, gadflies, and extremists would look like!". In mock surprise – "So this is it – its you is it?". Furrowed eyebrows – "Very disappointing, you lot". Pause. Resumed surprise. "You look *normal* to me!" More banter. Voice now serious. Smile gone. "But of course, you're not normal, you know that don't you". Pause. Crescendo. "Because you have just caused a major political applecart to be turned over in Britain". Jabbing finger at the audience – "*You* did that". Jabbing both fingers – "*You* did that, you panicked both the major old political parties, you *scared* them to death", dropping his voice in the last words.

Kilroy-Silk spoke without notes. There is no doubt that he was a star performer. Watching a videotape of the speech some nine months later I was almost convinced that, indeed, we had missed a historic opportunity. That speech was the apogee of the party's development, at least in the period covered by this book. It was a consummation of the struggling, unknown party activists with a media star who might have taken them into the history books, turning aspirations into reality. It was a brief emergence into the foothills of real influence.

He had been a lecturer in political science before he entered politics, so he knew all about these things, he said with heavy irony. "You weren't supposed to push *Her Majesty's Loyal Opposition* into fourth place!" He knew all about the lonely years of obscurity, those wet Wednesday evenings knocking on doors, he knew how they had struggled on, despite all the obstacles. Now success had come. And in a low, earnest voice - "and *this* success is yours and it is *right* that you should celebrate it".

Then he approached the issue that was waiting to be debated later that day, an issue on which he and Farage were completely at odds. What should the party's strategy be in the General Election coming up? Should we fight as many seats as possible, irrespective of the views on "Europe" of the incumbents, or should we give "true" Eurosceptics an easy ride? Kilroy-Silk said that he wouldn't be acting honestly if he didn't give his listeners his views on that subject. Leaning again on the lectern, absolutely still and with a fixed gaze on the audience: "It would be wrong to make alliances with the old parties". Applause and shouts of "yes!". Shaking his head and raising his voice: "That is not what you are about, you have gone beyond that now!". He denounced the prospect of shoddy deals reached in smoke-filled rooms with the old parties. That was "old politics". UKIP was the new politics. Voice rising in a crescendo: "You should not be having any truck with any kind of deals with any other parties. You will be besmirched, tainted by association. What can they give us?" And then the quote that hit the headlines, the dream quote for the media:

> *The Conservative Party is dying – why would you want to give it the kiss of life? What we have to do is KILL IT!*

The opportunity for UKIP, said Kilroy, was there that day, not the day after, not the week after. The chance had to be taken then and the party could not afford to go AWOL for another three months as it had done, he claimed, for the previous three.

Political punch ... Robert Kilroy-Silk outside the
UKIP conference hall, where he set out his vision
of killing off the Tories,
The Guardian, 4th October 2004, picture by Martin Godwin

After lunch the conference reconvened to debate the issue of strategy for the General Election. The motion for debate was:

This conference resolves to fight the General Election in every constituency in the United Kingdom, but should reserve the right, subject only to the approval of the Constituency Association in question, to reach an accommodation with the sitting Member of Parliament of another party on receipt of an irrevocable undertaking that he/she will oppose further EU integration and will support Britain's withdrawal from the European Union.

Farage and Mike Nattrass spoke in favour of the motion. Gerard Batten and Lawrie Boxall spoke against. It was the old dilemma – whether to potentially split the Eurosceptic vote and let in a Europhile candidate, or whether to stand down and not oppose a sitting candidate judged sympathetic to the cause. And then, of all times, when a General Election was looming and when it was likely that Labour would be re-elected and when a Bill to start the introduction of the EU Constitution would most likely be introduced, the question was – should we potentially increase the size of the Labour majority and thus assist the EU Constitution on its way in the United Kingdom? Farage gave a passionate speech and implored the members present "not to make the classic mistake and put party before country". Batten and Boxall argued that there could be no such thing as an irrevocable undertaking – whatever a candidate might say in the hustings and to the media during the campaign they would be under the control of the party whips once re-elected and would have to follow party policy.

Party members present were in no mood for compromise. Farage later spoke of what he thought was a certain feeling of euphoria in the hall that day which had, he implied, clouded people's judgement. So the vote was lost. Members voted over-whelmingly, almost unanimously, against the motion. There would be no compromise. It would be a fight to the bitter end.

The Kilroy battle call to "kill the Tories" and the vote that followed, which he certainly influenced by his speech, had serious fall-out however. Within days, Paul Sykes announced that he would not fund the party's General Election campaign. He was said to think that the party had "blown it" by deciding to fight as many seats as possible at the General Election. Also, the Conservative Party had, in very short order after the European Elections, toughened up its policy on 'Europe' – and immigration – and Sykes now gave it more credibility on the European issue. Indeed, the Conservative Party conference, held immediately after the UKIP conference, sent out even stronger messages on 'Europe'. The *Daily Telegraph* claimed that the Conservatives had been in secret talks with Sykes for several weeks. Speaking on Radio 4's *Today* program, Sykes said that there was little chance under the first-past-the-post system of UKIP getting any MPs elected and that there was now only one major party that was anti-Brussels – the Conservatives. He was "at least warming" to what he was hearing from the Conservatives and he had no intention of "upsetting their applecart". They now seemed to understand that "it's not a bad idea to make our own laws in our own Parliament by our own people, rather than importing them from unelected Brussels". Having said that, he denied having been in negotiations with the Conservatives and said that he had not decided to switch his funding to the party.

On the same program, Nigel Farage admitted that UKIP had lost sight of its key objective amid the euphoria over its recent election results, adding "We have never been about UKIP as a party, as a tribe, being the most important thing. The most important thing to us is we get out of the EU and get back to simply a free trade agreement".

So the broad parameters of our General Election campaign were set: there would be no deals, money would be tight, it would obviously be a first-past-the-post election and we would be up against a seemingly more Eurosceptic Conservative Party. And Kilroy went on to spend the rest of the year dragging the party through an ugly attempted leadership coup, played out in front of the national media – and the electorate watching at home.

The North East Says 'No'

I have already said that there were three crucial battles to be won in the war against the federalist forces: the single currency; the EU Constitution; and regionalisation. The single currency battle was fought over a number of years – it was a slow-burn, underlying battle that culminated in the declaration by the Chancellor of the Exchequer that his five tests for UK membership of the euro had not been met. The battle ended (for the time being, at least) in something of an anti-climax, not proclaimed openly, but buried deep in thousands of pages of Treasury documents and an announcement from the Chancellor based on apparently technical, economic issues. But, nevertheless, the battle had been won.

The battle against the EU-sponsored regionalisation policy, was won (partly and, again, perhaps temporarily) almost without anyone noticing or appreciating the significance of what had happened. Although a few commentators in the tabloid newspapers had savagely attacked the plans for regional assemblies when they were first published, and made their EU dimension clear, media coverage of the referendum campaign in the North East was scant until just before the vote, at least in the national press. When the referendum campaign *was* covered it was generally presented along government lines – that it was about devolving government to the regions and taking the political process closer to the people. Otherwise, the media reported on the government's climbdown over its original plan to hold referenda in three Northern regions to just one in the North East and, rumbling along just beneath the surface, the idea that regional assemblies were largely the brainchild of John Prescott, and the supposed lack of enthusiasm for the plans on the part of the Prime Minister.

Why was this issue, and this particular vote, so important? What significance could there be in whether a few counties in the North East of England might or might not have an elected regional assembly? The answer is that the entire antifederalist movement was united in believing that this was the first step towards the balkanisation of Britain into twelve regions, each with its own miniparliament, which would most probably be warring with each other, and which would increasingly be responsive and responsible to Brussels. The Westminster parliament would, in our opinion, be increasingly by-passed as the regions were given responsibility for implementing EU policies, initially in such areas as transport, the environment and planning. A phrase had even been coined for this process by the theorists of European union – "perforated sovereignty".

Could this really be true or were we in the antifederalist forces working ourselves up into a conspiracy theory frenzy? But it wasn't just the die-hards of the movement who thought this. When the White Paper on regional assemblies was published in May 2002, a number of newspaper commentators identified the EU connection and fiercely attacked it. Richard Littlejohn in the *Sun* said that the regions were:

> *Specifically designed to break up England into administra -tive units in preparation for our absorption into a federal Europe. The regional assemblies correspond exactly with a map drawn up by Brussels for the government of a fully integrated European Union. Stage one was devolution in Scotland, Northern Ireland and Wales. This is stage two. Stage three is the abolition of the English counties. Stage four is the abolition of England.*

At the *Daily Mail*, Simon Heffer was equally scathing and, noting that Peter Mandelson had just appeared on the BBC's *Today* program emphasising that regional government was in accordance with the European model, went on to say:

> *The European Union, and avid pro-Europeans across Europe, hate nation states. They regard England as a persistent offender. It has been a nation of sorts since Roman times, its government formalised after the Norman conquest 936 years ago. The English national identity is the enemy of the European project, and Europe is keen to break it.*

After these initial reactions, the EU connection disappeared off the media radar screen. Individuals on the antifederalist side continued to attempt to bring the issue out through local newspapers and through demonstrations outside meetings of the assemblies. Whenever they did so the usual reaction from the members of the assemblies was – no reaction at all. It was the old tactic of simply ignoring the opposition. In the rare cases where a response was elicited, it was blanket denial of any European dimension and suggestions that the critics had a screw loose. Another line came from the academics in the Universities – the campaigners were ignorant fools who didn't understand that there had been administrative regions in Britain since after the second world war and, therefore, their ideas about the EU connection were so much Eurosceptic blather and conspiracy.

Referenda on whether to have elected regional assemblies (unelected regional assemblies already existed in England in every region outside London) were originally planned to take place in three regions – the North West, Yorkshire and the Humber, and the North East. The government plainly considered these three regions the most likely to vote 'yes'. Using the domino effect, they hoped to get a 'yes' vote in at least one of these regions and then hold referenda in the rest. In an attempt to increase voter turnout the referenda would be by all-postal voting. But postal voting trials in the European and local elections had raised doubts about the security and integrity of such a system (less than a year after those elections there were allegations of widespread postal voting fraud by Labour Party candidates across the whole of Birmingham). In late July the government postponed the referenda in the North West and the Yorkshire and the Humber regions. The North East was considered the most likely region to vote 'yes', so its referendum went forward.

Under the rules set out in the Political Parties, Elections and Referendums Act of 2000, there would be designated official 'yes' and 'no' campaigns, with £100,000 of public funding given to each. Neil Herron, the longstanding supporter of UKIP, had begun his 'no' campaign almost immediately after the European Election and he wanted his to be the official 'no' campaign. As a resident of the North East region and a well-known figure there, he had excellent credentials. We also wanted to fight the referendum, for the reasons explained above. But UKIP and Herron had fallen out after the latter stood as an independent in the North East in the European Elections. Harris told me that Herron now considered himself to be "too big" for the party. In the event, then, UKIP joined a coalition composed of the Conservative Party and local business and professional people, meaning that we and Herron were competitors in the bid to become the official 'no' campaign. Herron led the North East No Campaign (NENO), UKIP was in the North East Says No (NESNO) campaign. Herron and others complained that the NESNO group were a bunch of Johnny-come-latelys mostly from outside the region and that the presence of the Conservative Party in NESNO would be a liability in the North East where there was only one Conservative MP.

With just three weeks to go to the vote on the 4th November, the opinion polls still looked risky for the 'no' campaign. The *Times* reported that, in the months before, polls had shown a two-to-one majority for the 'yes' side but that a new poll had given 36 per cent to the 'no' side, 28 per cent to the 'yes' side, and 36 per cent undecided. These figures were certainly no guarantee of success now that the last three weeks of the campaign had arrived and voters would be starting to concentrate on the issue. Reporting on the composition of the 'yes' and 'no' sides, the paper said:

> The 'no' group is fronted by former members of the Business for Sterling campaign, which fought against the euro, and is backed by Tory and UKIP-supporting businessmen...The 'yes' group, backed by Labour and the Liberal Democrats

*and academics and regional artists, is more knowledgeable,
better organised, better financed but, so far, less aggressive
than its opponents.*

The 'yes' group was headed by Professor John Tomaney, a
Newcastle University academic and one of those who ridiculed
the Eurosceptic claims on regionalisation. Tomaney, in fact,
worked in the Centre for Regional and Urban Studies of the
University and was a member of the management board of the
Jean Monnet centre. Jean Monnet is counted as one of the
"founding fathers" of the European Union.

With two weeks to go the polls had turned further against the
'yes' side. The *Northern Echo* newspaper reported a MORI poll
showing 42 per cent intending to vote 'no' against 35 per cent
intending to vote 'yes'. Among those who said they were certain
to vote, the split was 54 per cent against and 31 per cent in
favour. John Prescott, backed by local MP and former Cabinet
minister Stephen Byers, said during a tour of the region: "If it fails
here, we won't be back for a considerable period of time..This
opportunity may be the last for a decade...It is up to the people
of the North East to decide whether to go with the building
blocks they have got now".

The 'yes' side had descended into calling their opponents RATS
– 'rather arrogant toff southerners' – in an attempt to paint them
as a pack of Tory outsiders. The 'no' campaign was lugging a
giant white elephant around the region as a symbol of what they
thought the assembly would be.

On the Monday before the Thursday vote the *Daily Telegraph*
reported that it seemed that turnout might be higher than
expected but that while that might encourage the 'yes' campaign,
the signs were that the plan would still be rejected, leaving
Prescott's dream of English regional government in tatters. Neil
Herron was typically direct – there was "not a cat in hell's chance
of a 'yes' vote". The turnout could be 10 or 100 per cent "it
wouldn't make any difference. The answer is still going to be no".

On the day of the poll, the *Northern Echo* reported on Prime
Minister's Questions in Parliament the day before, where Charles
Kennedy, Leader of the Liberal Democrats, had linked the
referendum in the North East to the expected referendum on the
EU Constitution. He wanted the Prime Minister to undertake

"early and full-blooded campaigning to make the case for the Constitution". The paper said that the North East Says No Campaign (NESNO) saw its campaign as a dry-run for the campaign against the EU Constitution. This was also on the part of Herron and NESNO, as Herron later publicly said.

The final result was a massive victory for the 'no' side. On a turnout of 48 per cent, much higher than expected, the 'no' vote was 78 per cent, an unprecedentedly decisive figure. All 23 council areas voted against the proposal and, in some areas, the margin of victory was seven to one.

The overwhelming 'no' vote in the North East torpedoed the regionalisation agenda below the waterline. Government ministers lamely insisted that the policy might continue but it was widely, realistically accepted that the project was at an end. Indeed, the antifederalist forces quickly moved the agenda on to the next step – the complete abolition of the assemblies which, it should be remembered, still existed, though not elected. In the months to come the Eurosceptic side widened the envelope, pushed their efforts into the salient that had been created, chipped away at the foundations and undermined the confidence of the members of the regional assemblies. Neil Herron, ever resourceful, took up the issue of the personal financial responsibility of members of the assemblies. The members, Herron said, could be personally liable for the financial commitments of the assemblies, such as future staff pensions, because they were unincorporated bodies. Some local councils, seeing the way the wind was blowing, and perhaps none too enthusiastic about the assemblies in the first place (their own councils would probably eventually be abolished if the assemblies ever gained real legitimacy) began to reconsider their subscriptions to the assemblies. In March 2004, in the South East England Regional Assembly, a motion was put that the assembly should dissolve itself. The motion was very nearly carried when 71 per cent of the seconded councillors voted for abolition. A vote of 75 per cent of those councillors plus, separately, 75 per cent of the so-called "social, environmental and economic partners" was required under the legislation for an assembly to dissolve itself. Clearly, the councillors were almost ready to shut up shop but the thirty seven 'social, environmental and economic partners' voted to keep the show on the road. It might be said that here was an example of how the European Union was actually intended to be run – unelected elites immune from electoral pressure, pushing their agenda on ordinary people in the belief that they know best, revelling in the power that it gives them, and snouts firmly in the trough.

The project has been halted, the situation is stalemate, the regional assemblies are still there. For the antifederalist forces it is unfinished business. The drive to abolish them completely will continue.

Return Of The Curse

In the age of mass democracy, publicity is all important. It may be distasteful, the public may not like it, but it is an imperative demand for all political parties. Academic discussions can be held aplenty, Manifestos can be drawn up, ideas debated, but if the public does not know that you exist, it is all a waste of time.

Our problem in late 2003 and early 2004 was that, still, many voters had not heard of us. The inertia of the media and the establishment had blocked wider knowledge of the party. Into this situation came Robert Kilroy-Silk, media superstar. As recounted in the previous chapter, Farage, along with others, had been instrumental in bringing Kilroy-Silk into the party and positioning him at the top of the party's list in the East Midlands region for the European Elections. It was an immense media coup that enabled us to break through the media barrier. But Kilroy-Silk was far more, or less, than the party thought he was. Indeed, when the final explosion happened, Farage apologised for having brought Kilroy-Silk into the party, saying in an email to South East chairmen: "It only remains for me to apologise to all of you. I recruited Robert Kilroy-Silk believing it would help UKIP. I got it badly wrong".

Robert Kilroy-Silk is an exceptional character, a truly *sui generis* individual. But does he belong in the pages of a Shakespearean tragedy or in the antics chronicled by Cervantes? The key to this difference is undoubtedly his ego. Quite possibly he was always thus, even in the days when he was a young Labour MP battling against the Militant Tendency in Liverpool. On being elected in 1974 he had, after all, declared that he would be Prime Minister within fifteen years.

It soon became clear that Kilroy-Silk was not satisfied with being part of a team. He wanted to be "head man", he wanted to be Leader of the party – and quickly. Lott was later to describe how Kilroy-Silk was offered, just before the 2004 party conference, the key position in a committee of four which Lott proposed should lead the General Election campaign of 2005. The team would consist of Kilroy-Silk, Lott, Paul Sykes, and Alan Bown. The first day of the party conference was to be the venue at which the team would be announced. On the day before the conference, and after two weeks of negotiations, Kilroy-Silk turned down the offer. Kilroy-Silk later claimed that he had been offered, during the European Election campaign, leadership of the party shortly after the election, when Knapman would step down. Lott said that what had actually happened was that, even before Kilroy-Silk had joined the party, Knapman had privately told Lott and Farage that he would probably step down at the next conference. Farage had then said to Kilroy-Silk that, of course, at some point Knapman *would* step down as Leader. It was a hint to Kilroy-Silk that, yes, he could expect to eventually have his chance to become Leader. But, Lott said, it *didn't* amount to a deal for the post-election leadership of the party.

Friction between Kilroy-Silk and the rest of the UKIP contingent in the European parliament eventually led, in late October, to Kilroy-Silk facing the threat of being expelled from the group. Lott described how he had telephoned Kilroy-Silk and asked him in a message that he had left whether there was any position within the party, short of the leadership, that would allow him to remain within the group and the party. Lott asked him to reply within 24 hours – the situation in the group was now becoming critical. Kilroy-Silk did not reply.

Lott recounted this offer, and the non-response, to myself and also to a meeting of the South East region branches in Woking in November. At the same meeting, Farage emphasised the difference between his own approach and the party's approach in general, and that of Kilroy-Silk. He said that, whenever he had the opportunity of speaking to the media, he always talked about "the party, the party, the party". In contrast, Farage asked, "have you heard Kilroy when he speaks? Its always 'I', 'I', 'I' ".

The first public sign of the split to come was in a gossip column in the *Daily Telegraph* in the middle of September. The article said that Kilroy-Silk had never been known to have a low opinion of his abilities but that it was surprised by quite how brazen he could be. According to the article, Kilroy-Silk had signed the visitor's book for a House of Commons lunch with the flourish "Robert Kilroy-Silk MEP, UKIP Leader de facto, Brussels". The article also said that Paul Sykes wanted Kilroy-Silk as Leader or he would withdraw his funding.

On the day after the party conference, Kilroy-Silk was interviewed by David Frost on his Sunday *Breakfast With Frost* program. Kilroy-Silk made a naked bid for the leadership of the party. In the interview he claimed that the vast majority of the party wanted him as Leader. He made public his claim that there had been a deal over the leadership and that Knapman had agreed to stand down in his favour. He said that "what everybody tells me they want is for the current Leader to accept the inevitable and to stand down. We have a very short period between now and the General Election – we need to start now".

His approach to party colleagues and the spirit of working together as a team was shown by his comment about the reason why he thought Knapman had reneged on the supposed deal. He said "but then, of course, he got a massive election result and probably he liked the size of his new train set". Knapman immediately denied that there had been a deal, "there was no deal. Even if there was, there is no mechanism to change Leader in the middle of a term". Knapman said he had no intention of resigning: "I am here to serve. I have done my best for the party and I am happy with my record. We are on a high and have no problems. Robert has so much to offer the party. I am sure he will see we have to pull together".

The *Daily Mail*, reporting the comments above, said that Kilroy-Silk was trying to "grab the leadership of the party" and, as the newspapers like to do, said that the battle was "threatening to tear the fledgling right-wing party apart". On this occasion, at least, the prognosis was true. The ambition of Kilroy-Silk to be the Leader of the party and the aggressive, unrelenting campaign that he waged to that end over the following three months, did indeed polarise opinion within the party for and against him, with some constituency associations coming out for him and a demand for an EGM at which a motion of no confidence in the Leader would probably be put. Long-term associates and colleagues within the party found themselves bitterly opposed to each other.

Interviewed by *BBC News Online* two days after Kilroy-Silk's *Breakfast With Frost* declaration of his aim, Knapman said that Kilroy-Silk would:

> ..*make his own luck over the next short while. I hope he will settle down and be a team player...Nobody is bigger than the party. We are a political party and not a chat show party...he needs to be a team player...I will take the party definitely into the General Election...on the other hand I don't say I will go on and on and on.*

But Kilroy-Silk clearly did not intend to be a team player and events slid towards open warfare. In a *Sunday Telegraph* interview four days later, he called on party members to put up or shut up, claiming that he had considerable support within the party and that moves were being made to make him Leader. He complained that:

> *I'm treated as the Leader, I'm asked by the Leader of the party to be the spokesman for the party, then he comes and asks me will I be Deputy Leader, then he comes and asks me will I run the General Election campaign. I can't carry on dissembling. I can't carry on like that. It has to be sorted out.*

Kilroy-Silk was asked what financial backing he had, now that Paul Sykes had deserted him and the party after his "kill the Tories" comment at the Bristol conference. He claimed to have over £100,000, enough for the full election expenses of ten constituencies. When asked why he thought he should be Leader he said:

> *The flatness of the landscape. There isn't anybody else, that's all. Perhaps I'm the best they've got. I'm no good but that is what we have got to work with. If the party wants to be more than just a pressure group, then that is the choice it should make. Its up to you [UKIP members] – if you want me to be Leader, you must find a way of it happening.*

All eleven of the party's MEPs, including Kilroy-Silk, met in Brussels three days later to try and resolve the situation. But the result was inconclusive, partly reflecting the fact that it was not a clear case of ten against one. Jeffrey Titford, now the party's chief whip in the European parliament, told the press that there had been a "long and amicable discussion in which, on both sides, strong views were expressed. All those involved were, however, concerned that although there were legitimate differences on the direction the party should take, nothing should be done to damage its long-term prospects. It was therefore decided that the discussions would continue in order to arrive at a position that would be in the long-term interests of the party".

By this time, the possible game plan of the Kilroy-Silk camp was beginning to emerge. It was to gather the support of a sufficient number of branch committees to call an EGM under the party's Constitution and to then pass a motion of no-confidence in the Leader and thereby to precipitate a leadership election. Without going into the arcana of constitutional clauses, a detailed reading of the document indicates that there was, in fact, simply no constitutional way of replacing the Leader at that stage unless he were to stand down voluntarily. As always happens, the meaning of this or that clause was disputed and, again in the usual way, there were threats of legal proceedings.

Also beginning to emerge was the question of whether the party's leading members and older members might take a different view on the desirability of Kilroy-Silk as Leader than newer members. The MEPs were said to be almost ten-to-one against Kilroy-Silk as Leader. But would ordinary members think the same? Our membership had now climbed to around 27,000, many of these having joined during or after the European campaign. Perhaps they had joined because of Kilroy-Silk. Perhaps, if a leadership election were held, many of these new members would vote enthusiastically for him. Nobody really knew, but the suspicion on the part of the anti-Kilroy side was that this was what he was banking on.

Damian Hockney emerged as the most high-profile party member to openly support Kilroy-Silk's ambition to lead the party. It was to be the final disagreement between Hockney and the party leadership in a three-year series of disagreements on almost every substantive issue. Commenting on the meeting in

Brussels, Hockney said "there was talk about reading the riot act to him and that hasn't happened. I have a better chance of winning an election if Kilroy is Leader than if Roger is. That's a fact". Those supporting Kilroy-Silk's bid for the leadership had this, at least, as their motivation. As Rodney Howlett, chairman in Kilroy-Silk's own constituency put it to me, the 2005 General Election would be a case of "shit or bust".

But Kilroy-Silk's leadership bid was running into the sands. It was reported that he had admitted defeat, that he had been slapped down, that there was "blood on the carpet". The party said that his attempt to hijack it had led to a flood of resignations and that "it should be clear by now that his leadership bid isn't going anywhere and he needs to shut up for a while...not behave like a spoilt child who hasn't got the toy he wanted".

In retrospect, it is clear that this must have been the point at which Kilroy-Silk decided to declare open warfare. Two days later he issued a letter and email to all branch chairmen in which he put ten issues before them. The "ten issues" email asked "What Kind of Party Do You Want?". The text of the letter, which also went to the media, had been toned down from the email. The email asked whether UKIP should be a serious political party or just a pressure group. It claimed that the leadership was not democratically elected. It implied that the party was willing to make "shoddy electoral deals" with the Conservatives. It asked whether principles were paramount to the party or whether the cheque book was king – presumably a reference to Paul Sykes. It claimed that the party was a single-issue party and had no other policies. It referred to "paid foreign advisors and self-confessed lying PR men" – presumably references to Dick Morris and Max Clifford, his fellows in the "three outsiders". It implied that the party lacked vision and a sense of where it wanted to go. Ending the email, Kilroy-Silk said:

These are 'legitimate differences'. Only by discussing them openly and fearlessly, without rancour, can we arrive at a decision that will be in the long-term interest of the party and, most important, enable Britain to govern itself. If we cannot have an honest, open public debate about these important issues and decide them democratically, then we have no right to ask the British people to support or indeed to trust us.

In response to this clear declaration of war, Knapman immediately mounted a counter-attack. On the 18th October, two days after the 'ten issues' letter was released, Knapman launched a snap poll of party chairmen, asking them "do you want a leadership election before the next General Election?". This was a sounding exercise and no constitutional validity was claimed for the poll. Probably, Knapman wanted to gauge opinion within the party before deciding how to proceed. Farage, in an email to all South East chairmen asking their opinion, said what they all probably already knew:

> *I am afraid that I have to alert you to the fact that unless we act quickly and decisively UKIP may be in for a period of turbulence once again, as has followed previous successes...One cannot disguise the fact that this is potentially hugely damaging and the press may choose to have a field day at our expense. Many of you may consider that these are not actions putting party and our crusade to lead this country out of the EU above personal ambition. Others may detect a left-wing agenda within a party which seeks to draw support [from] across the political spectrum. The main concern, however, must be UKIP unity in the coming months to capitalise on our new-found influence in the fight to save our country in the short time that remains.*

Farage said that he had hoped that Kilroy-Silk would have worked within the party to establish his suitability to lead it and, in due time, could have qualified to run for the leadership. He said that, once Kilroy-Silk had learned more about the party he had so recently joined – that it was a party that put country before "party people" and that it was not in the business of "wrecking" the European Union or killing other political parties, he could well have taken over as Leader. Farage was under no illusions about the gravity of the situation - "whatever the motivation, we now have to deal with what can only be seen as a potentially terminal threat, caused by the upheaval of a leadership crisis a few short months before a General Election".

The route of officially polling branches for their decisions on whether they wanted an EGM, the notice period for an EGM, a leadership election if the EGM passed a vote of no-confidence in the Leader – and the fact that the leadership disputed that the Constitution allowed such a decision, and the possibility that court cases could result from that disagreement – would have devastated our preparations for the General Election. At the end of November Lott, as General Election Campaign Manager, pleaded with the membership to let him get on with the job. He recounted the original plan for the General Election campaign committee. That committee, with the formidable communication skills of Kilroy-Silk, the financial backing of Sykes and Bown, and the experience that Lott had accumulated in running national campaigns, would have put the "fear of God" into the opposition. By the time of his plea, said Lott, the party would probably have been showing in the polls if the squabble had not erupted. Instead, two precious months had been lost. "Please unshackle me" he asked, because, if the infighting continued, then he would have no hope of building momentum for the General Election campaign. He went on:

> *The enemy is out there: wounded, debased, corrupt, weak and vulnerable, propped up by fragile loyalties. In all my life there has never been a greater opportunity for a new party with radical and exciting policies to capture the imagination of a disgruntled and despairing electorate.*

On the Tuesday after the weekend declaration of war, the *Times* reported the unofficial poll, calling it a counter-attack by Knapman against Kilroy-Silk. Regional Organisers had been instructed to contact all branch chairmen at home, to "test their loyalty" to him. All 400 party chairmen would, the following day, be receiving a personal letter from Kilroy-Silk attacking Knapman and Farage as a "self-selecting cabal".

A Kilroy-Silk supporter said "It is open warfare now, each camp is organising". The article suggested that Kilroy-Silk was preparing a tour of the branches to try and bolster support among the mass membership of the party. The following day the paper reported that the telephone survey of the party's 235 constituency associations had resulted in 75 per cent of them backing Knapman. Knapman's supporters were saying that Kilroy-Silk should accept defeat or face the prospect of expulsion from the party's MEP group, the paper said. Alan Bown, who had contributed £400,000 to the party's European Election campaign, and who was now the party's biggest donor, called on Kilroy-Silk to abandon his leadership bid - "if Robert decides to continue with his leadership challenge, I will reluctantly have to reconsider the funding that I have promised for his personal election campaign in the East Midlands".

The results of the telephone survey were disputed by the Kilroy-Silk camp, but the unofficial vote, whichever way it was cut, was clearly against him. Knapman declared that the question of the leadership was now settled. There were more hints that Kilroy-Silk would be expelled from the MEP group if he persisted with his challenge. Eight of the party's MEPs, Alan Bown, and others in the leadership of the party, wrote to Kilroy-Silk saying that his talents were welcome but that "instead you have repeatedly promoted your own leadership and must be aware of the damage done to the party by your public comments...we will take firm action against further attempts to foment dissent which we would not tolerate".

Knapman denied that Kilroy-Silk was about to be expelled from the parliamentary grouping but also said that "we are asking him to make up his mind either to support the party or plough a single furrow...if he can't be a good team player, he owes it to himself and the party to consider his future carefully".

The infighting within the party enabled our political opponents to make political capital out of the situation. The *Guardian* recounted the party's history of internal conflicts, saying that "for those observers who have followed the party's fortunes since it was founded more than a decade ago, the dispute is nothing new. Over the past seven years the disasters – many of them self-made – have come thick and fast. UKIP has seen at least three leadership challenges, been infiltrated by racists, had a mass walkout of its national executive committee, faced allegations of intimidatory tactics, fought off claims of financial wrongdoing and battled threats of expensive legal action".

Alan Sked and Michael Holmes were contacted for comments and both obliged with vitriol for their old party.

Confusion over the poll of branch chairmen increased. The party had to issue an apology over earlier figures it had given.

Final issued figures showed 205 of the 233 branches had been contacted. Kilroy-Silk had majority support in the Yorkshire region and was level-pegging with Knapman in the East Midlands region. In contrast, the South East and South West regions were solidly against Kilroy-Silk. The overall figure was 159 to 27 with 32 undecided. On the release of these final results, Knapman again called on Kilroy-Silk to desist:

> It is clear that there is no appetite amongst branch chairmen either for a leadership election or for a change of Leader. Mr Kilroy-Silk has a valuable contribution to make as part of the UKIP team, but as a member, not as its Leader...It is likely that the next General Election will take place in less than 30 weeks and that must be our next target. I will not allow 10 weeks and thousands of pounds to be squandered on a clearly pointless leadership election merely to further humiliate one person.

The conflict between Kilroy-Silk and most of the rest of the leadership of the party was now so intense that discussions had begun on whether to expel him from the MEP group. In the event, with discussion of this possibility on the agenda of the monthly meeting of the MEPs, Kilroy-Silk chose to jump before he was pushed. Calling it a "kangaroo court" he made the somewhat bizarre comment that:

> They needed to dig themselves out of a hole and I have helped them by saying that these people in effect have wanted to hang me for the last week or more and now they're suddenly saying 'come and have dinner with us tonight'. Well, I don't think I can do that.

Commenting on the news report, a party spokesman welcomed the news:

> If he has withdrawn from the whip then to a certain extent he ceases to be our problem. But we would remind him that the people of the East Midlands voted for a UKIP MEP and not a maverick independent. We welcome the peace that will hopefully return to UKIP and [which] will allow us to get on

with the task of fighting the EU rather than fighting Kilroy-Silk.

Despite resigning from the European parliament group, Kilroy-Silk, crucially and bizarrely, said that he would remain a member of the party. Clearly, to challenge for the leadership, still his ambition, he would have to be a party member. Peace was not yet to return to the party. This was only the end of act one.

On the same day and in the European parliament, he caused uproar by continually barracking other MEPs, banging on his desk and shouting "oi!", in a debate on the new line-up of the European Commission, in particular in the debate on the appointment of Rocco Buttiglione as a member of the Commission. He was threatened with ejection from the chamber of the parliament. Martin Schulz, Leader of the Socialist group in the parliament, after repeated interruptions from Kilroy-Silk, sarcastically suggested that "perhaps medical services could despatch some tranquillisers". The British Leader of the Liberal group said, no doubt with delight at the opportunity to bring out the latest wheeze of the pro-EU camp to equate antifederalists with the *Sun* and beer-sodden football fanatics, "I'm quite ashamed that Britain is known for its football hooligans and even more so when I see their political representatives here in parliament".

Whether through anger or as a deliberate decision, Kilroy-Silk began to make increasingly outrageous criticisms of the party. On quitting the parliamentary group, he depicted himself as a moderating force and claimed that the party was extremist, adding that he was "relieved and happy to leave a group which engaged in barmy politics".

On the Sunday after his resignation from the group, Kilroy-Silk used his regular column in the *Sunday Express* to attack the party and set out his reasons for the disagreement. It is worth quoting his article extensively because it set out the core of his case:

Immediately after UKIP's victories in the European Elections in June, I suggested a meeting of party leaders so that we could build on our success and develop future strategy. UKIP Leader, Roger Knapman, the European parliamentary Leader, Nigel Farage, the two main financial backers, Paul Sykes and Alan Bown, my wife Jan and I met in the Goring hotel, London, on Monday June 13th. We agreed that we needed to establish a London HQ, assemble a research team, develop policies, draw up the Manifesto for the General Election, appoint spokespersons and plan a series of initiatives throughout the summer, leading to the October party conference which, I anticipated, would unveil the Manifesto.

Nothing happened. Weeks passed, nothing happened. Several times I told the party leadership that we were losing the political initiative that we had gained in June. We should, I stressed, be exploiting the panic we had occasioned in the Tory party and the alarm felt by the Prime Minister about his project to create a superstate called Europe being wrecked. Nothing happened. The leadership of the party went AWOL for three long summer months. We wasted precious time. We threw away our advantage. It was unforgivable, criminal. The British people had placed their trust in us and we were letting them down.

Here was more "we, we, we" than "I, I, I" so perhaps we should accept this analysis at face value. There *is* an argument to be made that we could have used our breakthrough to seize the agenda immediately after the European Election and continue the momentum, instead of winding down after an exhausting campaign as is all too natural. But other factors need to be taken into account. Lott stood down from the position of Party Chairman just after the campaign. In an email to activists on the 20th June he said that "for my part I find that I have over-extended myself in the pursuit of success...I have decided to stand down as Party Chairman from yesterday". Lott, by then 64, had undergone major surgery for cancer in 1996. Had it returned? When I asked Nigel Farage about this he said no, but also said that Lott had had medical problems during and after the campaign, though nothing serious. Most of all, Farage said, Lott was simply exhausted after 14, 16, 18 hour days.

Farage himself was under strain from the fallout of the Ashley Mote affair. Plans had been made in which Farage would lead the party's campaign in 'Europe' and Mote would lead the campaign in the UK. This was now impossible. Steve Harris, one of Farage's closest colleagues, told me that Farage was, for six weeks, almost *hors de combat* because of the pressures.

The conspiracy theorists around the party, those disgruntled by past arguments, were hard at work claiming that the party didn't really want to achieve real success in the General Election to come. As always, the target of the disgruntled ex-members was Farage. Farage, they said, was the real force in the party, the "kingmaker" who always ensured that the party Leader was under his control and would follow his direction. Farage was really engaged in a pact with the Conservative Party. Farage might even be, in the more extreme versions, a deliberate plant to ensure that the secessionist forces would always be blunted.

Richard North, in his blog, railed against what he claimed was the poor education and anti-intellectualism of Farage. Farage was against policy development, Farage was blocking the articulation of a developed philosophy for Britain outside the EU: "It has taken someone like Kilroy to expose the flaws at the heart of UKIP, but the problems were there long before he arrived. And, until they are sorted, UKIP cannot go anywhere. After all, politics is about ideas – the vision thing. Sadly, when push comes to shove, UKIP – or its leadership – doesn't want to know. But I cannot share Kilroy's optimism. The chance – for UKIP – has come and gone".

The task – and the loneliness – of leadership, is to provide direction to an organisation, to lead the organisation to success through all the difficulties that it meets along the way. Everyone has their own ideas, often mutually exclusive, sometimes unrealistic. A Leader must choose and does not have the luxury of espousing ideas that they will not have to act upon immediately.

The dispute between Kilroy-Silk and UKIP had now reached the end of Act One. Act Two of the schism now began. Act Two was the attempt by Kilroy-Silk to gain the support of a sufficient number of branches to call an EGM that would pass a vote of no-confidence in the Leader.

The dissident faction of the party was centred around what some termed "the London set", which had been progressively following its own path, and Damian Hockney in particular, Leader of the UKIP group in the London Assembly. Others in favour of Kilroy-Silk gravitated to the "London set". These included Craig Mackinlay, Gerard Batten, Tony Scholefield, John de Roeck and Michael Harvey. Underlining the gravity of the dispute was the fact that Mackinlay, Batten and Scholefield were among the founder members of the party.

Throughout November and the weeks leading up to Christmas, Kilroy-Silk and his supporters ratcheted up the pressure for an EGM by signing up local branches to a petition demanding such a meeting. Speaking to a local paper in Berkshire on the 12th November he said "it isn't over yet. Believe me, it isn't over":

> *I'm going around the country, we have people organising the branches, we already have far more branches than are necessary to force an election signed up. But we want more, and we want to choose our time. The members have to have a revolution in which they take control of the party.*

The war of the emails erupted again. The Kilroy-Silk camp reported on the progress of their petition. The party leadership reminded members of the long-drawn out procedures involved in getting to a leadership election. And for what? To have a new Leader in place two weeks before a General Election or two weeks after? There was a scramble to check the status of every branch. Were they all properly constituted and registered? Had they had local EGMs of their own to be able to add their name to the petition? Accusations of dirty tricks, of pressure being brought to bear. On the 29th November, the dissident camp submitted a schedule of 50 branches who had called for an EGM. A week later the call was rejected. In the intervening week both sides had consulted legal opinion to check their position. Both sides received the advice they wanted (some things, at least, are constant).

The dissident camp continued their efforts all the way up to Christmas Eve. A renewed attack was expected, but it never came. Farage told me then that he thought the threat was receding. The New Year of 2005 arrived and still no new attempt appeared. Then the news began to appear that 'Kilroy' was about to start his own party. A new, rival party would be a serious threat, but at least it would be outside UKIP and would take away the dissension to a separate arena where it could, hopefully, be extinguished in the future. With luck, internal arguments within the new party would lead to its rapid demise. Relief, relief. It was over.

So the schism ended, the end of a bad dream when the dreamer wakes with a start. During the squabble the Conservatives were said to be fearful that Kilroy-Silk would become Leader of UKIP and delighted when the short marriage ended in acrimonious divorce. They didn't know the half of it, in my opinion. Kilroy-Silk as Leader of UKIP would have been a nightmare from which there would have been no waking. Kilroy-Silk would have destroyed the party within a year.

9

The 2005 General Election Campaign

Great Hopes

After the great success of the European Elections, we hoped to go on to win representatives at Westminster, where we *really* wanted to be, where we knew we really *had* to be, to have any chance of achieving our political objectives. The talk was of five or six MPs. A historic breakthrough was beckoning.

But, in total contrast to the European election campaign, we were locked out of the national media. We were barely visible. The main parties didn't want to talk about 'Europe' – they all had their reasons for not doing so – and the media didn't raise the issue either. Iraq and public services dominated the campaign. It wasn't Farage or Knapman or Mahon who was the shock surprise, but George Galloway, leading an eclectic coalition of the hard left and Muslim activists.

It wasn't a case of nemesis after hubris. We did our best within what we had. But the Conservative party, by that time, had moved much closer to our policies on the European Union and the asylum and immigration issue. Other aspects – the damaging schism with Robert Kilroy-Silk, the overall image problem of the party, perhaps – led to a result far below what we had aimed for. But there was a consolation prize: over 620,000 votes were eventually won by almost 500 candidates and a toehold in national politics was gained with, perhaps, the message established that the party was not just a one-issue outfit. It was a base for the future.

Despite the quarrels, despite the loss of Paul Sykes, despite the dire media coverage, the party got up from its wounded position and carried on. By mid-November 2004, 262 candidates had been approved for the 2005 General Election. But funds were short. At a South East counties meeting of candidates and agents in Woking in that month, Lott explained that the candidates would have to find their own money. There would be no free election addresses as there had been in the European Elections when Paul Sykes had stumped up the cash. No deposits would be paid, it was up to individual candidates to put their own money where their beliefs were.

There would be no funds for a billboard campaign such as the one that had covered the country earlier that year. Posters left over from the European Elections could be reused. John Moran, in charge of the Ashford call centre, revealed that the Ashford and Preston call centres had phoned 23,000 people in Hartlepool during the by-election campaign there. Well over a half had said that they wouldn't give any more money because of the "Kilroy factor". There was a serious cashflow problem and 9,000 members had been lost since April, though Moran thought that 40 per cent of those could be re-recruited. Fortunately, Alan Bown, sitting on the platform, had agreed to put up £150,000 to pay for leaflets and a million of them had already gone out.

In a New Year message to members Knapman congratulated them on their tenacity in battle. They had withstood disregard, disdain, slander, lack of money and, sometimes, lack of friends. But they had stood firm and 2004 had brought them their just rewards. The established parties had been humbled, one by one, and UKIP itself had moved out of the "others" category and into the history books. Turning to the future, Knapman reminded the members that the party had to put together a Manifesto of credible policies that would withstand exacting scrutiny. He then sketched out some of the areas that the Manifesto would cover: against ID cards, the tool of big government; keeping the nation's historic army regiments, not dissolving them in the new battlegroups of the EU's common defence policy; a renewal of local government with local referenda to back that up and insulate the process from politicians following their own agenda and ignoring the will of the people.

Knapman signed off with thanks to the membership and a wish for even greater success in the year to come; in fact, to the party's first Westminster MPs.

Despite all the problems, the time had come when we were finally in the position to fight the campaign that we had been set up to fight – a General Election where we had, we thought, a realistic chance of winning seats. The dream was finally in view.

Organisation For The Campaign

At a strategy meeting for candidates in Exeter in mid-January, Dick Morris, still onboard as the party's political advisor, set out how he thought the campaign could turn to our advantage. It would be the exact inverse of the European election campaign. In the European campaign we had needed to use our strong regions to help the weaker regions, in order to get the percentage of the vote up nationally. In the General Election, we needed to focus our resources on a few winnable seats. The party should aim to show early electoral promise in these seats. If that were achieved, then the media would report it and these reports would strengthen the desire of wavering voters to vote for the party in our weaker areas. It would be a kind of ricochet effect. Morris also thought that UKIP could benefit hugely if the Conservative Party started to fall behind in the polls. The media might then focus on the improbability of the Conservatives winning the election and this might, in turn, convince normally Conservative voters to switch to UKIP. Morris's view leaned towards the idea of UKIP as a rival to the Conservatives. Farage, on the other hand, felt that we should try to tempt back those who hadn't voted since 1992, not in chasing a "bombed-out" Tory vote.

In a side-meeting for South East candidates, Steve Harris explained some of the technicalities of the campaign. As much as possible would be done online. Election addresses would be placed online and candidates could make corrections online before giving the go-ahead for printing. Those turned down as General Election candidates should consider standing in the local elections. Leaflets would be available in their millions – the first 100,000 through the South East office had been exhausted in 11 days, the second 100,000 in 13. Farage, even now looking beyond the General Election to the supreme battle everyone expected to have to fight, said that he wanted the party to grow substantially during the campaign to come because it was vital that we developed into the "shock troops" of the EU Constitution referendum campaign. On the money situation, he recalled that, back at the beginning of the European campaign, around the time of the Torbay meeting, the regional committees of the party had personally guaranteed £425,000 of liabilities to jump-start the campaign – "but hey, this *is* the UKIP"! He urged candidates to meet as many voters as possible – this was undoubtedly the way to gain hearts and minds – he knew, he had done it, just look at his record in the places where he had stood, he said. All candidates would be vetted and this would include a search on the internet. Posters from the previous campaign were still available. Any billboards would be targeted at the winnable seats. Special target voters were pensioners, small shops and businesses and the self-employed. The party had still not found a way to appeal to the young, he noted, thought it did have the appeal of *not* belonging to the established system.

Morris joined the meeting as Farage was speaking and sat with David Lott in the audience. Morris spoke of the American experience of bloggers and mass emailing and urged those present to take up the challenge – they should start their own campaign blogs and start to assemble a list of email addresses to which they could email. The internet was "the great equaliser".

Meanwhile, the national campaign office in Newton Abbot in Devon had been up and running for almost a month. Lexdrum House would be Lott's latest battle centre. Mark Croucher, the Director of Communications, thought they were magnificent offices that even Millbank and Central Office couldn't rival. A long way from the 'broom cupboard' that Lott had fought from in 1999. And this time he would have three lieutenants each covering a region of the country. After candidates had been interviewed and accepted they would be passed on to one of these three lieutenants, while still maintaining contact with their Regional Organisers.

A Press Office would be set up in London later in the campaign. It would be manned on a day-to-day basis by Clive Page, who had performed the same role in Hartlepool, and Quentin Williamson, with Mark Croucher coordinating. The draft Manifesto went before the party's NEC on the 6th December.

The Party's Policy Stance In The Campaign

The awkward boys of Brussels were making trouble again when

the EU Constitution came before the European parliament for approval on the 12th January. No surprises that the document was passed by 500 votes in favour with 137 against and 40 abstentions. Of the 70 British votes, 40 voted 'no', 29 voted 'yes' and there was one abstention. There were 9 UKIP 'no' votes and 24 Conservative. More dramatically, the UKIP MEPs, and others from the Conservatives and Polish and Czech parties, decided to mark the occasion with a demonstration. As the vote took place in the chamber seven of the UKIP MEPs hoisted placards saying "Not in my Name" and "The Death of Europe" while the other four, high up in the parliament building in their offices, unfurled Union Jacks and draped them from their windows. Outside the building, where Commission President Barroso and his entourage had assembled to speak to the world about the Constitution, the protesting MEPs surrounded him and hijacked the event. Inside the chamber, things were frosty indeed – the President of the parliament ordered the protesting MEPs to put down their placards or "they will be put away for you". UKIP MEPs complained that they were assaulted by ushers and that two UKIP staff were manhandled by security guards when they attempted to unfurl 'no' banners next to 'yes' banners.

Not in my Name protest

It hardly needs to be said that, policy-wise, the party made opposition to the EU Constitution a rock-solid, never-to-be-changed policy, for which we would fight till every last political breath had gone.

Asylum and immigration were again to play a prominent part in our campaign but somehow it didn't seem so risky as it had the previous year. The Conservative Party had shifted in our direction as a response to the European election result and Labour, in turn, had shifted to the Conservative position as they felt the electoral ground shifting beneath them. In fact, our policies on asylum and immigration were now almost mainstream and arguably less stringent than the Conservative position.

The draft policy on asylum and immigration was published in early February, with a foreword by Knapman. He said that the party would introduce stricter embarkation controls, a points system for immigrants and would withdraw from the EU's Common Asylum Policy. He pointed out that both Labour and the Conservatives had "cloned" UKIP policy but that they would never be able to implement their policies because the Labour government had signed up to various EU directives that outlawed what they wanted to do. This much had already been helpfully and clearly confirmed by the European Commission just a couple of weeks before. Knapman recalled that both Labour and the Conservatives had supported the expansion of the EU to the East, giving 70 million Eastern Europeans the right to come to the UK. They were further proposing that the EU should take in Turkey as well, giving another 80 million the right of unrestricted travel throughout the European Union. But, he said, the party accepted that legal immigration was necessary and acknowledged that Britain had a long tradition of accepting genuine refugees, which UKIP would continue. However:

> *What we do not accept is that immigration can continue without limit. The strains which are being placed upon our transport, health, education and housing resources are unacceptable, and we must deal with these problems first.*

The policy itself said that the aim would be to approach zero net immigration by imposing far stricter limits on legal immigration and at last getting a grip on the vexed problem of illegal immigration. In addition to the introduction of an Australian-style points system for legal immigration, the reintroduction of embarkation controls would enable a far better tally to be kept of who was actually in the country and, by extension, who had overstayed. Secondary immigration, through marriage and the granting of residency to family members, would be subject to stricter control as there was evidence of "widespread abuse" of the system. For those who settled in the country legally, the party wanted to move away from the multicultural settlement and "encourage those settling here to acquire knowledge of our language and culture and to assimilate fully into our society". On asylum, it should be the British government that determined who was granted asylum, no-one else. That *might* mean reinterpreting or renegotiating parts of the 1951 UN Convention on the Status of Refugees. The policy didn't say so, but this was something that Labour had suggested in its 2001 Manifesto. There would be no solution to the problem of illegal immigration until the country was prepared to deport more of those who had been refused the right to stay. The party wanted changes in human rights law so as to prevent applications being subject to apparently unending appeals and so that asylum was granted only for those who genuinely needed it.

When the full Manifesto was published in mid-April it contained a timetable to independence and a more nuanced consideration of a post-EU Britain than before. Formal withdrawal from the European Union would be achieved by repeal of the 1972 European Communities Act. Contributions to the EU budget would cease immediately and Britain would resume full and independent participation in international bodies such as the World Trade Organisation. Some EU regulations, like the Working Time Directive, would be scrapped without delay but the party recognised that the accumulated mass of EU law would have to be looked at over a longer period of time. A Cabinet committee would oversee a two-year process in which laws of EU origin would be examined for their usefulness and then they would either be scrapped or replaced with a British variant written for British interests. The nature of the post-EU relationship was also explored: the party was prepared to consider a temporary stay in the European Economic Area (EEA) where it would be free of most EU legislation but still within the single market.

Many of these ideas came out of a high-level 'exit strategy' group which had held several meetings in the last quarter of 2003. Chaired by David Lott, and with contributions from Ashley Mote, Petrina Holdsworth, Trevor Coleman, John Whittaker, John Harvey, Marcus Watney, and myself, the group explored the options available to Britain in the world, post-EU, and the legal situation as regards EU legislation after its founding legal base – the European Communities Act – had been repealed.

The Manifesto took an uncompromising stance on Regional Assemblies. The party totally rejected "the government's attempts to adopt the European Union's concept of regional government in England". The result in the North East referendum showed conclusively that the public didn't want them and the party would "scrap all English regional assemblies and dismantle other regional quangos". This was allied to promises to return powers and funding to local authorities and to provide for the possibility of referenda when there was sufficient demand for them. The latter policy, in particular, would provide protection from "misuse of office by professional politicians" and was born from our experience of watching the governing classes ride roughshod over the public's will as it had successively transferred power to Brussels. It was also motivated by the spite of New Labour towards country people and its recent ban on foxhunting.

The Manifesto set out policies in every important and not-so-important area. It covered our central policy goal as regards the EU; trade; the budget and taxation; health; schools and universities; law and order; immigration and asylum; agriculture and fishing; defence and foreign affairs; energy; the environment and transport; and regional and local government. There isn't space here to describe all these policies but a measure of what the party is about can be gained from the concluding section on British society.

It said that Britain was a prosperous society but that the state was too big. Along with state provision came state control and the state always thought it knew best. The home-grown nanny-state and the other government in Brussels had made far too many rules to protect people against too many things. The rights culture seemed to favour criminals and the anti-social element. It fostered tension in society, emphasised differences, and set society against itself. All these rules were killing off the virtues of trust, initiative, responsibility and respect that enabled society to function properly. Government expenditure could no longer meet people's expectations for healthcare, education and pensions. Government could only spend what it taxed or borrowed and high taxes were killing the economy. A change of mindset was necessary – the regulatory culture, the dependency culture, the compensation culture all had to go.

Once upon a time all this was called liberalism. Burke's 'little platoons' and John Stuart Mill's strictures on the liberty of the individual spring to mind. In the Britain of the early 21st century, it was called 'extremist'.

A Final Parting Of The Ways

In David Lott's first campaign bulletin, on the 22nd December 2004, Lott commented on the ongoing Kilroy-Silk affair. It had been reported in the *Guardian* that Kilroy-Silk was in discussion with the new English Democrat party with a view to becoming their Leader. Lott said that there had been no denial of the report. He also reported that only two of the 49 branches who had put their names to the petition for an EGM were properly constituted under the party's rules. Another five had changed their minds and the party Secretary was not aware of much preparatory work taking place in the attempt to push the EGM demand further. Lott's implication was, clearly, that Kilroy-Silk was about to jump ship. Then there was the affair of the hoax email. Lott explained that, ten days prior to his report, a sensitive document (an early draft of the party's Manifesto, though Lott did not say so) had been leaked from the NEC. As a result "a carefully prepared trap was set to identify the person responsible". He said that he couldn't reveal more at that stage but candidates should be aware that there would probably be another round of ugly emails. He urged the candidates to speak up and make their views known to those "drearily threatening legal action for the umpteenth time". Three weeks later, at the candidates' meeting in Exeter, Farage revealed that Kilroy-Silk was expected to soon be leaving the party and setting up a rival organisation. Petrina Holdsworth thought that at least he would take a lot of the dissenters with him. In the margins of the meeting she told me that a source in the *Guardian* had claimed that the media had gone off Kilroy-Silk and were now out to get him. Perhaps it was just the reporter currying favour with a source or perhaps the media had tired of the game.

Petrina Holdsworth

The trap was sprung in mid-December when Mark Croucher circulated an email among some of the members of the NEC. The content of the email was fictitious – it claimed that a senior, non-political figure was prepared to offer a six-figure donation on condition that the party adopt the promise of a referendum on EU membership. But buried within different copies of the email were various differences in punctuation and spelling errors and these led to the identification of those leaking from the NEC. Croucher claimed Damian Hockney and Daniel Moss were the culprits. The *Guardian* reported Croucher as saying "that the NEC members concerned, Hockney and Moss, were taken in so completely simply demonstrates their own lack of political judgement in their rush to damage the party which they supposedly support. Had they any integrity, they would resign immediately and save themselves further embarrassment".

On the 7th January, Tony Scholefield circulated a bitter email to branch Chairmen complaining about the lack of trust shown by such an act. The sting operation had, he said, damaged relationships among the members of the NEC and had destroyed the party's reputation for truthfulness among the media.

On the 17th January, Damian Hockney circulated a long email detailing what he saw as the many problems of the situation as it then was. He claimed that the party was facing "the deepest split in its history" but that he had been trying for months to avert that split by working for a leadership election. He said that he suspected that there had been a deal between UKIP and the Conservatives under which UKIP would give the latter an easy ride – referring to the motion that was debated, and lost, at the Bristol conference. Kilroy-Silk had been unjustly and unfairly sidelined by the leadership. Hockney's multiple complaints covered just about every area – the supposed failure to research policies and produce a full Manifesto, the refusal of the leadership to speak or coordinate with him as Leader of the UKIP group in the London Assembly, the affair of the hoax email, and the disciplinary procedures being invoked against him and others. His email was headed "If the leadership doesn't go then the party will go" and he ended it with the statement that, if the party leadership would not categorically confirm that they intended to fight every seat, then "I believe that we face the inevitable split and launch of a second Eurosceptic party…UKIP would suffer a serious blow from the launch of a new party".

The split had already begun. On the same day as Hockney's email, the *Daily Telegraph* reported that Kilroy-Silk was to set up a new party called Veritas. Just three days later Kilroy-Silk finally left UKIP altogether, apparently intent on leaving scorched earth behind him. He said that he was "ashamed" to have joined UKIP and that the party was a "joke" led by a "self-serving cabal". He rehearsed his claims that the party had "gone AWOL" after the European election campaign, that it had no real ambition to be a domestic political force or to seriously fight the General Election. Two weeks later, Hockney resigned from UKIP and became Deputy Leader of Veritas, with Peter Hulme-Cross, the party's second London Assembly member, following him. In an email to UKIP members Hockney spoke of his decision to resign. The last two years of his eight years in the party had seen a slow erosion of his trust in the party leadership, he said. He was going in sorrow and would take no part in any name-calling in the future. He had, he said, great respect for the vast majority of UKIP's members and wished to remain on good terms with them.

Two days later, Kilroy-Silk publicly launched Veritas.

The Penny That Didn't Drop

Ever since the summer of the previous year, the Conservative Party had been putting out a stream of press releases, articles and policy announcements on the immigration and asylum question. As the General Election campaign opened, the party decided to make immigration and asylum a central plank of its policy stance, with Michael Howard making a speech in late January saying that the Conservatives in government would put an annual limit on immigrant numbers, including a quota for asylum seekers.

It took only hours for the European Commission to step forward to say that no British government could do any such thing. As was well-known to many on the eurorealist side of politics, the Labour government had slowly been opting in to EU asylum and immigration policy since 2001. Now it emerged that a qualifications directive had assigned to Brussels the right to determine who was and was not a refugee. The directive also ruled out withdrawal from the 1951 UN Convention on the Status of Refugees, also a central plank in the Conservative proposals. It was reported that the intervention of the European Union in the electoral battle had taken "Westminster aback" and that many MPs and officials "were unaware of how much national sovereignty on immigration and asylum had been passed to Brussels".

The chief spokesman of the EU's Justice and Home Affairs

Commissioner slapped the proposal down – "there is nothing in these protocols that allows a British government to opt back out again" he said. But Howard insisted that, somehow, magically, he would indeed just opt out. And if that were blocked then he would insist on renegotiating the directives. Again, as in the previous year, there was no 'or else'.

It had always been an interesting question – what would happen when the twin *bêtes noires* of many voters, 'Europe' and immigration, came together and voters began to see that the one was controlled by the other. Many thought – anticipated, hoped – that this would be a galvanising moment. Certainly, Daniel Hannan thought so, writing in a centre-page article in the *Daily Telegraph*. Hannan opened his article with the words:

> *The penny is finally dropping. Thirty-two years after we joined, we are at last waking up to the nature of our subjection to Brussels. It was always going to take a big issue to jolt us from our narcolepsy, and immigration is that issue.*

Well, up to a point. It didn't feature much in the campaign after that. The media train moved on, the subject was put back in its box and no more has been heard of it. Robert Kilroy-Silk used the issue of immigration to launch his new party on the 2nd February. Were some of the UKIP members who had jumped ship with him feeling uncomfortable as Kilroy concentrated on asylum and immigration at the expense of the European issue? In a grand room at the Institute of Civil Engineers, with the new party's leadership sitting at the front table, including Damian Hockney, Kilroy bounced up with a scroll of paper detailing what he called the 100 lies of British politics. And then into the standard Kilroy mode:

> *Lies, lies, lies! Lies, evasions and spin. One after another. A whole pack of lies! And that's what the parties do! They lie to us about Europe. They lied about the weapons of mass destruction. They lie on immigration. They lie on asylum. They lie all the time. They are still at it today.*

Asylum and immigration seemed to be at the top of the Veritas agenda, with Kilroy-Silk railing against uncontrolled immigration, multiculturalism, the way in which immigration was changing the face of British society, and how the country had been stolen from the people without their permission. The party said that it aimed to contest over a hundred constituencies and to have a party political broadcast. The new party gained extensive coverage in the media: national newspapers published major articles on the launch. No other new party, and there are more than most people think, would gain even a single sentence.

On the following Monday it was the turn of UKIP and the Labour Party to set out their stalls on the immigration and asylum front. There didn't seem to be that much difference between us.

At Westminster, Knapman launched the UKIP policy by unveiling the party's poster on the theme. The poster featured a giant European bureaucrat crumpling up a document with the title "UK immigration policy" while Tony Blair, Michael Howard and Charles Kennedy looked on, bound and chained and cowering. Labour promised a five year plan in which they would get tough on secondary migration, introduce a points system for all migrants, make it harder for migrants to get permanent residence in Britain and promised (again) to increase the numbers of failed asylum-seekers deported. But the mood music of Labour was softer – the numbers of migrants would, overall, not change much and, of course, there was nothing they could do about immigration from EU countries.

Asylum and immigration was a major and ongoing theme in the election campaign but it isn't clear that it had any significant effect in changing how people voted. The Conservatives closed the gap on Labour by a few percentage points, perhaps four or five, and it didn't produce a great leap in UKIP votes. Daniel Hannan's hopes that the penny was finally dropping seemed to be optimistic, or perhaps premature.

The Question Unveiled

In the midst of the European election campaign of the previous year, the Labour government had made an astonishing U-turn by announcing that, after all, the electorate *would* have their chance to vote on the EU Constitution. No date had been fixed, the specific question to be asked had not been framed. But Tony Blair had defiantly thrown down the gauntlet and opened a full-scale challenge to the Eurosceptic forces in the country. Ending his speech to the House of Commons on the 20th April 2004, he declared:

> *It is time to resolve once and for all whether this country, Britain, wants to be at the centre and heart of European decision-making or not; time to decide whether our destiny lies as a leading partner and ally of Europe or on its margins. Let the Eurosceptics, whose true agenda we will expose, make their case. Let those of us who believe in Britain in Europe, not because we believe in Europe alone but because, above all we believe in Britain, make ours. Let the issue be put. Let the battle be joined.*

Nine months later, as the 2005 General Election campaign was about to take off, the government brought that battle one step closer. On the 26th January the European Union Bill was announced in the House of Commons. The Bill began the process by which a referendum would be held and included the wording of the question that would be put to the electorate: "should the United Kingdom approve the treaty establishing a Constitution for the European Union". The question seemed fair, apparently confounding expectations that the government would try to rig the question. All parties, even UKIP, pronounced themselves satisfied with the question. But after a few days it dawned on the 'no' side that they might have been had.

On the very day that the Bill was announced to Parliament, the *Daily Telegraph* commissioned a YouGov poll using the question decided upon by the government. The result, although substantially against accepting the Constitution, was far down on earlier polls: 45 per cent would say 'no', 24 per cent would say 'yes', 25 per cent said they didn't know. Polls in the previous year had consistently shown a 'no' vote of around 60 per cent. Worse than that, an ICM poll for the Vote No campaign less than two weeks later showed support and opposition level-pegging at 39 per cent if the official question was asked but 54 per cent against and 26 per cent in favour if a more neutral question was asked. The wording of the question was clearly having a very significant effect – so significant that victory for the 'no' side was far from assured. New cheer was breathed into the 'yes' side while Neil O'Brien, speaking for Vote No, admitted that "there is no sense in which the referendum is in the bag. I have always thought that it is going to be closer than a lot of people expect". Indeed, there was at that time a growing sense of assurance on the 'no' side that it *was* almost in the bag. The new poll results were a wake-up call.

Like the immigration and asylum issue, the Constitution then disappeared from the domestic political scene.

But the stage had been set, the parameters of the battle had been fixed. The timing was more-or-less known. All that remained was to martial the forces. This would take place after the election when breath could be drawn and the various groups could coordinate with each other, or not, as the case might turn out.

In fact, the battle never took place. Without knowing it, the Eurosceptics had already won. Shortly after the General Election, referenda were held in France and the Netherlands. Both countries rejected the Constitution and plunged the European Union into disarray.

We played our part in that. We weren't solely responsible but, in the clash of opinions and parties in individual countries and in the effects beyond their borders, in a Europe in flux and debate and uncertainty, our electoral showing in the 2004 European Elections had panicked the Labour government into promising a referendum. That, in turn, had, many agree, obliged President Chirac of France to promise a referendum to the French – thinking that it could easily be won, as opinion polls suggested at the time. The French referendum was not won and the Dutch, three days later, delivered the *coup de grace*.

To Sir James Goldsmith and the Referendum Party, the euro scalp and to UKIP, perhaps, the constitution scalp.

The Elephant In The Room

Opinion polls stretching back to January 2003 showed support for "others" slowly declining from around 8 per cent in that month to 5 per cent at the end of the year. From the beginning of 2004 the gentle decline was reversed and "others" reached 7 per cent in April. From May it jumped to 12 per cent and then again began a long decline to May 2005 when it stood again at around 8 per cent. As UKIP had again disappeared into the "others" bucket, at least for the General Election, it was difficult to judge what our share of that beleaguered 8 per cent was. One poll at the beginning of January gave us a derisory 1 per cent with the Greens on 3 per cent. Another gave us 4 per cent and the Greens 2 per cent. Whatever, we weren't going to win a General Election on 4 per cent of the vote. But there was still the prospect of that percentage going up as the campaign progressed – providing we got fair publicity. And within that increased vote share, there was the further possibility of hotspots, especially in the South West and South East. Such hotspots had the potential to bring in some shock results. At the end of January, the incumbent Labour government was at around 38 to 40 per cent in the polls with the Conservatives around 32 per cent and the Liberal Democrats at 18 per cent. This was close to the scenario that Dick Morris had identified as optimum for UKIP under a first-past-the-post system. Close, but not quite enough. Could the Conservatives close that gap? As the campaign progressed, the gap was indeed substantially closed, so the media kept their focus on the Labour/Tory fight.

The annoyance of the established parties at incursions into 'their' territory was shown, once again, by Bruce Anderson writing in the *Times*. Anderson, a biographer of John Major, announced that "in stagnant pools, scum thrives". No surprises for guessing which party was the object of his column. It was akin to Lord Kinnock's description of the party as "disgusting" in a letter to the *Financial Times* the previous year.

In mid-February we lost one of our founding members. Tony Scholefield, there from the founding of the Anti-Federalist League and who had provided the party with office space up to 1998, had lost confidence in Knapman and the party's NEC. In his letter of resignation from the NEC and the party he spoke of a "whole series of mistakes" by Knapman, a failure to produce attractive policies and to address the concerns of the public. He also said that he felt that the party was wrong to make any EU Constitution referendum a referendum on Britain's continued membership of the EU. Finally, he said:

To sum up, I no longer believe that UKIP is the best vehicle for the cause. It has been irredeemably damaged by mistrust in the leadership and its mania for control. It has wasted the momentum of the euroelections, has been unable to break out of the box of its anti-EU core stance and address the other concerns of the electorate.

Scholefield had circulated, just two weeks before his resignation, his own proposals on immigration and asylum and in the past had been associated with an attempt to heighten the immigration issue within the party.

It was reported in late February that it had originally been the intention of President Bush, during a speech to European leaders in Brussels, to signal approval for the EU Constitution. The *Sunday Telegraph* reported that the passage had already been written when Conservatives in both Washington and Britain, including UKIP officials and Daniel Hannan, began a lobbying campaign to get the offending passage removed. They were successful, according to the newspaper, convincing the President to tone down his remarks to general support for the "democratic unity" of Europe and "a strong Europe".

In the area of money and material, Alan Bown made a donation of £400,000 to the party in January. Half of this was used to produce ten million leaflets and other publicity material while £110,000 was allocated to the regions of the party and £90,000 was earmarked for target seats. The three staple leaflets of the campaign focussed on pensioners, immigration and GM foods. Over four million of them had been delivered by the last week of March and six million by mid-April. The distribution system was simple: come and get 'em before another branch does. Also available for street stalls and street campaigning was a pamphlet "Give Us a Better Future" which reprised the five freedoms theme of the European campaign, including that of "freedom from overcrowding".

In that last week of March it was also decided to beef up the election address so that it put immigration right up-front on the leaflet. The intention was to again highlight that neither a Labour nor a Tory government could now claim full freedom of decision in that area.

But the campaign never really took off for any party. It was a dull affair of Blairite slickness and a wooden Michael Howard with his one-and-only hand gesture slugging it out over immigration and bread and butter issues, with the Liberal Democrats looking smug away in a corner. And apart from them, the media, with no Kilroy celebrity to sell their papers with, almost completely ignored UKIP. Indeed, at the beginning of the campaign, at least, we only seemed to be mentioned because of the latest antics of Kilroy and Veritas.

And the great, undiscussed issue, the elephant in the room was, again, the question of Britain's membership of the European Union. None of the establishment parties wanted to talk about it. They all had their reasons not to. Even the media, not normally displaying such thoughtfulness, began to ask where the issue was. Even foreign media noticed. *Libération* said that Europe was the "terra incognita" of the British electoral debate. CNN said that Europe was "no star" as an election issue. In Britain, the *Daily Telegraph* complained in an editorial that "Europe is Missing". The BBC asked "what's happened to Europe?" their correspondent noting that the issue had "virtually disappeared from the agenda". John Whittaker, speaking to the BBC for the party, said that it was a "phoney election" and that the main parties were steadfastly ignoring the fact that the real government of Britain was in Brussels. Roger Knapman called for an end to the conspiracy of silence. One of the few times that the issue was raised was when Jeremy Paxman, in his *Newsnight* program, interviewed Michael Howard late in the campaign. Howard confirmed the position that he had given to Andrew Marr in late 2003:

Paxman: "Are there any circumstance under which you could contemplate withdrawal from the European Union?"

Howard: "No, I want to be a member of the European Union – that's very clear."

Creating an electoral bubble proved difficult for us. Where was the 'dry timber' of 2004? We had three aims: put up 500 candidates, get at least one of them elected and get the message across properly for the first time that we were not a single-issue party. These three aims were referred to by Knapman when he talked to the BBC in early April. He said that we would field 500 candidates, that we were "about Britain, not just about Europe", and that we had a full Manifesto of quite radical ideas. He also mentioned the 21 constituencies where we had come first in the European Elections and said that he hoped the party's straight-forward message would produce a good vote in many of those constituencies.

By the time of that interview the polls were showing Conservative and Labour neck and neck at around 36 per cent each. Not the Morris scenario at all. Although this proved to be a high point for the Conservatives, their poll showing retreating after this date, the gap never became a chasm. Still, the option was there for the media to change their line. That they did not was probably helped by the conspiracy of silence. The media-establishment nexus managed to keep hold of the agenda this time.

Interviewed by David Frost on the Sunday TV show *Breakfast With Frost* a couple of days after the Knapman interview, Farage kept up the optimism by again saying that the party had a fighting chance in those twenty seats where it had done so well the previous year. Farage was sitting, as Frost reminded him, in the very seat where Kilroy-Silk had started his leadership challenge the year before.

With 480 candidates signed up and the election addresses now being printed, Knapman, Farage, Holdsworth, Whittaker and Titford launched the Manifesto at a press conference in Westminster on the 15th April. Knapman's foreword in the Manifesto emphasised again the non-politician self-perception of the party: "None of us in UKIP see ourselves as politicians. Our members are people from all backgrounds who feel deeply what the majority of British people feel – that it is not right to have our country run by institutions across the channel. We are not *anti-European*; we just believe the best people to run Britain are the British".

There was good media coverage of the launch and then, to the end of the campaign three weeks later, a trickle of stories but no great breakthrough.

In further blows for the Europhile forces, those of them left anyway, both the Chancellor and the Prime Minister effectively declared that, for the time being at least, British entry into the single currency was off the agenda. Of course, it probably did no harm to Labour's election prospects to make those statements just one week before the General Election but the statements were nevertheless made.

On the day before the 5th May election, Lott emailed his valedictory message to candidates. Although all positive in tone there was something between the lines that revealed that he knew the historic breakthrough would not be achieved. Expressing his admiration, and that of his staff, for all the candidates out in the field, he noted that they had had to find their own deposits and money for their campaigns. He said that they deserved great tribute for contesting those nearly 500 seats and that:

> I have my fingers firmly crossed for your success tomorrow. You deserve it. Whatever the outcome, you can always look with pride upon the part you have played in the service of your country.

The 490 UKIP candidates passed the finishing line in a disciplined formation helped by the party's grass-roots strength, but it wasn't the massive battering ram that the party had wielded the previous year. No seats were won, no seats were even nearly won. But 620,000 votes were gained, maintaining the party in its overall position of fourth place in terms of the number of votes cast. But still, that so vitally important first seat at Westminster. Just one, only one, would do. One would be enough to start the ball rolling.

Alas, it would have to be for another time.

Postscript

"No More Europe"?

We failed in our bid to gain MPs in 2005 but a great consolation was ours just weeks later – victory in the Constitution battle. In popular referenda in France and the Netherlands, the people voted 'no' to the EU Constitution. The European project crashed into a wall and an unparalleled crisis in EU politics began.

We can claim our share in that great success. Those 2.7 million votes in June 2004 contributed to the decision by Tony Blair to promise a referendum, thus, in turn, obliging President Chirac of France to offer the same to the French people. And, just as that referendum approached, a long-running dispute, almost personal, between Nigel Farage and José Manuel Barroso, came to a head in the European parliament. The affair was widely reported in France and both Farage and Philippe de Villiers of the Mouvement Pour La France believe that it contributed to the French 'no'.

In August 2004 Barroso had taken a six-day holiday on board the yacht of the billionaire Greek businessman Spiros Latsis, whose companies were involved in many EU-funded construction projects. At this time Barroso was President-elect of the European Commission. Just a few weeks later, the Commission gave permission to the Greek government to grant £10 million of state aid to modernise a shipyard in which Latsis had substantial business interests.

It also came out that Peter Mandelson had spent time in the Caribbean over the New Year of 2005 with businessmen whose companies were in dispute with the Commission. Mandelson met Paul Allen, the billionaire co-founder of Microsoft, on board his yacht, for a drinks party.

In February 2005, Farage tabled a question in the European parliament asking for details of all hospitality that Commissioners had received since they were nominated to the

Commission. In a collective reply in April they said that it was their business and their business only. Not willing to let the matter drop, and annoyed by the disdain that the Commission had shown for his request, Farage set out to gather the signatures of 10 per cent of the parliament's MEPs in order to force a confidence motion on the Commission. The motion was finally debated in the European parliament on the 25th May, three weeks after the British General Election and just four days before the French referendum. With Farage being booed in the chamber, Barroso said that the motion was "unjustified, illegitimate and absurd", claiming that it was only being brought forward to undermine the credibility of the European institutions. To Farage, he said bitterly "of course Mr Farage, this will never happen to you – you will never be invited onto a yacht – because you have no friends".

Graham Booth MEP, UKIP, in Paris helping the
French campaign against the EU Constitution

There was scant chance of the motion being passed, as the inbuilt pro-European majority rallied around the standard. Hans-Gert Pöttering, Leader of the EPP group in the parliament, was adamant: "no one, but no one, must be allowed to shake our resolve as we continue to build European integration". But in France there were now growing doubts about whether the French would approve the Constitution. Over twenty consecutive polls had, by the end of April, shown that the French were about, apparently, to do the unthinkable, and turn against the project that its politicians, at least, had always seen as their own. Worse, even the Dutch, traditionally one of the most federalist-minded countries, who were due to vote two days after the French, also looked as though they were going to vote 'no'. Former European Commission President Romano Prodi said that rejection of the Constitution by the French would be the "fall of Europe" and that there would be "no more Europe" if that happened.

In the event, both the French and the Dutch voted 'no', dealing a double hammer blow to federalist ambitions.

Thus, for now, the three battles recounted in this story have been fought and, possibly, won. 'Europe', post-election, has faded from many people's minds. The single currency, for Britain, has been postponed to at least, we are told, 2010. Regional assemblies remain, but unelected, unloved and unregarded. The Constitution, many think, has been defeated.

But we should remember the determination of the federalist forces to achieve their goals.

On the evening of the Dutch vote on the EU Constitution, Farage was among fifty or sixty eurosceptic MEPs watching the voting in the press bar of the European parliament. A huge cheer went up as the final result came in. Champagne bottles were opened. Just at that moment, Jo Leinen, a senior German Socialist MEP, happened to walk through. Leinen had worked closely with Valéry Giscard d'Estaing in the Convention which had drafted the Constitution. Farage walked up to Leinen and asked, with a note of triumph in his voice, whether he would like to have a glass of champagne with them. "Nigel", said Leinen, "you have had your little triumph tonight. But remember, we have fifty ways to get it through".

One year after that momentous double blow, after a so-called "period of reflection", the extent of federalist determination to get their Constitution, come what may, is evident. European politicians constantly discuss new ways to achieve it. The project continues, whatever the people of Europe may think.

The collapse of the Constitution brought to an end the period that began with Maastricht. Here our story ends. We shall see what the future will bring. But one thing is sure – the fight is not yet over.

References

I have not provided reference numbers in the text of the book but it should be easy to locate a given article by the chapter section, the date, the publication named, and the title of the articles, as given in the listing below. The listings prefixed by 'see also' relate to the full chapter, not the chapter section. They are not used in the text of the book but serve as additional background information.

Counter Revolution

A Disillusioned European

1   Margaret Thatcher: The Downing Street Years, Harper Collins 1993, (The Babel Express – The Bruges Speech)
2   *The Times*, "Thatcher Sets Out Her Five Guiding Principles", 21st September 1988
3   *The Times*, "Europe Fears Battle Ahead With Thatcher", 22nd September 1988
4   *The Times*, "Europe Delivers Unity Message", 16th October 1988
5   *The Times*, "Rome, Brussels – or Bruges", 8th February 1989
6   *The Times*, "A Vision of Europe", 20th September 1988
7   *The Times*, "Bruges to Rhodes", 26th September 1988

Ideals, Despair, Treachery

8   Peter Shore: Separate Ways, Duckworth 2000
9   Hugo Young: This Blessed Plot, Macmillan 1998
10   Harold Macmillan: Tides Of Fortune, Macmillan 1969
11   Harold Macmillan: Riding The Storm, Macmillan 1971
12   Harold Macmillan: Pointing The Way, Macmillan 1972
13   Richard J. Aldrich: The Hidden Hand: Britain, America and Cold War Secret Intelligence, John Murray, 2001
14   Lindsay Jenkins: Britain Held Hostage – The Coming Euro-Dictatorship, Orange State Press, 1997
15   Douglas Jay: Change and Fortune: A Political Record, Hutchinson, 1980

16 Anthony Forster: Euroscepticism in Contemporary British Politics, Routledge 2002

17 Gavin Smith: The European Court of Justice: Judges or Policy Makers? Bruges Group Pamphlet, July 1990

18 National Archives, FCO 26/1215

19 National Archives, FCO 30/1048

See also:

20 National Archives, FCO 26/1213

21 National Archives, FCO 30/1574

22 National Archives, FCO 26/1212

23 National Archives, FCO 30/1573

24 National Archives, FCO 26/1214

25 National Archives, FCO 26/797

26 National Archives, FCO 30/1061

27 National Archives, FCO 30/1065

28 National Archives, FCO 30/3066

29 National Archives, FCO 30/3067

30 National Archives, CAB 193/126

Born at Bruges

The Bruges Group

1 *The Times*, "Bruges Boy Fights Back", 9th February 1989

2 *The Times Higher Education Supplement*, "Intellectual Arguments Over the Train Fare" 30th August 1991

3 *The Times*, "Tory MPs Group to Fight EEC Federalism", 21st March 1989

4 *The Times*, "Tory Joins Fight to Curb Power of European Court", 17th July 1990

5 Alan Sked, "Time For Principle", Bruges Group pamphlet, March 1992

6 *The Times*, "Denning Backs Attempt to Curb EC Law", 14th July 1990

7 *The Independent on Sunday*, "The Boy Against Brussels", 16th June 1991

8 *The Times Literary Supplement*, Letters, John Campbell, 10th February 1989

9 *The Times*, "Federalism Denounced: Norman Tebbit", 26th January 1990

10 "Bruges Revisited", Bruges Group pamphlet, full text of Bruges speech, 1998

REFERENCES

Maastricht And The Establishment Parties

11   Commons Hansard, 20th May 1992

The Anti-Federalist League

No references

The UK Independence Party

12   Mark Daniel: Cranks and Gadflies – The Story of UKIP,
Timewell Press, 2004

The 1994 European Elections

13   *The Times,* "Why Tory Leadership Should Not Pass the Buck",
10th May 1994

14   *The Times,* "Tories Snipe at Lib Dems", 28th May 1994

15   *The Times,* "Rotten Ballots", 8th June 1994

16   *Sunday Telegraph*, "Dear Tory, Don't Vote Tory On Europe",
24th April 1994

17   *The Times,* "Lamont Sees No Reason to Stay in Federal Europe",
12th October 1994

See also:

18   *Daily Telegraph*, "Britain May Face Prospect of Leaving the EU Claims
Lamont", 12th October 1994

19   *The New Statesman*, Interview with Alan Sked, 11th April 1997

20   *The Times,* "Think Tanks Go Into Action Against Delors",
21st August 1989

21   *The Times,* "Past the First Post", 16th January 1993

22   *The Times,* "Europe Needs a Mandate", 15th January 1993

23   *The Times,* "Nation Undermined by Supreme Act of Folly",
7th February 1994

24   *The Times,* "No Turning Back the Euro Tide", 29th April 1994

25   *The Times,* "Tories Redraft Euro Poll Manifesto", 29th April 1994

26   *Daily Telegraph*, "Don't Mention Europe", 15th October 1994

27   *The Independent*, "Major Opens Door to Referendum",
13th December 1994

Building a Nationwide Party – 1994 to 1997

Grass Roots Rising

1   *Daily Telegraph*, "Black Country Omens That Reflect The National Gloom", 15th December November 1994

2   *Wolverhampton Express And Star*, "Anti-Europe Groups Enter The Poll Race", 26th November 1994

Coming Together

3   *Daily Telegraph*, "Anti-EU Party Loses Limelight to Electrician", 30th October 1995

The 1997 General Election

4   *Sunday Telegraph*, "Minority Parties Fight to Keep TV Broadcast Slots", 19th February 1996

5   *The Guardian*, "Tory MPs 'Tried to get Poll Deal' ", 23rd March 1996

6   *The Guardian*, "The Other Anti-Europe Party Unveils 100 Candidates", 24th July 1996

7   *The Independent* on Sunday, "Major Tells Euro-MPs: Go Boil Your Heads", 13th October 1996

8   *The Guardian*, "Save Us from the Saviours of England", 30th December 1996

9   *The Times,* "Eurosceptics Want Manifesto Pledge to Boycott Single Currency", 8th June 1995

10   *The Independent*, "Britain and Europe: A Proposal", 3rd June 1996

11   *Daily Telegraph*, "Beware the Real Euro Crisis", 12th October 1998

12   *The Financial Times*, "Visions of a 'Monster' Rouse the Independence Party", 3rd February 1997

13   *Daily Telegraph*, "Why the Tories Fail to Gain from the Continental Drift", 18th April 1997

14   *Daily Telegraph*, "Britain '£20bn Better Off Outside European Union'", 8th April 1997

15   *Daily Telegraph*, "On the Fringe", 2nd May 1997

16   *The Times,* "Genial Don Gives Britain a Lecture on Lone Survival", 8th April 1997

17   *Daily Telegraph*, "Fighting Pound for Pound", 21st April 1997

18   *The Times,* "The Good Eurosceptic's Guide to Making the Most of a Tactical Vote", 28th April 1997

19   *Daily Telegraph*, "The Only Serious Choice", 30th April 1997

UKIP And The Referendum Party

20 James Goldsmith, The Trap, French edition – Editions Fixot (Paris) 1993,
    English edition – Macmillan (London) 1994

21 *The Independent*, "Why This Man is Major's Nightmare",
    12th March 1996

22 *The Times,* "Splinter Party Will be Waste of Time and Money",
    24th October 1995

23 *The Sunday Times*, "Look…its that Hugh Grant Moment", 27th April 1997

24 *Daily Telegraph*, "Free Lunch on Jimmy Costs £750,000",
    20th October 1996

25 *The Guardian*, "Goldsmith Party 'An Empty Shell' ", 1st January 1997

26 *Sunday Telegraph*, "Table Talk", 5th January 1997

27 *The Independent*, "Leading Actor Joins Anti-EU Campaign",
    31st December 1996

See also:

28 *The Times,* "Did Heath Deceive Britain Over Europe", 11th January 1997

29 *The Times Higher Education Supplement*, "Singular Man of Sceptical
    Faith", 11th April 1997

30 *The Times Higher Education Supplement*, "A European Superstate
    Would Cause International Tension and War", 16th April 1997

31 *Daily Telegraph*, "The Single Issue", 15th April 1997

32 *The Times Higher Education Supplement*, "Making a Big Decision",
    18th April 1997

33 *The Times,* "Principle Not Party", 29th April 1997

34 *The Times,* "Sir James Goldsmith: Obituary", 21st July 1997

Internal Conflict and Recovery I – 1997 to 1999

The First Fracture Of UKIP

1   *The Guardian*, "The Outsiders", 26th February 2001

"Tirez Le Rideau"

2   *Notes From The Borderland*, Issue 4, Winter 2001-2002,
    BM Box 4769, London, WC1N 3XX

3   *The Sunday Times*, "MI5 Foiled National Front Plot to Wreck
    Referendum Party", 27th July 1997

4   *The Spectator*, Letters: "Sked and Tory Spin", 17th February 2001

5   *The Times*, "UK Party in Squabble Over Plan for Merger", 6th June 1997

6   *Sunday Telegraph*, "Civil War Erupts in Anti-EU Party", 6th June 1997

7   *Sunday Telegraph*, "Sir James in Secret Pact", 15th June 1997

8   *These Tides* is now managed by the Research Centre Free Europe,
     Estonia pst 1-406, Tallinn B-101, Estonia

9   *Daily Telegraph*, "Anti-Europe Party Chief Quits Politics", 8th August 1997

Rebuilding The Party

10   *Daily Telegraph*, "Tebbit Will Not Sail in the Euro-Titanic",
     20th March 1998

11   *York Evening Press,* "Soap Boxes Are Back", 20th March 1998

12   *York Evening Press,* "York Relaunch for Anti-Euro Party",
     20th March 1998

13   *Daily Telegraph*, "Bosses Back Campaign Against 'EMU Myth' ",
     12th June 1998

14   *Daily Telegraph*, "Businessman Gives £20m to Fight Euro",
     25th September 1998

The 1999 European Elections

15   *Daily Telegraph*, "30 Groups Campaign Against the Euro",
     4th January 1999

16   *The Times,* "Trouble is in Store as Euro Splits the Sainsbury Family",
     1st March 1999

17   *Daily Telegraph*, "Hope for EU Opponents", 13th February 1999

18   *Daily Telegraph*, "Tory Rebels Accused of 'Wrecking Campaign'",
     23rd March 1999

19   *Daily Telegraph*, "Poll Blow for Tories", 26th March 1999

20   *Daily Mail,* "A Vote for Independence", 15th May 1999

21   *The Times,* "Hague Lays into Blair 'Double-Talk' on Europe",
     19th May 1999

22   *Daily Telegraph*, "Which Tories to Vote For?", 31st May 1999

23   *The Times,* "BNP Link Allegation Hits Euro Party", 5th June 1999

24   *The Times,* Correction, 21st July 1999

25   *Daily Telegraph*, "Written-off UKIP Bounces Back with Three Seats,
     14th June 1999

26   *The Times,* "UKIP is Surprise Winner of Three Seats", 14th June 1999

See also:

27   *Sunday Times,* York demonstration photograph, 22nd March 1998

28   *Sunday Business,* "Protestors Wave The Flag For Sterling",

22nd March 1998

29   *Daily Telegraph,* "Owen Plans Comeback to Fight The Single Currency",
     12th February 1998

30   *Daily Telegraph,* " 'Ich Bin Ein Londoner' For Kohl", 19th February 1998

31   *Daily Telegraph,* "Eurosceptics Mean Business", 6th April 1998

32   *The Times,* "Ex-Minister May Head Campaign Against The Euro",
     25th April 1998

33   *Daily Telegraph,* "Blair Tells His Team To Bat For Brussels",
     15th December 1998

34   *The Times,* "The Euro School Of Thought That Is Inevitably Wrong",
     5th January 1999

35   *Daily Telegraph,* "Euro Stays Firm On Thin First Day", 5th January 1999

36   *The Independent,* "Pro-Europe Group Aims To Halt EMU",
     2nd March 1999

37   *The Times,* "Tory MEPs Quit Party Over Euro", 20th January 1999

38   *Daily Telegraph,* "Tories Step Up Fight To Keep Pound", 1st June 1999

39   *The Times,* "The Real Choice", 10th June 1999

40   *The Times,* "UKIP Will Vote Only for Less Power", 15th June 1999

41   *The Guardian,* "This is Just the Beginning, say Greens and UKIP",
     15th June 1999

42   *Daily Telegraph,* "A Tribute to Goldsmith", 14th June 1999

43   *Daily Telegraph,* "EU Spanish Junket Drove Retired Tycoon into Politics",
     15th June 1999

44   *Daily Telegraph,* "Vote to Save the Pound", 9th June 1999

45   *Daily Telegraph,* "Blair's PR 'Present' May Produce First Labour Setback",
     11th June 1999

46   *The Times,* "I Would Advise People Voting on Thursday to Help the
     Tory Revival" (Alan Sked), 8th June 1999

47   *BBC News Online,* "What Next For the UKIP?", 13th July 1999

48   Rodney Atkinson and Norris McWhirter, Treason at Maastricht,
     Compuprint Publishing, 1994

Internal Conflict and Recovery II – 1999 to 2001

Breaking The Consensus

1   *The Guardian,* "Letter to the Leader", 21st June 1999

2   *The Times,* "Tory Quitters", 18th September 1999

3   *The Times,* "Sceptics Demand that EU Treaties are Renegotiated",
    5th October 1999

4   *The Times,* "Blair Picks Up Gauntlet for Europe", 27th July 1999

5   *The Times*, "Blair and Clarke in New Euro Alliance", 28th July 1999

6   *The Times*, "Pro-European Tories Seal Pact With Blair", 14th October 1999

7   *The Times*, "Pro-Euro Group 'Acted Like Goebbels' to Distort Figures", 19th February 2000

8   *Financial Times*, "Economic Price of Quitting EU 'Would be Small' ", 20th February 2000

9   *The Times,* "Hague Must Come Clean on Europe", 7th October 1999

10   *Daily Telegraph*, "Leading Us to Withdrawal", 30th August 1999

11   *The Times*, "UKIP Will Only Vote for Less Power", 15th June 1999

12   *Sunday Telegraph*, "Broadcasters 'Show Pro-Europe Bias'", 18th July 1999

The Second Fracture Of UKIP

13   Debate in the European Parliament, 21st July 1999

14   *The Guardian*, "UKIP in Turmoil as Leadership is Ousted", 15th October 1999

15   *The Guardian*, "High Life Bites into UKIP's anti-Europe Fighting Fund", 20th October 1999

16   *The Times,* "Independence Party Throws Out Leader and Executive", 24th January 2000

17   *The Times,* "Don't Laugh", 26th February 2000

18   *The Times,* "Party Rocked as MEP Resigns", 21st March 2000

19   *The Financial Times*, "Would-be Leader Quits Over 'Extremist Infiltration'", 27th April 2000

20   *The Times,* "'Far-Right' Fear Splits UKIP as 200 Leave Party", 29th April 2000

21   *The Guardian*, "Hague Off the Hook as Tory MP Denies Plans to Defect", 4th January 2000

22   *Daily Telegraph*, "Anti-Europe Party Hopes to Recruit Allason", 4th January 2000

23   *The Independent*, "Now MEPs Round on Hague", 6th January 2000

24   *The Independent*, Letters: "Tories in Europe", 7th January 2000

25   *Daily Mail*, "Tories Warned: Stop the Constant Carping", 7th January 2000

26   Debate in the European Parliament, 2nd February 2000

27   *Daily Telegraph*, "UKIP's Unwitting Allies", 22nd February 2000

28   *Daily Telegraph*, "BBC Accused of Bias by Labour Eurosceptics", 25th January 2000

29   *The Independent*, "Lib Dem Councillor is Candidate for Rivals", 17th April 2000

30   *Daily Telegraph*, "Tory Defects Over Hague's 'Bogus' European Policy", 30th May 2000

REFERENCES

Preparing For The 2001 General Election

31 *The Times*, "UK Eurosceptics 'Have the Power'", 30th September 2000

32 *Sunday Telegraph*, "No Wonder the Premier Could Hardly Keep Himself From Crying", 1st October 2000

The 2001 General Election

33 *Daily Telegraph*, "Anti-EU Party Targets Labour and Lib-Dems", 8th December 2000

34 *The Times,* "Perks Protest MEPs Face Legal Action", 27th January 2001

35 *Daily Telegraph*, "Tories Outraged at Fringe Party's £1m 'Blackmail'", 30th January 2001

36 *The Spectator*, "Sceptics Who Betray Britain", 10th February 2001

37 *Daily Mail*, "A Vote for Blair Will Cost You the Pound", 11th February 2001

38 *The Guardian*, "The Outsiders", 26th February 2001

39 *Daily Telegraph*, "Eurosceptic Tories Round On UKIP 'Rabble'", 31st March 2001

40 *The Guardian*, "Pint-Sized Party Proud to be a Rabble", 15th May 2001

41 *Daily Mail*, "Pack It In Before the Cause Is Lost", 20th April 2001

42 *The Guardian*, "Football Tycoon Joins and Funds Anti-EU Party", 30th April 2001

43 *The Guardian*, "Sacked Tory to Back UKIP Candidate", 8th May 2001

44 *The Guardian*, We Can Win 1m Votes and Three Seats, Claims UKIP", 15th May 2001

45 *The Spectator*, "UKIP: Is There a Hidden Agenda?", 26th May 2001

46 *Daily Mail*, "Down Here, Europe is Hated Like an Occupying Power", 25th May 2001

47 *Evening Standard*, "The Anti-Euro Vote at Euan Blair's School", 25th May 2001

48 *Daily Telegraph*, "Tories Playing With Fire on EU, Says Blair", 26th May 2001

49 *Daily Telegraph*, "Sykes Pours Cash Into UKIP", 26th May 2001

See also:

50 *Sunday Telegraph*, "Briton Bankrolled Danish No Campaign", 1st October 2000

51 *The Guardian*, "Sympathy For the Europhobes", 9th February 2000

52 *Private Eye*, "Focus On UKIP", 28th January 2000

53 *The Times,* "Tories Lose Knapman to UKIP", 31st May 2000

REFERENCES

54   *The Times,* "How Euro-plot Was Born Among the Heather",
     2nd March 2001

55   *The Times,* "Tory Peer Offered Anti-EU Party £2m to Drop Candidates",
     2nd March 2001

56   *The Guardian,* "'£2m deal' to Shield Tory Marginals", 3rd March 2001

57   *The Times,* Letters: "UKIP Strategy to Effect Change", 19th March 2001

58   *The Independent,* "Welcome to Little England – A Metropolitan Liberal's
     Adventures in Eurosceptic Land", 1st May 2001

59   *Daily Telegraph,* "Push Comes to Shove for Bexhill's Squabbling Tories",
     9th May 2001

60   *Birmingham Post,* "Jack Flies Flag for UKIP", 1st May 2001

61   *Daily Telegraph,* "Quit EU and Save £20bn, Says Independence Party",
     15th May 2001

62   *Daily Telegraph,* "Millionaire Finances Campaign to Quit EU",
     18th May 2001

63   *BBC News Online,* Interview with Nigel Farage, 22nd May 2001

64   *Daily Telegraph,* "Blair to Launch Fightback Against Euroscepticism",
     27th July 1999

65   *Daily Telegraph,* "Eurosceptic Campaign to Put Pressure on Tory MPs",
     29th October 1999

66   *The Times,* "Odd Couple Set Out on Blair's EU Line", 2nd December 1999

67   *Daily Telegraph,* "Blow to Blair Over 'Silly' EU Job Scare",
     19th February 2000

68   *Daily Telegraph,* "Anger As Labour Eurosceptics Take Sykes Cash",
     21st February 2000

69   *Daily Telegraph,* "Our Challenge to Nigel (Keith) Vaz", 24th February 2000

70   *The Times,* "Sceptic Website Sets Out to Topple Hague",
     28th February 2000

71   *Daily Telegraph,* "Campaign Aims to Block Euro Vote",
     4th September 2000

72   *Daily Telegraph,* "Blair Accused of Treason Over Europe",
     21st September 2000

73   *The Times,* "Resignation Shakes Euro Group", 4th November 2000

74   *The Times,* "Royal Mail 'is Delivering Euro Propaganda'",
     15th November 2000

75   *Daily Telegraph,* "Eurosceptic Peer Attacks BBC's 'Raging Europhiles' ",
     6th December 2000

76   *The Times,* "Report Shows European Movement in Crisis", 8th May 2001

77   *The Times,* "Young People Oppose the Euro", 4th September 2000

78 *Daily Telegraph*, "Britain Was Ready to Pay Any Price to Join EEC",
    7th September 2000

General Election to European Election – 2001 to 2004

A Long Preparation

1   *Daily Telegraph*, "Brown Orders Start On Euro Criteria",
    12th August 2001
2   *Daily Telegraph*, "New Currency For A New World", 3rd October 2001
3   *The Guardian*, "Silence is Golden For The Conservatives",
    16th December 2001
4   *BBC News Online*, "Tories Set To Break Euro Silence", 4th April 2003

People And Places

5   *ePolitix.com*, "Expelled Welsh Tory May Join BNP", 26th August 2001
6   *Daily Telegraph*, "Traders Appeal Against Imperial Measures Ban",
    21st November 2001
7   *Daily Telegraph*, "Peers Use Magna Carta to Oppose EU Charter",
    7th February 2001

Moving Into Pavement Politics

No references

Moving Onto Risky Ground

No references

Goodbye Euro, Hello Constitution

8   *The Guardian*, "Battle Pledge From Euro 'No' Leader", 26th July 2002
9   *Daily Telegraph*, "Blair Could Win Euro Vote by Blurring the Question",
    9th September 2002
10 *The Guardian*, "Anti-Euro Lobby in Disarray as Tycoon Bids to Hijack
    Official No Campaign", 3rd September 2002
11 *The Times*, "Euro Campaigners are Ready to Give Up", 10th May 2003
12 *Daily Telegraph*, "MPs Talk of Blair Quitting in Spring",
    5th December 2003
13 *The Business*, "Euro Lobby Switches Focus After 'No' Vote Win",
    29th September 2003

REFERENCES

See also:

14 *The Times,* "Anti-Euro Group Keeps Distance From Tory Leader,
    31st May 2001

15 *Daily Mail*, "Dave the Butcher's Imperial Crusade", 4th February 2000

16 *Daily Telegraph*, "Greengrocer Faces Court for Refusing to go Metric",
    7th September 2000

17 *The Times,* "MEPs' Expenses Fund Case", 14th December 2000

18 *Daily Telegraph*, "Grocer Case Puts Metric Law on Trial",
    16th January 2001

19 *Daily Telegraph*, "Blair Accused of Treason Over Europe",
    21st September 2000

20 *The Observer*, "Clarke Win Will 'Purge' Tory Right", 26th August 2001

21 *Daily Telegraph*, "No, No, Stop it – This is All Too Confusing",
    24th August 2002

22 *The Scotsman*, "Europe is the Ghost at the Feast as Tories Stay Silent",
    10th October 2002

23 *Daily Telegraph*, "Why 'Biased' BBC News Team Stands Accused of Selling
    its Soul to Euroland", 27th December 2002

24 *Daily Telegraph*, "Tory Chief 'Had Talked of Defecting to UKIP'",
    20th February 2003

25 *Daily Telegraph*, "Eurosceptic Fury Over EU Plans to Limit Party Funding",
    20th February 2003

26 *The Guardian*, "British MEPs Accused of Interfering in Malta Poll",
    6th March 2003

27 *House of Commons Select Committee on "The UK and the Euro",*
    Examination of Witnesses, 18th March 2003
    Questions to Mark Damazer and Anne Sloman of the BBC

28 *BBC News Online*, "Call to Scrap 'Wasteful' Assembly", 9th April 2003

29 *The Scotsman*, "A Growing Chorus of Radical Voices and Alternative
    Causes", 28th April 2003

30 *BBC News Online*, "Polls Dominate Commons Exchanges",
    30th April 2003

31 *The Business*, "Sterling Crisis for Pro-Euro Pressure Group",
    12th May 2003

32 *Daily Mail*, "Now Will You Listen, Mr Blair", 17th June 2003

33 *Daily Telegraph*, "Euro Group Gives Blair Warning on Referendum",
    10th May 2003

34 *EUObserver.com*, "Pan-European Funding Law Discriminatory,
    Say MEPs", 29th January 2004

35 *Daily Telegraph*, "UKIP Pins its Hopes on Former Clinton Spin-Doctor",

29th May 2003

36 *The Times,* "Battle for Independence", 27th June 2003

37 www.thisisthenortheast.co.uk, "Candidate for Europe Withdraws as Party Feud Escalates", 28th May 2003

38 *The Guardian,* "UKIP Applauds Tony Martin", 10th October 2003

39 *BBC News Online,* "Tories Take EU Vote Call to N⁰ 10", 23rd October 2003

40 www.congressfordemocracy.org.uk, Minutes of the Congresses

41 *Daily Telegraph,* "Britons Want to Stop Brussels Juggernaut on Road to Federalism", 15th May 2003

42 *Sunday Telegraph,* "New Campaign Launched for Referendum on EU 'Superstate'", 18th May 2003

43 *The Times,* "Blair Rules Out Referendum on New Europe", 31st May 2003

44 *Daily Telegraph,* "Pressure Grows for Vote on EU Constitution", 20th May 2003

45 *Daily Telegraph,* "Hain Sparks Furore Over EU 'Liars'", 19th May 2003

The Opening Of The Second Battle

No references

The 2004 European Election Campaign

Crash

No references

Three Outsiders

1 *BBC News Online,* "UKIP and Greens Gear Up for Vote", 2nd January 2004

2 *The Times,* "Why I, an American, Have Championed the UK's Independence from Europe", 15th June 2004

3 *BBC News Online,* "Clifford Joins UKIP Election Bid", 16th January 2004

4 www.ukip.org, "Max Clifford to Help UKIP in European Elections", 7th February 2004

5 www.varsity.cam.ac.uk, "Feature: The Agent Provocateur", March 2000

6 *The Times,* "Momentum Builds as UKIP Casts its Net Beyond the Fringe", 3rd June 2004

7 *The Guardian,* "Smooth Operator", 8th June 2004

8 *Sunday Express,* "We Owe Arabs Nothing", 4th January 2004

9 *Sunday Express,* "Backing Britain is Not a Black or White Issue",

23rd May 2004

10   www.ukip.org, "A Personal Message From Robert Kilroy-Silk",
     10th May 2004

11   *The Scotsman*, "Kilroy Was Here: Up Close and Personal", 29th May 2004

Organisation For The Campaign

12   *BBC News Online*, "UKIP Boasts £2m Election Campaign",
     30th April 2004

The Party's Policy Stance In The Campaign

13   *The Observer*, "Why 10th June Could be Independents' Day",
     30th May 2004

A Pensioner Fires The Opening Shot

14   *ITV*, 20th February 2004

15   *BBC*, "Breakfast With Frost" , 22nd February 2004

16   *Western Morning News*, "UKIP Denies Its in a Spin", 24th February 2004

17   *The Guardian*, "How an 83-year-old Woman Became a Council Tax Martyr
     (With a Little Help), 24th February 2004

18   *Commons Hansard*, 20th November 2000, Column 90WH

19   *House of Lords Select Committee on the European Union*,
     Minutes of Evidence, Memorandum from the Foreign and Commonwealth
     Office, 19th December 2000

20   *The Economist*, "A Constitution for Europe", 11th October 2002

21   *Commons Hansard*, 22nd November 2000, Column 92WH

22   *Daily Mail*, "Minister of Arrogance", 19th May 2003

23   *Sunday Telegraph*, "I Won't Be Your Leader, 6ft 4in Lesbian Tells UKIP's
     Gay Members", 29th August 2004

24   *Daily Telegraph*, "UKIP Candidate Maloney Provokes Gay Backlash",
     30th April 2004

Kilroy-Silk Brings Up The Heavy Artillery

25   *Sunday Express*, "Britain Must Quit EU, Says Kilroy", 9th May 2004

26   *BBC News Online*, "Kilroy Predicts EU Disintegration", 9th May 2004

27   *Daily Telegraph*, "Voters Fed-Up With Lying Elite, Says Kilroy-Silk",
     13th May 2004

28   *The Guardian*, "Kilroy Boost for Anti-EU Cause", 13th May 2004

29   *Yorkshire Post*, "Yorkshire Tycoon Backs UK Independence Party on
     Europe", 18th May 2004

REFERENCES

30 *Western Morning News*, "Return to Fold, Letwin Urges UKIP Voters",
    20th May 2004

31 *The Observer*, "The United Kilroy Party?", 17th May 2004

32 *The Times,* "Kilroy Chats Up Anti-EU Vote", 21st May 2004

"Our Time Has Come"

33 *Daily Telegraph*, "Why the Rapid Rise of UKIP Will Spread Alarm Among
    Big Three", 24th May 2004

34 *Daily Telegraph*, "UKIP Scoring On the Anti-Brussels Card",
    24th May 2004

35 *The Guardian*, "This Euro-Fraud Must be Exposed", 24th May 2004

36 *Daily Mail*, "Anti-EU Party Races Ahead of Lib-Dems", 25th May 2004

37 *Daily Telegraph*, "Voters 'Are Losing Faith in Immigration Policy'",
    26th May 2004

38 *The Guardian*, "A Silky Start", 25th May 2004

39 *Le Monde*, "Tony Blair Veut Faire des Elections Européennes un Tour de
    Chauffe, Avant de Briguer un Troisième Mandat", 27th May 2004

40 *Financial Times* Deutschland, "Rein ins Parlament, Raus Aus der EU",
    1st June 2004

41 *Evening Standard*, "Independence Day", 27th May 2004

Of Cranks And Gadflies

42 *Daily Telegraph*, Letter: "UKIP is a Pointless Protest Vote", 27th May 2004

43 *Daily Telegraph*, "Be Careful, Mr Howard", 30th May 2004

44 *Daily Telegraph*, "Howard Rages at UKIP 'Gadflies'", 31st May 2004

45 *The Times,* "Tories Denounce Rivals as 'Little Englanders'", 31st May 2004

46 *Daily Telegraph*, "Conservatives Need To Find Some Inspiration",
    24th May 2004

47 *BBC News Online*, "Tory Peers in UKIP Support Row", 29th May 2004

48 *The Observer*, "Tories Throw Out Rebel Peers for Backing UKIP",
    30th May 2004

49 *Sunday Telegraph*, "As Founder of the UKIP, I Will Vote Tory",
    30th May 2004

50 *Mail On Sunday,* [title], 6th June 2004

51 *The Guardian*, "UKIP Leaders Round on Defiant Kilroy",
    21st October 2004

52 *Mail On Sunday*, "Cameron Stands By UKIP 'Racist' Jibe", 5th April 2006

53 *The Scotsman*, "Postmen Can Refuse to Deliver 'Extreme' Euroelection
    Leaflets, 30th May 2004

REFERENCES

54   *The Scotsman*, "To Brussels With Love?", 30th May 2004

Coming To The Boil

55   *BBC News Online*, "Howard Makes His Pitch for Europe", 1st June 2004

56   *The Independent*, "Howard Launches Fierce Attack on UKIP 'Extremists'", 2nd June 2004

57   *The Guardian*, "Amidst the Sour Self-Seeking, Europe is Falling into Decay", 2nd June 2004

58   *Sunday Telegraph*, "Hello, I'm From UKIP And I Want to Take Us Out of the EU", 6th June 2004

59   *Evening Standard*, "Senior Tories 'in Talks to Defect'", 2nd June 2004

60   *ePolitix.com*, "Backing Grows For EU Poll Reform", 4th June 2004

61   *Sunday Telegraph*, "UKIP is Just a Stunt: I'm a Celebrity…Get Me Out of Europe", 6th June 2004

62   *The New Statesman*, "Pleased to Bow to Uncle Sam", 5th June 2004

63   *Daily Telegraph*, "The Predator Snapping at Howard's Heels", 7th June 2004

64   *The Times*, "Kilroy-Silk Ponders Leadership of UKIP", 7th June 2004

65   *ePolitix.com*, Interview with Nigel Farage, 9th June 2004

66   *The Times*, "Decision Day", 10th June 2004

67   *The Guardian*, "Euro Fear For Tories As UKIP Eyes Top Slot", 12th June 2004

Champagne And Then To Wreck?

68   *Sunday Telegraph*, "Blair's Crisis Deepens As UKIP Raid's Labour Vote", 13th June 2004

69   *The Independent*, "Tories and Labour Crushed Under the Wheels of UKIP's Bandwagon", 14th June 2004

70   *Daily Mail*, "A Big 'No' to Europe and a Big 'No' to Tony Blair", 14th June 2004

71   *Evening Standard*, "A Wake-Up Call From UKIP", 14th June 2004

72   *Daily Telegraph*, "Sparkling Moment for Men Who Want to Say No", 15th June 2004

73   *BBC News Online*, "Kilroy-Silk Win Crowns UKIP Night", 14th June 2004

74   *The Times*, "UKIP Turns to Domestic Agenda for By-Elections", 14th June 2004

75   *The Independent*, "Britain Has An Allergy to Europe, and Even Tony Blair Knows He Cannot Cure it", 14th June 2004

REFERENCES

See also:

76 *Daily Telegraph*, "Eastern European Migration 'Far Exceeds Estimate'",
11th November 2004

77 *The Observer*, "Doing the Splits Again at UKIP", 6th January 2004

78 *The Guardian*, "Fury at UKIP Letter Bomb Jibe", 6th January 2004

79 *York Evening Press*, "BNP Euro 'Plot' Foiled", 6th January 2004

80 *Bath Chronicle*, "UKIP Chief Expelled Over BNP Claims",
7th February 2004

81 *Searchlight*, "BNP Challenges UKIP in Bid for European Glory",
February 2004, www.searchlightmagazine.com

82 *Daily Telegraph*, "I'll Go to Prison, Says 83-year-old Council Tax Rebel",
20th February 2004

83 *The Times,* "Prescott Praises Pensioner's Stand Over Council Tax",
23rd February 2004

84 *Daily Telegraph*, "Anger as 83-year-old Council Tax Rebel Sells Story
to Paper", 25th February 2004

85 *Daily Mail*, "Prescott Doesn't Frighten Me", 27th February 2004

86 *The Guardian*, "Accentuating the Negative", 11th April 2004

87 *BBC News Online*, "Kilroy-Silk to Stand for UKIP", 6th May 2004

88 *The Guardian*, "UKIP: Our Moment Has Come", 12th May 2004

89 *BBC News Online*, "UKIP Launches London Mayoral Bid", 13th May 2004

90 *The Times,* "Eurosceptics Hope to Win Balance of Power at Polls",
14th May 2004

91 *The Times,* "Jasper Gerard Meets Robert Kilroy-Silk", 16th May 2004

92 *The Guardian*, "Poll Shows UKIP is Gaining on Lib Dems", 24th May 2004

93 *Daily Telegraph*, "Surge by UKIP Hits Big Parties", 24th May 2004

94 *Daily Telegraph*, "Big Guns Turn Their Fire on UKIP Policies",
25th May 2004

95 *The Independent*, "Established Parties fear Advance of UKIP",
25th May 2004

96 *The Times,* "Joan Collins is Independent Again", 26th May 2004

97 *The Times,* "Tories Rattled by UKIP's Appeal to Eurosceptics",
1st June 2004

98 *The Guardian*, "A Vote For UKIP is a Wasted Vote", 1st June 2004

99 *The Scotsman*, "Challenge of the UKIP", 3rd June 2004

100 *The Independent*, Letters: "UKIP Extremism" (Aidan Rankin),
3rd June 2004

101 *Financial Times*, Letters; "Without a Clear European Engagement, UK Runs
Risk of Believing in a Cost-Free Withdrawal", (Neil Kinnock),
4th June 2004

102 *The Times,* "Labour Stokes UKIP Fire at its Own Risk", 4th June 2004

103 *Financial Times*, "Party Splits Reopen With Legal Threat Over Ballot",
4thJune 2004

104 *The Sunday Times*, "Howard Aide Revealed as the Man From UKIP",
6th June 2004

105 *Sunday Express*, "Post Vote Will Hit UKIP But Boost Labour",
6th June 2004

106 *The Guardian*, "Why Robert Kilroy-Silk Could Kill or Cure the Tories",
7th June 2004

107 *The Times,* "Howard Urged to Revise Strategy", 7th June 2004

108 *The Guardian*, "Smooth Operator", 8th June 2004

109 *Evening Standard*, "Mystery Ban on UKIP Man", 8th June 2004

110 *The Independent*, "The Self-Styled Saviour of Britain", 5th June 2004

111 *The Times,* "Labour and Tories Hit by Fringe Parties", 8th June 2004

112 *BBC News Online*, "UKIP 'Taking Support From Labour'", 8th June 2004

113 *The Guardian*, "A Seismic Change", 7th June 2004

114 *The Times,* "Poll Places UKIP as Top EU Sceptics", 11th June 2004

115 *The Independent*, "You British, the Elections, and Your Special Brand
of European Hatred", 10th June 2004

116 *Daily Telegraph*, "Main Parties Rattled by UKIP Surge in Euro Vote",
14th June 2004

117 *Le Monde*, "Les Europhobes Réussissent Une Spectaculaire Percée en
Grande Bretagne", 14th June 2004

118 *Le Monde*, "Un Seul Mot d'Ordre: 'Quittons l'Union Européenne'",
14th June 2004

119 *The Independent*, "UKIP Aims For Every Seat at General Election",
14th June 2004

120 *Financial Times*, "UKIP in EU Poll Success", 14th June 2004

121 *The Times,* "UKIP Leads Charge of the Eurosceptics", 14th June 2004

122 *Evening Standard*, "Independence Day", 14th June 2004

123 *Daily Mail*, "Kicked in the Teeth", 14th June 2004

124 *Daily Telegraph*, "Party Leaders Start to Flex Their New Muscles",
14th June 2004

125 *Daily Mail*, "The Death of the Great Euro Dream", 14th June 2004

126 *Daily Telegraph*, "The Lunatic Mainstream Had Better Start Worrying
Fast", 15th June 2004

127 *The Independent*, "The True Face Of a Party That Wants Us Out of
Europe", 15th June 2004

128 *The Times,* "Blair Calms Labour Nerves as Howard Reshuffles Pack",
15th June 2004

129 *The Guardian*, "These Are No Swivel-Eyed Xenophobes", 18th June 2004
130 *BBC News Online*, "Blair Hails EU Constitution Deal", 19th June 2004

European Election 2004 to General Election 2005

The End Of The Beginning

No references

The House On The Rhine

1 *Daily Telegraph*, "New MEP for UKIP Faces Fraud Charges",
   15th June 2004

2 *BBC News Online*, "UKIP Suspends Fraud Trial Euro MP", 16th July 2004

3 *The Guardian*, "UKIP MEP: Pregnant Women Should Resign",
   20th July 2004

4 *BBC News Online*, UKIP MEP in Row Over Working Women",
   21st July 2004

5 *Daily Telegraph*, "UKIP's Spokesman for Women Says They Should Get
   Back in the Kitchen", 21st July 2004

6 *The Guardian*, "Godfrey's Bloomer Leaves Village Aghast", 22nd July 2004

7 *Daily Telegraph*, "Cheering MEPs Welcome Barroso Climb-Down",
   28th October 2004

8 *Sunday Telegraph*, "This Was No Triumph for European Democracy",
   31st October 2004

9 Nigel Farage, Report from Plenary Session of the EU Parliament,
   October 2004

10 *Financial Times*, "EU Commissioner Faces Flak Over Conviction",
    18th November 2004

11 *Daily Telegraph*, "Euro Team Are Crooks And Liars, Says UKIP",
    19th November 2004

12 *UKIP Press Release*, "Did Barroso Know of Barrot Conviction, And If Not,
    Why?" 19th November 2004

13 *UKIP Press Release*, "Sack Barrot, Says UKIP, as Barroso Admits
    Ignorance", 19th November 2004

14 *UKIP Press Release*, "Conviction Politics: Anti-Fraud Commissioner
    Has Criminal Record", 19th November 2004

15 *Daily Telegraph*, "New Row at EC Over Funding Conviction of MEP",
    20th November 2004

16 *Financial Times*, "Barrot Faces Questions On Conviction",
    20th November 2004

17   *Sunday Telegraph*, "Barroso Under Pressure to Fire Commissioner Over Past Crime", 21st November 2004

18   *Libération*, "La Chasse au Barrot Continue au Parlement Européen, 23rd November 2004

Kill The Tories

19   *The Times*, "UKIP Will Not Stand Against Anti-EU Tories", 27th July 2004

20   *Daily Telegraph*, "UKIP Leadership Blocks Kilroy's Westminster Bid", 8th August 2004

21   *Daily Telegraph*, "Kilroy-Silk Will Not Stand in Hartlepool", 10th August 2004

22   *Hartlepool Mail*, "Ex-Councillor to Stand for UKIP", 12th August 2004

23   *News of the World*, "Sleaze At It Again", 12th September 2004

24   *BBC News Online*, "UKIP Drops Concession to Tories", 2nd October 2004

25   *Sunday Telegraph*, "Robert Kilroy-Silk Stakes Claim to Leadership of UKIP", 3rd October 2004

26   *Sunday Telegraph*, "I've Been Dying to Meet You Lot...But You Look Pretty Normal to Me", 3rd October 2004

27   *Daily Telegraph*, "Millionaire Backer Drops UKIP", 5th October 2004

28   *BBC News Online*, "UKIP Donor Pulls Plug On Funding", 5th October 2004

29   *Daily Telegraph*, "Sykes Dangles Prospect of UKIP Cash", 6th October 2004

The North East Says 'No'

30   *The Journal (Newcastle)*, "Eurosceptic Bid to Derail Home-Rule Move", 15th August 2002

31   *The Journal (Newcastle)*, "Drive for 'No' Vote Boosted", 5th September 2003

32   *The Guardian*, "North-West MPs Line Up Against Local Assemblies", 11th May 2004

33   *BBC News Online*, "Blair to Make EU Poll Statement", 19th April 2004

34   *The Independent*, "'No' Campaigners Desperate to Sideline Hardline Eurosceptics", 23rd April 2004

35   *Daily Telegraph*, "Blair is Staring Poll Defeat in the Face", 30th April 2004

36   *The Times*, "Vote No Campaign Ready for Quick Start", 21st May 2004

37   *BBC News Online*, "Delay Possible for Regional Votes", 22nd June 2004

38   *BBC News Online*, "Regional Assembly Votes Postponed", 22nd July 2004

39   *The Times*, "North East Turns Against 'White Elephant' Assembly",

13th October 2004

40   *Sunday Telegraph*, "The Invisible Official Campaign", 3rd October 2004

41   www.thisisthenortheast.co.uk, "Prescott: 'This is Your Only Chance' ", 22nd October 2004

42   *Daily Telegraph*, "There's a No in the Post Say Critics of Prescott's Assemblies", 1st November 2004

43   *BBC News Online*, "Backing the Ref", 1st November 2004

44   *The Times*, "Prescott Rides to Aid Of Assembly", 3rd November 2004

45   *The Times*, "Assembly Vote Turnout Grows", 5th November 2004

46   *BBC News Online*, "No Camp Hail 'Resounding' Victory", 5th November 2004

47   *BBC News Online*, "North East Votes 'No' to Assembly", 5th November 2004

48   *BBC News Online*, "Is This the End for Regional Devolution?", 5th November 2004

49   *BBC News Online*, "MPs Call to Scrap Assembly Vote", 5th November 2004

50   *Sunday Telegraph*, "A Resounding No for Prescott's Big Scheme", 7th November 2004

Return Of The Curse

51   *Daily Telegraph,* "UKIP Backer Threatens to Withdraw Support", 10th September 2004

52   *BBC News Online, "UKIP Money Man Wants New Leader",* 10th September 2004

53   *Daily Telegraph, "Kilroy – A Leader Who's Not Waiting",* 15th September 2004

54   David Lott, "Campaign Director's General Election Update", 28th November 2004

55   *Daily Mail*, "Kilroy Tries to Grab Leadership of UKIP", 4th October 2004

56   *The Times*, "They Talk About a War and There's a Leadership Challenge in Prospect, But This Time it's the UKIP Party Conference", 4th October 2004

57   *The Guardian*, "Cheers Greet Kilroy, The Man Who Would be UKIP King", 4th October 2004

58   *BBC News Online*, "Kilroy Warned to Get Back in Line", 6th October 2004

59   *Sunday Telegraph*, "If You Want Me As Leader, Then Do Something About It", 10th October 2004

60   *ePolitix.com*, "UKIP Fails to Resolve Leadership Split", 13th October 2004

61   *The Independent*, " 'Blood On The Carpet' As Kilroy-Silk Slips in leadership

Challenge", 14th October 2004

62   *Daily Telegraph*, "Kilroy-Silk Fights On After Slapdown",
14th October 2004

63   *Financial Times*, "UKIP in Brussels Row Over Leadership Challenge",
14th October 2004

64   *The Times*, "Kilroy-Silk Admits Defeat in the Bitter Competition for
Leadership of UKIP", 14th October 2004

65   Robert Kilroy-Silk, Letter to all Branch Chairmen: "Ten Issues",
16th October 2004

66   Nigel Farage, email to all South East Branch Chairmen, 18th October 2004

67   *Daily Telegraph*, "Open War as Kilroy-Silk Condemns UKIP 'Cabal' ",
18th October 2004

68   *The Times*, "Knapman Calls Snap Poll to Halt Kilroy-Silk",
19th October 2004

69   *Daily Telegraph*, "UKIP Snub for Kilroy-Silk", 20th October 2004

70   *The Times*, "Kilroy-Silk Could Lose UKIP Whip in Leadership Battle",
20th October 2004

71   *BBC News Online*, "UKIP Branches 'Reject Kilroy Bid' ",
20th October 2004

72   *BBC News Online*, "Kilroy Says He Won't Keep Quiet", 20th October 2004

73   *The Times*, "Kilroy Loses Poll On UKIP Leadership Bid",
20th October 2004

74   *The Times*, "Kilroy Turns Up The Heat in His Fight to be Leader of UKIP",
21st October 2004

75   *Daily Telegraph*, "Kilroy-Silk Faces Moves to Force Him Out of UKIP",
21st October 2004

76   *The Guardian*, "UKIP Leaders Round on Defiant Kilroy",
21st October 2004

77   *ePolitix.com*, "Kilroy-Silk 'Facing Humiliation' Over UKIP Leadership
Bid", 23rd October 2004

78   *BBC News Online*, "Kilroy Quits UKIP Group of MEPs",
27th October 2004

79   *ePolitix.com*, "Kilroy-Silk Resigns UKIP Whip", 27th October 2004

80   *The Guardian*, "'You're All Barmy' – Exit Kilroy from UKIP Group",
28th October 2004

81   *The Times*, "Kilroy Quits UKIP Group in Europe", 28th October 2004

82   *Daily Telegraph*, "Kilroy-Silk Leaves UKIP in Turmoil", 28th October 2004

83   *BBC News Online*, "Is UKIP Better Off Without Kilroy?",
28th October 2004

84   *BBC News Online*, "UKIP Leadership Vote is Rejected",

REFERENCES

7th December 2004

See also:

85   *The Guardian*, "Sykes Moves Up the UKIP Ladder", 19th June 2004
86   *Yorkshire Post*, "UKIP Takes a Breather Before its 12 MEPs Go to Work", 15th June 2004
87   Robert Kilroy-Silk, Maiden Speech to European Parliament, 22nd July 2004
88   *The Guardian*, "Kilroy-Silk Returns to Haunt 'Lazy, Lying Elite' ", 10th September 2004
89   *Daily Telegraph*, "Tories Suspended Over UKIP Video", 3rd August 2004
90   *ePolitix.com*, "Pro-Europeans Slam UKIP as a 'Waste of Space' ", 12th October 2004
91   *BBC News Online*, "UKIP Demands Pamphlet is Pulped", 12th October 2004
92   *The Scotsman*, "Tory Congratulates UKIP on EU 'Corruption' Expose", 22nd July 2004
93   *Le Figaro*, "Les Eurosceptiques Eparpillés", 23rd July 2004
94   *La Libre Belgique*, "Les Mastodonts aux Commandes", 24th July 2004
95   *euobserver.com*, "European Political Life at Risk of Fossilisation", 14th October 2004
96   *Sunday Times*, "In One Bloody Bout Brussels Reveals its True Hypocrisy", 31st October 2004
97   *The Scotsman*, "Ban on Far-Right Party 'Will Incite Extremism' ", 15th November 2004
98   *ePolitix.com*, "Britain, 'Should Stand Aside from EU' ", 15th November 2004
99   *Daily Telegraph*, "The Euro Parliament is no Longer a Joke for Bored Hacks", 28th October 2004
100 Ashley Mote, Speech in European parliament, 15th November 2004
101 *Le Monde*, "La Commission Européene s'efforce de Tuer La Menace d'Une 'Affaire' Barrot", 22nd November 2004
102 *Le Monde*, "Un Antieuropéen Britannique Fait Scandale en Rappelant à Jacques Barrot l'Affaire du CDS", 20th November 2004
103 *The Times*, "Barroso's New Team Gets to Work", 22nd November 2004
104 *Sunday Telegraph*, "The Prophet Mohammed Was a Paedophile, Says Kilroy-Silk Aide", 26th September 2004
105 *Sunday Telegraph*, "Shame Nobody Noticed", 10th October 2004
106 *Sheffield Today*, "Eurosceptic Spurs Tories' Election Bid", 15th November 2004
107 *The Guardian*, "UKIP Opens Seaside Souvenir Shop", 9th December 2004

REFERENCES

108 *The Scotsman*, "UKIP to Target Tory Eurosceptic MPs",
9th December 2004

109 *The Times*, "High Cost of UKIP's Poll Win Revealed", 23rd December 2004

110 *Daily Telegraph*, "Labour Plans £1m New Year Poster Blitz",
23rd December 2004

111 *The Scotsman*, "UKIP Glad to be Rid of 'Negative' Kilroy-Silk",
28th October 2004

112 *The Independent*, "Kilroy is Silenced After Split From UKIP's MEPs",
28th October 2004

113 *Private Eye*, "Is it a Crime to Mock Robert Kilroy-Silk?",
29th October 2004

114 *The Guardian*, "We Won't Miss Kilroy for Long: UKIP",
29th October 2004

115 *Yorkshire Post*, "I Won't Give the Tories a Penny, Says Paul Sykes",
15th November 2004

116 *Western Morning News*, "UKIP Leaders Don't Need This",
6th December 2004

117 www.thisisthenortheast.co.uk, Your Views, 22nd October 2004

118 *The Times*, "Regional Assembly Campaigners Spent £400,000 and Lost",
4th March 2005

119 *BBC News Online*, "Keep Politicians Out of EU Vote", 21st June 2004

120 *The Independent*, "Why I Can No Longer Sell Europe to the British",
5th July 2004

121 *The Times*, "UKIP Plans Alliance to Scupper Constitution", 20th July 2004

122 *The Times*, "Brussels Chief Takes On Eurosceptics", 22nd July 2004

123 *The Times*, "UKIP Recruits Allies to Wreck Legislation", 22nd July 2004

124 *BBC News Online*, "EU Constitution Battle Restarts", 9th September 2004

125 *euobserver.com*, "Tories and UKIP Link Up for Constitution Campaign",
9th September 2004

126 *BBC News Online*, "Roger Knapman on the EU Constitution",
29th October 2004

127 *BBC News Online*, "Europe Vote 'Early 2006' – Straw", 29th October 2004

128 *The Times*, "Europe Woos Sceptics on Rocky Route to Ratify the
Constitution", 29th October 2004

129 *ePolitix.com*, "Straw Hints at EU Referendum Date", 29th October 2004

130 *Daily Mail*, "Battle for Europe is Just Starting", 30th October 2004

131 *Daily Mail*, "Blair Signs Away Our Birthright", 30th October 2004

132 *Daily Telegraph*, "Rome May Prove to be Fatal for Another Leader",
30th October 2004

133 *Daily Telegraph*, "Britons Can Vote on Treaty in 2006", 30th October 2004

134 *Daily Telegraph*, "Britain Can't Pick and Choose Which Bits of Law it Will Obey, 25th November 2004

135 *The Times*, "'No' Campaign Raises its Profile, and £0.5m, With Dinner at Savoy", 25th November 2004

136 *The Sun*, "Mr Europe Didn't Like Euro", 10th December 2004

137 *The Times*, "Will Blair Never Learn? Its Sure to be Third Time Unlucky With Mandelson", 26th July 2004

138 *Daily Telegraph*, "Uproar in Labour Ranks Over Mandelson Comeback", 24th July 2004

139 *BBC News Online*, "UKIP Mulls Truce for Eurosceptics", 27th July 2004

140 *Daily Telegraph*, "Howard Rejects UKIP's Truce", 28th July 2004

141 *The Times*, "Tories Face Discipline Over UKIP Video Party", 30th July 2004

142 *Daily Telegraph*, "Tories Suspend Local Chiefs Over UKIP Video", 3rd August 2004

143 *Daily Telegraph*, "Just Like the Rest of Us, Howard Has a Poor Summer", 27th August 2004

144 Daily Telegraph, "We Will Work With UKIP, Says Ancram", 9th September 2004

145 BBC News Online, "UKIP Out to Change the Face of Politics", 9th September 2004

146 *Daily Telegraph*, "Euroscepticism Encourages Britain's Dark Streak of Racism", 7th August 2004

147 *ePolitix.com*, "UKIP's 'Twisted Reality' Comes Under Fire", 21st September 2004

148 *Daily Telegraph*, "Tories Want to Renegotiate EU Laws", 22nd September 2004

149 *The Guardian*, "Kinnock Joins Europe Campaign", 24th September 2004

150 *The Guardian*, "Today Hartlepool, Tomorrow...", 28th September 2004

151 *Daily Telegraph*, "UKIP Voters Can Make a Lame Protest of Join Us", 3rd October 2004

152 *The Observer*, "Whatever the Tories Do, They're Doomed", 3rd October 2004

153 *The Observer*, "Howard: Trouble to the Left, Trouble to the Right", 3rd October 2004

154 *Sunday Times*, "Howard is Warned Heads Must Roll", 3rd October 2004

155 *Sunday Times*, "Will the Real Opposition Please Stand Up", 3rd October 2004

156 *Sunday Times*, "The Tories Are at Rock Bottom – And Falling", 3rd October 2004

157 *BBC News Online*, "UKIP Stakes its Claim", 3rd October 2004

REFERENCES

158 *BBC News Online*, "TV Chef to Stand as MP For UKIP", 4th October 2004

159 *Financial Times*, "Howard Aims to Woo Voters With 'Timetable For Action' ", 4th October 2004

160 *Daily Telegraph*, "Tories Must Win Back the Right to be Believed", 4th October 2004

161 *Daily Telegraph*, "Howard is Doomed Unless He Sticks to the Centre Ground", 4th October 2004

162 *Daily Mail*, "Last Chance for Tories to Tell Us What They're For", 4th October 2004

163 *The Times*, "All The Parties Are Losing", 4th October 2004

164 *The Times*, "Supporters Say A Tougher Line On Europe Will Win More Votes", 4th October 2004

165 *The Times*, "UKIP Protest Vote Counter-Productive", 5th October 2004

166 *Daily Telegraph*, "For All Our Sakes, France Must Say No", 5th October 2004

167 *Daily Telegraph*, "Campaigner Closes His UKIP Chequebook", 5th October 2004

168 *Daily Telegraph*, "Howard Pledges Action Not Words", 6th October 2004

169 *The Times*, "Big Donor Returns to Tories From UKIP", 6th October 2004

170 *The Independent*, "Pro-Europeans Fear Deal With UKIP After Defection of Sykes", 6th October 2004

171 *The Guardian*, "BBC's Religious And EU Coverage Comes Under Scrutiny", 8th October 2004

172 *The Spectator*, "UKIP Is Mad, Bad And Nasty, And Intends Real Harm", 9th October 2004

173 *The Scotsman*, "Howard 'Deluded' On EU Power – UKIP", 6th October 2004

174 *Sunday Times*, "Tories Pick the Wrong Enemy...And a Right-Wing Suicide", 10th October 2004

175 *Scotland On Sunday*, "UKIP Are Like Hitler's Appeasers", 10th October 2004

176 *The Independent*, "Patten Blasts Tories For Flirting With UKIP", 11th October 2004

177 *The Guardian*, "We'll Bin EU Treaties, Redwood Tells UKIP", 16th October 2004

178 *Sunday Times*, "Intolerance Is At Its Most Dangerous On The Left", 17th October 2004

179 *BBC News Online*, "Major Warns Tories Against UKIP", 24th October 2004

180 *The Business*, " 'No' Vote For Europe Grows In ICM Poll",

20th November 2004

181   *The Mail On Sunday*, "Sceptics Are The Only True Europeans",
      31st October 2004

182   *The Business*, "Twilight Of The Elites And The BBC Dwarfs",
      7th November 2004

183   *The Northern Echo,* "Figures Reveal True Cost Of Assembly Vote",
3rd March 2005

The 2005 General Election Campaign

Great Hopes

No references

Organisation For The Campaign

1   *BBC News Online*, "UKIP's Secret Weapon?", 14th January 2005

The Party's Policy Stance In The Campaign

2   *PA News,* "Immigration Initiatives 'Pointless' Says UKIP",
      7th February 2005

3   *The Guardian*, "UKIP Launches Manifesto", 15th April 2005

4   *BBC News Online,* "Call For Scots MPs to Downgrade", 15th April 2005

5   *BBC News Online,* "UKIP Aim Is To 'Reclaim' Nation", 15th April 2005

6   *The Guardian,* "UKIP Accentuates The Negative", 16th April 2005

A Final Parting Of The Ways

7   *The Guardian,* "Putsch Time", 16th December 2004

8   *Daily Telegraph*, "Kilroy-Silk Ready to Quit UKIP And Set Up His Own
      Rival Party", 17th January 2005

9   *Daily Mail*, "Kilroy 'Starting Rival Party To UKIP' ", 18th January 2005

10   *Financial Times*, "Kilroy-Silk Expected To Quit UKIP And Form Rival
      Party", 18th January 2005

11   *Daily Telegraph*, "Kilroy-Silk Party Is His Idea Of Truth",
      18th January 2005

12   *BBC News Online*, "The End Of The Affair", 20th January 2005

13   *BBC News Online*, "Kilroy Hints At Political Rebirth", 21st January 2005

14   *BBC News Online*, "Kilroy-Silk Quits 'Shameful' UKIP", 21st January 2005

15   *The Guardian*, "End Of The Affair As Kilroy-Silk Storms Out Of
      'Self-Serving' UKIP", 21st January 2005

16   *The Times*, "UKIP Linked To BNP As Kilroy-Silk Finally Quits",

21st January 2005

17　*Daily Telegraph*, "Kilroy-Silk Leaves UKIP, Saying Party Is A 'Joke'",
21st January 2005

18　*BBC News Online*, "New UKIP Defection To 'Veritas'", 30th January 2005

19　*The Times*, "Kilroy-Silk Claims Monopoly On The Politics Of Truth",
3rd February 2005

20　*Daily Telegraph*, "Kilroy-Silk Puts Immigration At The Top Of New Party's
Agenda", 3rd February 2005

21　*Daily Mail*, "Not-So-Silky Kilroy", 3rd February 2005

22　*The Independent*, "In A One-Man Crusade For The Truth, Kilroy Can Get
Rid Of The Facts", 3rd February 2005

23　*The Guardian*, "Kilroy Was There", 3rd February 2005

24　*The Guardian*, "Kilroy-Silk Colleague Linked To ex-National Front
Leader", 3rd February 2005

The Penny That Didn't Drop

25　Conservative Party Press Release, "New Conservative Plans to Combat
Immigration Abuse", 7th July 2004

26　Conservative Party Press Release, "Conservatives Pledge Controlled
Immigration", 24th January 2005

27　*Daily Telegraph,* "Brussels: We'll Halt Howard's Curbs On Migrants",
25th January 2005

28　*Daily Telegraph*, "Blair's Asylum Switch Gives Europe The Key To Britain",
26th January 2005

29　*Daily Telegraph*, "Howard: Why Britain Must Set Quotas On
Immigration", 24th January 2005

30　*Daily Telegraph*, "The EU's Four-Stage Strategy To Reduce Britons To
Servitude", 26th January 2005

31　*Daily Telegraph*, "UKIP Shuns Kilroy As It Talks Tough On Migrants",
8th February 2005

32　*The Guardian*, "No Truth Behind Veritas", 6th February 2005

33　*ePolitix.com*, "Kilroy-Silk Targets Migrants", 14th February 2005

34　*Daily Mail*, "Kilroy Pledges A Total Asylum Ban", 14th February 2005

35　*BBC News Online*, "UKIP Could Sue Veritas Defectors",
24th February 2005

36　*BBC News Online*, "Kilroy Attacks 'Liberal Fascism' ", 14th April 2005

37　*The Scotsman*, "Kilroy-Silk Blames Media For Veritas Party's Election
Lows", 15th April 2005

38　*The Times*, "Seeking Truth On A Shoestring", 15th April 2005

39   *Daily Telegraph*, "Kilroy The Charmer Hands Out A Lesson In
      Canvassing", 20th April 2005

The Question Unveiled

40   *Daily Telegraph*, "Simple Yes Or No For Voters On EU Constitution",
      27th January 2005
41   *BBC News Online*, "EU Referendum Question Unveiled",
      26th January 2005
42   *The Times,* "Facts For Voters In Referendum Drive", 29th January 2005

The Elephant In The Room

43   *The Times*, "The Day Of The Anoraks", 1st February 2005
44   *The Times*, "Labour Rises To Post-Iraq War High As Lib Dems Slip",
      8th February 2005
45   *Sunday Telegraph*, "How British And American Conservatives United To
      Stop Bush Endorsing The EU Constitution As Favour To Blair",
      27th February 2005
46   *BBC News Online*, "UKIP To Run 500 Poll Candidates", 5th April 2005
47   *BBC News Online*, "UKIP 'Fighting Chance' Of 20 MPs", 10th April 2005
48   *BBC News Online*, "UK Independence Party", 10th April 2005
49   *The Times*, "UKIP Trumpets Its Claim To Be The Best Of British",
      16th April 2005
50   *CNN.com*, "Europe No Star As Election Issue", 19th April 2005
51   *BBC News Online*, "What's Happened To Europe?", 20th April 2005
52   *BBC News Online*, "UKIP Dismisses 'Phoney' Election", 20th April 2005
53   *Le Temps*, "Le Royaume Uni En Campagne Ignore L'Europe",
      23rd April 2005
54   *BBC News Online*, "UKIP Seats Within Reach – Knapman",
      27th April 2005
55   *Libération*, "L'Europe Terra Incognita Du Débat Electoral Britannique",
      2nd May 2005

See also:

56   *ePolitix.com,* "Labour EU Divisions Surface", 7th January 2005
57   *Yorkshire Post*, "Row Over £2,000 'Political' Grant For Euro-MP",
      11th January 2005
58   *Le Monde,* "Le Parlement Européen Plébiscite La Constitution",
      13th January 2005
59   *The Guardian*, "A Defence Against Glossy Rightwing Demagoguery",

REFERENCES

20th January 2005

60   *The New Statesman*, "1 in 5 Britons Could Vote Far Right",
     24th January 2005

61   *BBC News Online*, "UKIP Candidate Suspended In Probe",
     29th January 2005

62   *BBC News Online*, "Space Launch For EU Constitution",
     11th February 2005

63   *The Times*, "Senior Tory Faces a David Versus David Battle For His Seat",
     15th February 2005

64   *ePolitix.com*, "MacShane Attacks Eurosceptic Press", 15th February 2005

65   *Daily Telegraph*, "Letwin Tries To Head Off Challenge From UKIP",
     22nd February 2005

66   *The Times*, "Euro MP Facing Fraud Case", 24th February 2005

67   *ePolitix.com*, "Labour Election Launch A'Failure' ", 5th March 2005

68   *Daily Telegraph*, "Save Your Constitution Cash, Urge Politicians",
     17th March 2005

69   *BBC News Online*, "Profile: UK Independence Party", 5th April 2005

70   *Financial Times*, "Business Individuals Dig Deep To Provide Vital Party
     Funding", 5th April 2005

71   *BBC News Online*, "Election Issues: Europe", 5th April 2005

72   *Daily Telegraph*, "UKIP Offers Deal to Anti-EU Candidates",
     11th April 2005

73   *ePolitix.com*, "Union Chief: BNP A Threat North Of Border",
     19th April 2005

74   *FT.com*, "Matthew Engel: Voter Apathy or Antipathy?", 19th April 2005

75   *ePolitix.com*, "UKIP Hopeful Contests Eight Seats At Once",
     20th April 2005

76   *Daily Telegraph*, "3,500 Candidates Run The Risk Of Losing Their
     Deposit", 20th April 2005

77   *BBC News Online*, "Election Draws 3,500 Candidates", 20th April 2005

78   *Daily Telegraph*, "Conservatives Are Paddling Furiously But Struggle To
     Go Against The Flow", 22nd April 2005

79   *Sunday Times*, "The Tories Undone By Their Victor Meldrew Manifesto",
     24th April 2005

80   *BBC News Online*, "UKIP Wants Freedom From Brussels", 25th April 2005

81   *The Guardian*, "It Is Racist To Target The Bigot's Vote", 26th April 2005

82   *BBC News Online*, "Police Warn Parties 'On Race Ads' ", 26th April 2005

83   *BBC News Online*, "Protest After Candidate Arrested", 26th April 2005

84   *The Guardian*, "Wandering In The Wilderness – How Tories Stole UKIP's
     Political Clothes", 29th April 2005

85 *The Spectator*, "Parliament Of Eunuchs", 30th April 2005

86 *The Business*, "Tories Get Business Readers' Vote, But Do Little To Earn It", 1st May 2005

87 *BBC News Online*, "UKIP In Call For 'Patriot Votes' ", 3rd May 2005

88 *abc.es*, "Verdes y UKIP, Sin Opción a Escaño", 3rd May 2005

89 *ePolitix.com,* "Smaller Parties Seek Election Breakthroughs", 5th May 2005

Postscript: "No More Europe"?

1 *The Times*, "EU Fears For Future As French And Dutch Threaten 'No' Vote", 25th May 2005

2 *Sunday Telegraph*, "Anything To Declare, Mr Barroso?", 24th April 2005

3 *Sunday Times*, "Mandy's Island Holiday Was With Beatles Manager", 24th April 2005

4 *The Times*, "Mandelson Faces Sleaze Claim Over Caribbean Hospitality", 19th April 2005

5 *Daily Telegraph*, "Mandelson's Holiday Secrets Revealed", 21st April 2005

See also:

6 *Daily Telegraph*, "Europe Faces Up To Double Rejection Of Treaty, 25th May 2005

7 *The Times*, "France Votes NON", 30th May 2005

8 *The Times*, "D-Day For Europe As Dutch Vote", 1st June 2005

9 *Daily Telegraph*, "Now The Dutch Say No", 2nd June 2005

10 *The Times*, "Fight To Save Constitution After Dutch Vote 'Nee' ", 2nd June 2005

11 *The Times*, "Europe Turmoil As Treaty Collapses", 14th June 2005